Stochastic Sorcerers: Transformer Models

Jamie Flux

https://www.linkedin.com/company/golden-dawn-engineering/

Collaborate with Us!

Have an innovative business idea or a project you'd like to
collaborate on?
We're always eager to explore new opportunities for growth and
partnership.
Please feel free to reach out to us at:

https://www.linkedin.com/company/golden-dawn-
engineering/

We look forward to hearing from you!

Contents

Chapter 1

Text Classification with Transformers

Common use cases include categorizing emails, news articles, or support tickets into predefined labels. To construct the algorithm, begin by collecting a labeled dataset, ensuring each text sample has an associated category. Preprocess the dataset by converting text into tokens using a pre-trained tokenizer (e.g., BERT tokenizer). Next, load the corresponding pre-trained Transformer model (e.g., BERT or RoBERTa) and add a classification head—a feedforward layer—on top of the final Transformer layer. Fine-tune the model end-to-end using cross-entropy loss, adjusting hyperparameters such as learning rate, batch size, and maximum sequence length to optimize performance. For innovative approaches, consider using domain-adaptive pre-training, where you further pre-train on domain-specific text before fine-tuning. Additionally, explore label smoothing or focal loss for better handling of class imbalance in real-world data.

Python Code Snippet

```python
import torch
import random
from torch.utils.data import Dataset, DataLoader, random_split
from transformers import BertTokenizer,
 ↪  BertForSequenceClassification
from transformers import TrainingArguments, Trainer, logging
import numpy as np
```

```python
# For reproducibility
random.seed(42)
np.random.seed(42)
torch.manual_seed(42)

logging.set_verbosity_warning()

# ------------------------------------------------------------
# 1) Synthetic Data Creation
# ------------------------------------------------------------
def create_synthetic_data(num_samples=1000):
    """
    Create synthetic text data and corresponding binary labels (0 or
    ↪  1).
    """
    texts = []
    labels = []
    vocab = ["transformers", "classification", "email", "news",
             "support", "ticket", "customer", "feedback",
             "label", "domain", "text", "fine-tune", "model"]
    for _ in range(num_samples):
        length = random.randint(4, 10)
        # Randomly choose words
        words = [random.choice(vocab) for __ in range(length)]
        text_sample = " ".join(words)
        # Assign a random label
        label = random.randint(0, 1)
        texts.append(text_sample)
        labels.append(label)
    return texts, labels


# ------------------------------------------------------------
# 2) Custom Dataset
# ------------------------------------------------------------
class TextDataset(Dataset):
    """
    Custom Dataset to store text samples and their labels.
    """
    def __init__(self, texts, labels, tokenizer, max_length=32):
        self.texts = texts
        self.labels = labels
        self.tokenizer = tokenizer
        self.max_length = max_length

    def __len__(self):
        return len(self.texts)

    def __getitem__(self, idx):
        text = self.texts[idx]
        label = self.labels[idx]
        # Tokenize the text
        encoding = self.tokenizer.encode_plus(
```

```python
            text,
            add_special_tokens=True,
            max_length=self.max_length,
            padding="max_length",
            truncation=True,
            return_tensors="pt"
        )
        return {
            "input_ids": encoding["input_ids"][0],
            "attention_mask": encoding["attention_mask"][0],
            "labels": torch.tensor(label, dtype=torch.long)
        }

# --------------------------------------------------------------
# 3) Main Execution (Data Prep & Model Configuration)
# --------------------------------------------------------------
def main():
    # Step A: Create synthetic dataset
    texts, labels = create_synthetic_data(num_samples=1000)

    # Step B: Initialize a pre-trained tokenizer
    tokenizer = BertTokenizer.from_pretrained("bert-base-uncased")

    # Step C: Build the custom dataset
    dataset = TextDataset(texts, labels, tokenizer, max_length=32)

    # Split into train and test sets (80/20 split)
    train_size = int(0.8 * len(dataset))
    test_size = len(dataset) - train_size
    train_dataset, test_dataset = random_split(dataset, [train_size,
    ↪    test_size])

    # Step D: Initialize a BERT model for sequence classification
    # num_labels=2 for binary classification
    model = BertForSequenceClassification.from_pretrained(
        "bert-base-uncased",
        num_labels=2
    )

    # Step E: Define training arguments
    training_args = TrainingArguments(
        output_dir="./results",
        num_train_epochs=3,
        per_device_train_batch_size=8,
        per_device_eval_batch_size=8,
        evaluation_strategy="epoch",
        logging_dir="./logs",
        logging_steps=10,
        load_best_model_at_end=False
    )

    # Step F: Create Trainer object
    trainer = Trainer(
```

```
        model=model,
        args=training_args,
        train_dataset=train_dataset,
        eval_dataset=test_dataset
    )

    # Step G: Train the model
    trainer.train()

    # Step H: Evaluate the model on the test set
    test_metrics = trainer.evaluate(eval_dataset=test_dataset)
    print("Test Metrics:", test_metrics)

if __name__ == "__main__":
    main()
```

Key Implementation Details:

- **Synthetic Data Creation**: We generate random text from a small vocabulary in `create_synthetic_data` to illustrate a binary classification objective.

- **Dataset Class**: The class `TextDataset` wraps text samples and labels, performing tokenization via the BERT tokenizer within its `__getitem__` method.

- **Pre-Trained Model**: `BertForSequenceClassification` incorporates a Transformer encoder and an additional classification head on top.

- **Trainer API**: The Hugging Face `Trainer` class orchestrates training and evaluation. We specify `train_dataset` and `eval_dataset` alongside training hyperparameters in `TrainingArguments`.

- **Evaluation Strategy**: Setting `evaluation_strategy="epoch"` triggers an evaluation loop at each epoch. This can be configured further for more frequent checks.

- **Usage**: Running this script will tokenize the input, fine-tune the pre-trained BERT model, and print out test metrics such as loss and accuracy.

Chapter 2

Sentiment Analysis with Transformers

Commonly used for gauging opinions on social media posts, product reviews, or customer feedback, sentiment analysis identifies positive, negative, or neutral sentiments. To build a Transformer-based model, begin with a labeled dataset of text snippets paired with sentiment labels. Tokenize text using a pre-trained model (e.g., DistilBERT) to take advantage of language understanding. Stack a classification layer atop the Transformer's final hidden states, then fine-tune via standard backpropagation, optimizing a loss function like cross-entropy. For novel approaches, you can incorporate aspect-based sentiment analysis by extracting relevant keywords or entities first, then refining the classification to those aspects. Another advanced method includes using attention maps to visualize how the model focuses on specific words or phrases, helping interpret the sentiment detection process.

Python Code Snippet

```
import torch
import torch.nn as nn
import torch.optim as optim
from torch.utils.data import Dataset, DataLoader
import numpy as np
import random
from transformers import DistilBertTokenizerFast,
↪   DistilBertForSequenceClassification
```

```python
from transformers import AdamW

# To ensure reproducibility
torch.manual_seed(42)
np.random.seed(42)
random.seed(42)

class SentimentDataset(Dataset):
    """
    Custom Dataset for Sentiment Analysis tasks.
    Expects a list of text inputs and their corresponding sentiment
    ↪ labels.
    """
    def __init__(self, texts, labels, tokenizer, max_length=128):
        self.texts = texts
        self.labels = labels
        self.tokenizer = tokenizer
        self.max_length = max_length

    def __len__(self):
        return len(self.texts)

    def __getitem__(self, idx):
        text = self.texts[idx]
        label = self.labels[idx]
        encoded = self.tokenizer(
            text,
            add_special_tokens=True,
            truncation=True,
            max_length=self.max_length,
            return_tensors='pt',
            padding='max_length'
        )

        # Extract input_ids and attention_mask
        input_ids = encoded['input_ids'].squeeze()
        attention_mask = encoded['attention_mask'].squeeze()

        return input_ids, attention_mask, label

def collate_fn(batch):
    """
    Collate function to combine inputs and labels into a batch.
    """
    input_ids = torch.stack([item[0] for item in batch])
    attention_masks = torch.stack([item[1] for item in batch])
    labels = torch.tensor([item[2] for item in batch],
    ↪ dtype=torch.long)
    return input_ids, attention_masks, labels

def generate_synthetic_data(num_samples=2000):
    """
```

```
    Generate a simple synthetic dataset of text and random sentiment
    ↪    labels.
    Labels could be 0 (negative), 1 (neutral), or 2 (positive).
    """
    sample_texts = []
    sample_labels = []
    words_pool = [
        "great", "bad", "average", "transformers", "pytorch",
        ↪    "awesome",
        "terrible", "wonderful", "boring", "exciting", "useful",
        ↪    "questionable"
    ]

    for _ in range(num_samples):
        length = random.randint(5, 15)
        text_words = [random.choice(words_pool) for __ in
        ↪    range(length)]
        text = " ".join(text_words)
        # Random sentiment label in {0, 1, 2}
        label = random.randint(0, 2)
        sample_texts.append(text)
        sample_labels.append(label)

    return sample_texts, sample_labels

def train_model(model, data_loader, optimizer, device):
    """
    Train the DistilBERT model for one epoch.
    """
    model.train()
    total_loss = 0

    for batch in data_loader:
        input_ids, attention_masks, labels = batch
        input_ids = input_ids.to(device)
        attention_masks = attention_masks.to(device)
        labels = labels.to(device)

        optimizer.zero_grad()
        outputs = model(
            input_ids=input_ids,
            attention_mask=attention_masks,
            labels=labels
        )
        loss = outputs.loss
        loss.backward()
        optimizer.step()

        total_loss += loss.item()

    return total_loss / len(data_loader)

def evaluate_model(model, data_loader, device):
```

```python
    """
    Evaluate the DistilBERT model on the given data loader.
    """
    model.eval()
    correct = 0
    total = 0

    with torch.no_grad():
        for batch in data_loader:
            input_ids, attention_masks, labels = batch
            input_ids = input_ids.to(device)
            attention_masks = attention_masks.to(device)
            labels = labels.to(device)

            outputs = model(
                input_ids=input_ids,
                attention_mask=attention_masks
            )
            logits = outputs.logits
            predictions = torch.argmax(logits, dim=-1)
            correct += (predictions == labels).sum().item()
            total += labels.size(0)

    return correct / total

if __name__ == "__main__":
    # Device setup
    device = torch.device('cuda' if torch.cuda.is_available() else
    ↪  'cpu')

    # Generate synthetic data
    texts, labels = generate_synthetic_data(num_samples=3000)

    # Split into train and validation
    train_size = int(0.8 * len(texts))
    train_texts, val_texts = texts[:train_size], texts[train_size:]
    train_labels, val_labels = labels[:train_size],
    ↪  labels[train_size:]

    # Initialize a DistilBERT tokenizer
    tokenizer =
    ↪  DistilBertTokenizerFast.from_pretrained('distilbert-base-uncased')

    # Create Datasets
    train_dataset = SentimentDataset(train_texts, train_labels,
    ↪  tokenizer, max_length=64)
    val_dataset = SentimentDataset(val_texts, val_labels, tokenizer,
    ↪  max_length=64)

    # Dataloaders
    train_loader = DataLoader(train_dataset, batch_size=32,
    ↪  shuffle=True, collate_fn=collate_fn)
```

13

```
val_loader = DataLoader(val_dataset, batch_size=32,
↪    shuffle=False, collate_fn=collate_fn)

# Initialize DistilBERT for sequence classification (3 labels)
model = DistilBertForSequenceClassification.from_pretrained(
    'distilbert-base-uncased',
    num_labels=3
)
model = model.to(device)

# Optimizer
optimizer = AdamW(model.parameters(), lr=2e-5)

# Training loop
num_epochs = 3
for epoch in range(num_epochs):
    train_loss = train_model(model, train_loader, optimizer,
↪        device)
    val_accuracy = evaluate_model(model, val_loader, device)
    print(f"Epoch {epoch+1}/{num_epochs} - Loss:
↪        {train_loss:.4f} - Val Accuracy: {val_accuracy:.4f}")

print("Training complete. You can now use the model to predict
↪    sentiment on new texts.")
```

Key Implementation Details:

- **Data Handling**: The synthetic dataset and the
  SentimentDataset class demonstrate how to structure textual data and associated sentiment labels for use with a Transformer.

- **Tokenizer**: We use the DistilBERT tokenizer
  (DistilBertTokenizerFast) to convert text into input IDs
  and attention masks, aligning with the pre-trained model's
  vocabulary.

- **Model Architecture**: The core model,
  DistilBertForSequenceClassification, provides the Transformer backbone and a classification head for predicting sentiment.

- **Training** (train_model): We optimize the model with AdamW,
  computing cross-entropy loss from DistilBERT's outputs for
  labeled examples.

14

- **Evaluation** (`evaluate_model`): We compare predictions to ground-truth labels, calculating accuracy to gauge performance.

- **Aspect-Based and Advanced Methods**: While our example covers the basics, we can extend it with additional layers for aspect extraction, or use attention visualization techniques to understand which tokens influence the model's sentiment decisions.

Chapter 3

Question Answering with Transformers

Applications range from automated customer support to educational quiz generation. Begin by acquiring a dataset of context passages and corresponding questions, with exact spans or concise answers labeled. Use a pre-trained Transformer (e.g., BERT, RoBERTa, or ALBERT) adapted for QA by adding two output layers—one predicts the start index of the answer, the other predicts the end index. Tokenize the context passage and question together with special separators (e.g., [SEP]) so the model can focus on their relationship. Fine-tune using a span prediction loss, where the model learns to output the correct indices. To create more innovative algorithms, explore multi-passage retrieval: retrieve the most relevant text segments before applying the QA model, or incorporate cross-attention across multiple documents to address more complex questions.

Python Code Snippet

```
import torch
import torch.nn as nn
import torch.optim as optim
from torch.utils.data import Dataset, DataLoader
import random

# For reproducibility
torch.manual_seed(42)
```

```
random.seed(42)

#
↪    --------------------------------------------------------------------------
# 1) Synthetic Data Generation
#    We'll build a small dataset where each sample is:
#        - context: a string
#        - question: a string
#        - start_idx, end_idx: the span indices in the context that
↪ answer the question
#
↪    --------------------------------------------------------------------------
def generate_synthetic_qa_data(num_samples=100):
    """
    Generate a small synthetic QA dataset. Each example has:
      - context: random tokens from a limited set
      - question: a short question referencing a random word in the
      ↪   context
      - start_idx, end_idx: the indices in the context subword
      ↪   sequence that answer the question
    """
    possible_words = ["apple", "banana", "cat", "dog", "moon",
    ↪ "sun", "car", "plane"]
    contexts = []
    questions = []
    start_positions = []
    end_positions = []

    for _ in range(num_samples):
        # Random length of context from 8 to 14 tokens
        context_length = random.randint(8, 14)
        context_tokens = [random.choice(possible_words) for __ in
        ↪   range(context_length)]

        # Randomly pick one token to ask about
        answer_token_index = random.randint(0, context_length - 1)
        answer_token = context_tokens[answer_token_index]

        # Make a simple question referencing that token
        question_text = f"What is the special word? (Hint:
        ↪   {answer_token})"

        # The answer is exactly that one token
        context_str = " ".join(context_tokens)

        # For simplicity, the "start_idx" and "end_idx" each point
        ↪   to the single token
        # in subword-level, we treat each word as a single token
        contexts.append(context_str)
        questions.append(question_text)
        start_positions.append(answer_token_index)
        end_positions.append(answer_token_index)  # same index for
        ↪   single-token answer
```

17

```
        return contexts, questions, start_positions, end_positions

#
↪   --------------------------------------------------------------------------------
# 2) Simple Tokenizer
#   We define a naive tokenizer that just splits on whitespace and
↪   assigns IDs.
#
↪   --------------------------------------------------------------------------------
class SimpleTokenizer:
    """
    A basic tokenizer mapping each distinct token to an ID. Includes
    ↪   [CLS], [SEP], and [PAD].
    """
    def __init__(self, pad_token="[PAD]", cls_token="[CLS]",
    ↪   sep_token="[SEP]", unk_token="[UNK]"):
        self.pad_token = pad_token
        self.cls_token = cls_token
        self.sep_token = sep_token
        self.unk_token = unk_token

        self.token2id = {}
        self.id2token = {}

    def fit(self, texts):
        """
        Build vocabulary from a list of texts (contexts +
        ↪   questions).
        """
        unique_tokens = set()
        for txt in texts:
            for token in txt.split():
                unique_tokens.add(token)

        # Initialize with basic tokens
        self.token2id = {
            self.pad_token: 0,
            self.cls_token: 1,
            self.sep_token: 2,
            self.unk_token: 3
        }
        idx = 4
        for tok in sorted(list(unique_tokens)):
            self.token2id[tok] = idx
            idx += 1

        self.id2token = {v: k for k, v in self.token2id.items()}

    def encode_plus(self, question, context):
        """
        Encode question and context as:
        [CLS] question_tokens [SEP] context_tokens [SEP]
```

```python
        Return token IDs and also needed offsets for the model to
        ↪   locate answers.
        """
        question_tokens = question.split()
        context_tokens = context.split()

        # Convert tokens to IDs, falling back to [UNK] if not found
        def to_id(token):
            return self.token2id[token] if token in self.token2id
            ↪   else self.token2id[self.unk_token]

        input_ids = (
            [self.token2id[self.cls_token]] +
            [to_id(t) for t in question_tokens] +
            [self.token2id[self.sep_token]] +
            [to_id(t) for t in context_tokens] +
            [self.token2id[self.sep_token]]
        )

        # The position of context in the token sequence starts after
        ↪   [CLS] + question_tokens + [SEP]
        context_offset = 1 + len(question_tokens) + 1  # skip [CLS],
        ↪   question tokens, [SEP]
        return input_ids, context_offset

    def pad_batch(self, encoded_list, max_length):
        """
        Pad all input sequences to the same max_length with the
        ↪   [PAD] token ID.
        """
        padded = []
        for seq in encoded_list:
            if len(seq) < max_length:
                seq = seq + [self.token2id[self.pad_token]] *
                ↪   (max_length - len(seq))
            else:
                seq = seq[:max_length]
            padded.append(seq)
        return padded

#
↪   -------------------------------------------------------------------
# 3) QA Dataset (PyTorch)
#    Each item returns:
#        - input_ids: the token IDs for question+context
#        - start_positions, end_positions: the answer span in that
↪   sequence
#
↪   -------------------------------------------------------------------
class QADataset(Dataset):
    def __init__(self, contexts, questions, start_positions,
    ↪   end_positions, tokenizer, max_length=32):
        self.contexts = contexts
```

19

```python
        self.questions = questions
        self.start_positions = start_positions
        self.end_positions = end_positions
        self.tokenizer = tokenizer
        self.max_length = max_length

        # We'll build all encoded ID sequences up front
        self.encoded = []
        for i in range(len(self.contexts)):
            context = self.contexts[i]
            question = self.questions[i]
            start_idx = self.start_positions[i]
            end_idx = self.end_positions[i]

            input_ids, context_offset =
            ↪   self.tokenizer.encode_plus(question, context)

            # Convert the gold start/end (which refer to the context
            ↪   word indices)
            # to positions in the combined input_ids.
            # Each context word is offset by context_offset in the
            ↪   sequence.
            adj_start = context_offset + start_idx
            adj_end = context_offset + end_idx

            self.encoded.append((input_ids, adj_start, adj_end))

    def __len__(self):
        return len(self.contexts)

    def __getitem__(self, idx):
        return self.encoded[idx]

def qa_collate_fn(batch_data):
    """
    Collate function to pad sequences and gather start/end
    ↪   positions.
    """
    input_ids_list, start_list, end_list = zip(*batch_data)
    max_len = max(len(seq) for seq in input_ids_list)
    # For demonstration, let's limit to some max length
    max_len = min(max_len, 64)

    padded_input_ids = tokenizer.pad_batch(input_ids_list, max_len)

    return (
        torch.tensor(padded_input_ids, dtype=torch.long),
        torch.tensor(start_list, dtype=torch.long),
        torch.tensor(end_list, dtype=torch.long)
    )

#
↪   -------------------------------------------------------------------------------
```

```
# 4) Building a Transformer-based QA Model
#    We'll use a simple embedding + nn.TransformerEncoder + two
↪  linear heads
#    to predict start and end positions.
#
↪  --------------------------------------------------------------------
class SimpleTransformerForQA(nn.Module):
    def __init__(self, vocab_size, d_model=64, nhead=2,
    ↪  num_layers=2, dim_feedforward=128, dropout=0.1):
        super(SimpleTransformerForQA, self).__init__()
        self.embedding = nn.Embedding(vocab_size, d_model,
        ↪  padding_idx=0)

        encoder_layer = nn.TransformerEncoderLayer(
            d_model=d_model,
            nhead=nhead,
            dim_feedforward=dim_feedforward,
            dropout=dropout
        )
        self.transformer_encoder =
        ↪  nn.TransformerEncoder(encoder_layer,
        ↪  num_layers=num_layers)

        # Heads for predicting start and end index
        self.start_head = nn.Linear(d_model, 1)
        self.end_head   = nn.Linear(d_model, 1)

        self.dropout = nn.Dropout(dropout)

    def forward(self, input_ids):
        """
        input_ids: [batch_size, seq_len]
        The PyTorch transformer expects [seq_len, batch_size,
        ↪  d_model].
        We'll permute after embedding.
        """
        # [batch_size, seq_len, d_model]
        embedded = self.embedding(input_ids)
        # [seq_len, batch_size, d_model]
        embedded = embedded.permute(1, 0, 2)

        # Pass through the Transformer encoder
        encoded = self.transformer_encoder(embedded)  # [seq_len,
        ↪  batch_size, d_model]
        encoded = encoded.permute(1, 0, 2)  # back to [batch_size,
        ↪  seq_len, d_model]

        # Dropout
        encoded = self.dropout(encoded)

        # We produce a single logit per token for start and end
        ↪  classification
```

```
        start_logits = self.start_head(encoded).squeeze(-1)   #
        ↪  [batch_size, seq_len]
        end_logits   = self.end_head(encoded).squeeze(-1)      #
        ↪  [batch_size, seq_len]

        return start_logits, end_logits

#
↪  -----------------------------------------------------------------------
# 5) Training and Evaluation Routines
#
↪  -----------------------------------------------------------------------
def qa_span_prediction_loss(start_logits, end_logits,
↪  start_positions, end_positions):
    """
    Compute the cross-entropy loss for predicting start and end
    ↪  indices.
    """
    # Flatten the logits => [batch_size, seq_len]
    # Positions => [batch_size]
    loss_fn = nn.CrossEntropyLoss()
    start_loss = loss_fn(start_logits, start_positions)
    end_loss   = loss_fn(end_logits,   end_positions)
    total_loss = (start_loss + end_loss) / 2.0
    return total_loss

def train_one_epoch(model, dataloader, optimizer, device):
    model.train()
    total_loss = 0.0
    for batch_input_ids, batch_starts, batch_ends in dataloader:
        batch_input_ids = batch_input_ids.to(device)
        batch_starts = batch_starts.to(device)
        batch_ends   = batch_ends.to(device)

        optimizer.zero_grad()
        start_logits, end_logits = model(batch_input_ids)
        loss = qa_span_prediction_loss(start_logits, end_logits,
        ↪  batch_starts, batch_ends)
        loss.backward()
        optimizer.step()

        total_loss += loss.item()
    return total_loss / len(dataloader)

def evaluate(model, dataloader, device):
    """
    Returns the average loss and a rough measure of accuracy
    (whether both start and end match exactly).
    """
    model.eval()
    total_loss = 0.0
    correct_count = 0.0
    total_samples = 0.0
```

22

```python
with torch.no_grad():
    for batch_input_ids, batch_starts, batch_ends in dataloader:
        batch_input_ids = batch_input_ids.to(device)
        batch_starts = batch_starts.to(device)
        batch_ends    = batch_ends.to(device)

        start_logits, end_logits = model(batch_input_ids)
        loss = qa_span_prediction_loss(start_logits, end_logits,
        ↪   batch_starts, batch_ends)
        total_loss += loss.item()

        # Compare predicted starts/ends
        pred_starts = torch.argmax(start_logits, dim=1)
        pred_ends   = torch.argmax(end_logits,   dim=1)

        match_starts = (pred_starts ==
        ↪   batch_starts).sum().item()
        match_ends   = (pred_ends   == batch_ends).sum().item()

        # For a sample to be correct, both start and end must
        ↪   match
        # We'll treat that as a single "correct prediction"
        ↪   measure
        matches = ((pred_starts == batch_starts) & (pred_ends ==
        ↪   batch_ends)).sum().item()

        correct_count += matches
        total_samples += batch_input_ids.size(0)

avg_loss = total_loss / len(dataloader)
accuracy = correct_count / total_samples
return avg_loss, accuracy

#
↪   ----------------------------------------------------------------
# 6) Main: Putting It All Together
#
↪   ----------------------------------------------------------------
if __name__ == "__main__":
    # 1. Generate synthetic data
    contexts, questions, starts, ends =
    ↪   generate_synthetic_qa_data(num_samples=200)

    # 2. Build a tokenizer and fit on the entire text corpus (all
    ↪   contexts + questions)
    global_token_list = [c for c in contexts] + [q for q in
    ↪   questions]
    tokenizer = SimpleTokenizer()
    tokenizer.fit(global_token_list)

    # 3. Split data into train/test
    train_size = int(0.8 * len(contexts))
    train_contexts = contexts[:train_size]
```

```
train_questions = questions[:train_size]
train_starts = starts[:train_size]
train_ends = ends[:train_size]

test_contexts = contexts[train_size:]
test_questions = questions[train_size:]
test_starts = starts[train_size:]
test_ends = ends[train_size:]

# 4. Create Dataset and Dataloaders
train_dataset = QADataset(train_contexts, train_questions,
↪   train_starts, train_ends, tokenizer, max_length=32)
test_dataset = QADataset(test_contexts, test_questions,
↪   test_starts, test_ends, tokenizer, max_length=32)

train_loader = DataLoader(train_dataset, batch_size=8,
↪   shuffle=True, collate_fn=qa_collate_fn)
test_loader = DataLoader(test_dataset, batch_size=8,
↪   shuffle=False, collate_fn=qa_collate_fn)

# 5. Initialize Model, Optimizer
device = torch.device("cuda" if torch.cuda.is_available() else
↪   "cpu")
model =
↪   SimpleTransformerForQA(vocab_size=len(tokenizer.token2id)).to(device)
optimizer = optim.AdamW(model.parameters(), lr=1e-3)

# 6. Training Loop
epochs = 4
for epoch in range(epochs):
    train_loss = train_one_epoch(model, train_loader, optimizer,
    ↪   device)
    val_loss, val_acc = evaluate(model, test_loader, device)
    print(f"Epoch {epoch+1}: Train Loss = {train_loss:.4f}, Val
    ↪   Loss = {val_loss:.4f}, Val Acc = {val_acc:.4f}")

print("Training complete. Model is ready for inference.")
```

Key Implementation Details:

- **Synthetic Data Construction**: We generate a toy dataset
  where each context has a "special word" randomly placed,
  and the question references that token.

- **Tokenizer**: The SimpleTokenizer handles splitting of texts
  into tokens and assigns IDs to each distinct token. Questions
  and contexts are combined into the form [CLS] + question +
  [SEP] + context + [SEP].

24

- **Transformer Model (Question Answering):** SimpleTransformerForQA uses a Transformer encoder (nn.TransformerEncoder) to process the token embeddings and then produces start and end position logits by linear heads.

- **Span Prediction Loss:** We use a custom function qa_span_prediction_loss that calculates cross-entropy loss for both start index and end index predictions.

- **Training Loop:** train_one_epoch and evaluate illustrate an end-to-end workflow, training the transformer on labeled QA data and evaluating span accuracy (both start and end must match).

- **Putting It Together:** Inside the main block, we generate data, train the QA transformer, and validate model performance on a synthetic test set. This shows a complete pipeline for question answering with Transformers.

Chapter 4

Text Summarization with Transformers

Frequently used in news synopses, legal briefs, or meeting recaps, text summarization condenses lengthy documents into shorter, coherent paragraphs. To implement a Transformer-based summarizer, start with an encoder-decoder architecture such as BART or T5. Tokenize input documents and feed them into the encoder, which produces contextual embeddings. The decoder then generates the summary token-by-token, using a cross-attention mechanism that focuses on relevant encoder outputs. For training, employ a large corpus of document-summary pairs and use a standard seq2seq loss like cross-entropy at each predicted token. For a more innovative angle, experiment with reinforcement learning objectives that reward grammatically coherent and factually accurate summaries. Additionally, consider using contrastive training to encourage the summarizer to avoid repetitive phrases and produce more varied, human-like summaries.

Python Code Snippet

```
import random
import torch
from torch.utils.data import Dataset, DataLoader
import numpy as np
from transformers import T5Tokenizer, T5ForConditionalGeneration,
↪   Trainer, TrainingArguments
```

```python
# For reproducibility
random.seed(42)
np.random.seed(42)
torch.manual_seed(42)

# -------------------------------------------------------------
# 1) Synthetic Data Generation
# -------------------------------------------------------------
def generate_synthetic_summarization_data(num_samples=1000):
    """
    Generates synthetic pairs of (document, summary).
    Each 'document' is a random sequence of words,
    with a shorter 'summary' that is a truncated subset of that
    ↪ document.
    """
    word_bank = [
        "transformers", "summarization", "deep", "learning",
        ↪ "model",
        "efficient", "encoding", "decoder", "attention", "training",
        "reinforcement", "contrastive", "innovation", "variety",
        ↪ "analysis",
        "coherent", "condenses", "domain-specific", "data",
        ↪ "inference"
    ]
    documents = []
    summaries = []
    for _ in range(num_samples):
        doc_len = random.randint(10, 20)
        summary_len = random.randint(5, 8)
        doc_words = random.choices(word_bank, k=doc_len)
        summary_words = doc_words[:summary_len]  # naive approach
        ↪ for synthetic
        documents.append(" ".join(doc_words))
        summaries.append(" ".join(summary_words))
    return documents, summaries

# -------------------------------------------------------------
# 2) Custom Dataset
# -------------------------------------------------------------
class SummarizationDataset(Dataset):
    """
    PyTorch Dataset for text summarization.
    """
    def __init__(self, documents, summaries, tokenizer,
    ↪ max_input_length=64, max_target_length=32):
        self.documents = documents
        self.summaries = summaries
        self.tokenizer = tokenizer
        self.max_input_length = max_input_length
        self.max_target_length = max_target_length

    def __len__(self):
        return len(self.documents)
```

```python
    def __getitem__(self, idx):
        source_text = self.documents[idx]
        target_text = self.summaries[idx]
        # Tokenize input (document)
        source_encodings = self.tokenizer(
            source_text,
            truncation=True,
            padding="max_length",
            max_length=self.max_input_length
        )
        # Tokenize target (summary)
        target_encodings = self.tokenizer(
            target_text,
            truncation=True,
            padding="max_length",
            max_length=self.max_target_length
        )

        input_ids = source_encodings["input_ids"]
        attention_mask = source_encodings["attention_mask"]

        labels = target_encodings["input_ids"]
        # T5 often uses -100 for ignoring padding tokens in the loss
        labels = [
            (lbl if lbl != self.tokenizer.pad_token_id else -100)
            ↪   for lbl in labels
        ]

        return {
            "input_ids": torch.tensor(input_ids, dtype=torch.long),
            "attention_mask": torch.tensor(attention_mask,
            ↪   dtype=torch.long),
            "labels": torch.tensor(labels, dtype=torch.long),
        }

# ------------------------------------------------------------
# 3) Main Execution -- Data, Model, Training
# ------------------------------------------------------------
def main():
    # Generate synthetic dataset
    documents, summaries =
    ↪   generate_synthetic_summarization_data(num_samples=500)

    # Split data into train/test
    train_size = int(0.8 * len(documents))
    train_docs = documents[:train_size]
    test_docs = documents[train_size:]
    train_sums = summaries[:train_size]
    test_sums = summaries[train_size:]

    # Load a T5 tokenizer
    tokenizer = T5Tokenizer.from_pretrained("t5-small")
```

28

```python
# Create train/test datasets
train_dataset = SummarizationDataset(train_docs, train_sums,
↪ tokenizer)
test_dataset = SummarizationDataset(test_docs, test_sums,
↪ tokenizer)

# Load T5 base model
model = T5ForConditionalGeneration.from_pretrained("t5-small")

# Define training arguments
training_args = TrainingArguments(
    output_dir="./summarization_model",
    num_train_epochs=2,
    per_device_train_batch_size=8,
    per_device_eval_batch_size=8,
    evaluation_strategy="epoch",
    logging_dir="./logs",
    logging_steps=10,
    save_strategy="epoch",
    load_best_model_at_end=True
)

# Create Trainer instance
trainer = Trainer(
    model=model,
    args=training_args,
    train_dataset=train_dataset,
    eval_dataset=test_dataset
)

# Train the model
print("Starting Training...")
trainer.train()
print("Training Completed.")

# Evaluate the model on a small random subset
print("Sample Inference:")
sample_index = random.randint(0, len(test_docs) - 1)
test_doc = test_docs[sample_index]
test_sum = test_sums[sample_index]
print("Document:", test_doc)
print("Reference Summary:", test_sum)

# Prepare input for model
inputs = tokenizer.encode("summarize: " + test_doc,
↪ return_tensors="pt", truncation=True)
summary_ids = model.generate(inputs, max_length=40, num_beams=2,
↪ early_stopping=True)
generated_summary = tokenizer.decode(summary_ids[0],
↪ skip_special_tokens=True)
print("Generated Summary:", generated_summary)
```

```
if __name__ == "__main__":
    main()
```

Key Implementation Details:

- **Synthetic Data Generation**: A simple function
  `generate_synthetic_summarization_data` creates artificial
  document-summary pairs.

- **Custom Dataset**: The `SummarizationDataset` class tok-
  enizes inputs (documents) and targets (summaries). Labels
  are adjusted by replacing padding indices with `-100` so that
  the tokenizer's pad tokens are not counted toward the loss in
  T5.

- **Transformer Architecture**: We leverage the
  `T5ForConditionalGeneration` model, which follows an encoder-
  decoder Transformer design. T5 unifies multiple text-to-text
  tasks under a shared Transformer backbone.

- **Trainer and TrainingArguments**: The `Trainer` class man-
  ages the training loop, including backpropagation, optimization, evaluation, and checkpointing. Our script sets the number of epochs, batch sizes, and evaluation strategy.

- **Inference**: After training, we run the model's **generate**
  method on a sample test document to produce a concise summary, demonstrating how the encoder-decoder Transformer
  architecture effectively compresses lengthy text.

Chapter 5

Machine Translation with Transformers

Common applications include multilingual websites, global customer support, and international communication. Construct a Transformer-based translator by pairing large parallel corpora in a source language with a target language. Use an encoder-decoder model like the original Transformer architecture or Marian. The encoder reads source text tokens, producing context-aware embeddings, while the decoder processes the target tokens (shifted right) in tandem with cross-attention on the encoder output. Train the model on tokenized, parallel sentences, minimizing the cross-entropy loss for each predicted token. As an innovative approach, experiment with multilingual training, where a single model handles multiple language pairs by including language-specific tokens. You may also employ adapters—lightweight modules inserted into the Transformer layers—to allow efficient fine-tuning on new languages without retraining the entire model.

Python Code Snippet

```
import torch
import torch.nn as nn
import torch.optim as optim
from torch.utils.data import Dataset, DataLoader
import random

# For reproducibility
```

```
torch.manual_seed(42)
random.seed(42)

# -------------------------------------------------------------
# 1) Simple Tokenizer for Source and Target
# -------------------------------------------------------------
class SimpleTokenizer:
    '''
    A very basic tokenizer that splits words by spaces and
    limits the vocabulary to a specified size.
    '''
    def __init__(self, vocab_size=100, special_tokens=None):
        if special_tokens is None:
            special_tokens = ["[PAD]", "[UNK]", "[SOS]", "[EOS]"]
        self.vocab_size = vocab_size
        self.stoi = {}
        self.itos = {}
        self.special_tokens = special_tokens

    def fit(self, texts):
        # Count word frequencies
        freq = {}
        for t in texts:
            for w in t.split():
                freq[w] = freq.get(w, 0) + 1

        # Sort by frequency
        sorted_freq = sorted(freq.items(), key=lambda x: x[1],
        ↪  reverse=True)
        # Reserve space for special tokens
        truncated = sorted_freq[: self.vocab_size -
        ↪  len(self.special_tokens)]

        # Build stoi
        self.stoi = {}
        idx = 0
        for token in self.special_tokens:
            self.stoi[token] = idx
            idx += 1

        for word, _ in truncated:
            self.stoi[word] = idx
            idx += 1

        # Build itos
        self.itos = {v: k for k, v in self.stoi.items()}

    def encode(self, text):
        # Encode each word into an index
        tokens = text.split()
        encoded = []
        for w in tokens:
            if w in self.stoi:
```

```
                encoded.append(self.stoi[w])
            else:
                encoded.append(self.stoi["[UNK]"])
        return encoded

    def decode(self, indices):
        # Decode indices back to words
        tokens = []
        for idx in indices:
            tokens.append(self.itos.get(idx, "[UNK]"))
        return " ".join(tokens)

    def add_special_tokens(self, seq):
        # Helper to add [SOS] and [EOS] tokens around target
        ↪   sentences
        return [self.stoi["[SOS]"]] + seq + [self.stoi["[EOS]"]]

    def pad_batch(self, sequences, max_len):
        # Pad or truncate sequences to max_len
        padded = []
        for seq in sequences:
            if len(seq) < max_len:
                seq = seq + [self.stoi["[PAD]"]] * (max_len -
                ↪   len(seq))
            else:
                seq = seq[:max_len]
            padded.append(seq)
        return padded


# ----------------------------------------------------------------
# 2) Synthetic Parallel Data Generation
# ----------------------------------------------------------------
def generate_synthetic_parallel_data(num_samples=2000):
    '''
    Generate pairs of "source -> target" text for demonstration.
    Source will be pseudo-English, target will be pseudo-French.
    '''
    source_texts = []
    target_texts = []

    # Vocabulary pools
    eng_vocab = ["i", "you", "we", "like", "love", "eat", "speak",
                 "transformers", "python", "chips", "music", "and",
                 "to", "amazing", "great", "play", "football"]
    fr_vocab = ["je", "tu", "nous", "aimons", "mangeons", "parlons",
                "transformeurs", "python", "chips", "musique", "et",
                "pour", "génial", "super", "jouons", "football",
                ↪   "aimer"]

    for _ in range(num_samples):
        length = random.randint(5, 10)
```

33

```python
        eng_words = [random.choice(eng_vocab) for __ in
        ↪   range(length)]
        fr_words = [random.choice(fr_vocab) for __ in range(length)]

        source = " ".join(eng_words)
        target = " ".join(fr_words)

        source_texts.append(source)
        target_texts.append(target)

    return source_texts, target_texts


class ParallelDataset(Dataset):
    def __init__(self, src_texts, tgt_texts, src_tokenizer,
    ↪   tgt_tokenizer, max_len=15):
        self.src_texts = src_texts
        self.tgt_texts = tgt_texts
        self.src_tokenizer = src_tokenizer
        self.tgt_tokenizer = tgt_tokenizer
        self.max_len = max_len

        self.src_encoded = [src_tokenizer.encode(s) for s in
        ↪   src_texts]
        # Targets get [SOS] + tokens + [EOS]
        self.tgt_encoded =
        ↪   [tgt_tokenizer.add_special_tokens(tgt_tokenizer.encode(t))
                    for t in tgt_texts]

    def __len__(self):
        return len(self.src_texts)

    def __getitem__(self, idx):
        return self.src_encoded[idx], self.tgt_encoded[idx]


def collate_fn(batch):
    '''
    Collate function that pads source and target sequences
    to the same length in the batch.
    '''
    src_lists, tgt_lists = zip(*batch)
    max_src_len = max(len(seq) for seq in src_lists)
    max_tgt_len = max(len(seq) for seq in tgt_lists)

    max_src_len = min(max_src_len, 15)
    max_tgt_len = min(max_tgt_len, 15)

    # Pad
    padded_src = src_tokenizer.pad_batch(src_lists, max_src_len)
    padded_tgt = tgt_tokenizer.pad_batch(tgt_lists, max_tgt_len)

    src_tensor = torch.tensor(padded_src, dtype=torch.long)
```

```python
        tgt_tensor = torch.tensor(padded_tgt, dtype=torch.long)
        return src_tensor, tgt_tensor


# ----------------------------------------------------------------
# 3) Transformer Encoder-Decoder Model for Machine Translation
# ----------------------------------------------------------------
class TransformerTranslator(nn.Module):
    '''
    Basic Encoder-Decoder model using PyTorch's nn.Transformer.
    '''
    def __init__(self, src_vocab_size, tgt_vocab_size, embed_dim=64,
                 num_heads=4, ff_dim=128, num_layers=2,
                 ↪  dropout=0.1):
        super(TransformerTranslator, self).__init__()

        self.src_embedding = nn.Embedding(src_vocab_size, embed_dim,
        ↪  padding_idx=0)
        self.tgt_embedding = nn.Embedding(tgt_vocab_size, embed_dim,
        ↪  padding_idx=0)

        self.transformer = nn.Transformer(
            d_model=embed_dim,
            nhead=num_heads,
            num_encoder_layers=num_layers,
            num_decoder_layers=num_layers,
            dim_feedforward=ff_dim,
            dropout=dropout
        )

        self.output_fc = nn.Linear(embed_dim, tgt_vocab_size)
        self.embed_dim = embed_dim

    def forward(self, src, tgt):
        '''
        src: [batch_size, src_len]
        tgt: [batch_size, tgt_len], assumed to have [SOS] and [EOS]
        '''
        # Shape transformations: Transformer expects [seq_len,
        ↪  batch_size, embed_dim]
        src_embedded = self.src_embedding(src).permute(1, 0, 2)
        tgt_embedded = self.tgt_embedding(tgt).permute(1, 0, 2)

        # Generate source and target mask
        src_mask = None
        tgt_mask =
        ↪  self.make_subsequent_mask(tgt.size(1)).to(tgt.device)

        # We also provide padding masks (optional for demonstration)
        # to ensure the model doesn't attend to [PAD] tokens.
        src_key_padding_mask = (src == 0)  # True if pad
        tgt_key_padding_mask = (tgt == 0)  # True if pad
```

35

```python
    # Transformer forward pass
    outs = self.transformer(
        src_embedded,
        tgt_embedded,
        src_mask=src_mask,
        tgt_mask=tgt_mask,
        src_key_padding_mask=src_key_padding_mask,
        tgt_key_padding_mask=tgt_key_padding_mask
    )

    # outs => [tgt_len, batch_size, embed_dim]
    logits = self.output_fc(outs)  # => [tgt_len, batch_size,
    ↪  tgt_vocab_size]

    # Transpose back: [batch_size, tgt_len, tgt_vocab_size]
    return logits.permute(1, 0, 2)

def make_subsequent_mask(self, size):
    '''
    Generates a mask for the target so that position i can only
    ↪  attend to
    positions j <= i (preventing cheating in training).
    '''
    mask = torch.triu(torch.ones(size, size), diagonal=1).bool()
    return mask


# ---------------------------------------------------------------
# 4) Training and Inference
# ---------------------------------------------------------------
def train_model(model, dataloader, optimizer, criterion, device):
    model.train()
    total_loss = 0.0
    for src_batch, tgt_batch in dataloader:
        src_batch, tgt_batch = src_batch.to(device),
        ↪  tgt_batch.to(device)

        # Prepare inputs for next-token prediction
        # The model input is everything except the last token in
        ↪  target
        # The label is everything except the first token in target
        tgt_input = tgt_batch[:, :-1]
        tgt_labels = tgt_batch[:, 1:]

        optimizer.zero_grad()
        logits = model(src_batch, tgt_input)

        # Flatten to compute cross entropy
        logits_reshaped = logits.reshape(-1, logits.size(-1))
        tgt_labels_reshaped = tgt_labels.reshape(-1)

        loss = criterion(logits_reshaped, tgt_labels_reshaped)
        loss.backward()
```

36

```
        optimizer.step()

        total_loss += loss.item()
    return total_loss / len(dataloader)

def evaluate_model(model, dataloader, criterion, device):
    model.eval()
    total_loss = 0.0
    with torch.no_grad():
        for src_batch, tgt_batch in dataloader:
            src_batch, tgt_batch = src_batch.to(device),
            ↪   tgt_batch.to(device)
            tgt_input  = tgt_batch[:, :-1]
            tgt_labels = tgt_batch[:, 1:]

            logits = model(src_batch, tgt_input)

            logits_reshaped = logits.reshape(-1, logits.size(-1))
            tgt_labels_reshaped = tgt_labels.reshape(-1)

            loss = criterion(logits_reshaped, tgt_labels_reshaped)
            total_loss += loss.item()
    return total_loss / len(dataloader)

def translate_sentence(model, src_sentence, src_tokenizer,
↪   tgt_tokenizer, device, max_len=15):
    '''
    Greedy decoding of a single source sentence.
    '''
    model.eval()
    with torch.no_grad():
        src_encoded = src_tokenizer.encode(src_sentence)
        src_tensor = torch.tensor([src_encoded],
        ↪   dtype=torch.long).to(device)

        # Start with [SOS]
        sos_idx = tgt_tokenizer.stoi["[SOS]"]
        eos_idx = tgt_tokenizer.stoi["[EOS]"]

        tgt_indices = [sos_idx]

        for _ in range(max_len):
            tgt_tensor = torch.tensor([tgt_indices],
            ↪   dtype=torch.long).to(device)
            output = model(src_tensor, tgt_tensor)
            # output shape => [batch_size, tgt_len, vocab_size]
            next_token_logits = output[0, -1, :]  # Last step of
            ↪   sequence
            next_token_id = torch.argmax(next_token_logits).item()

            tgt_indices.append(next_token_id)
            if next_token_id == eos_idx:
                break
```

```python
        # Remove the initial [SOS]
        decoded_tokens = tgt_tokenizer.decode(tgt_indices[1:])
        return decoded_tokens

# -----------------------------------------------------------------
# 5) Main Execution (Data Prep, Model Init, Training)
# -----------------------------------------------------------------
if __name__ == "__main__":
    # 1) Generate synthetic parallel dataset
    src_texts, tgt_texts =
    ↪   generate_synthetic_parallel_data(num_samples=3000)

    # 2) Fit tokenizers
    src_tokenizer = SimpleTokenizer(vocab_size=120)  # Slightly
    ↪   bigger vocab
    src_tokenizer.fit(src_texts)
    tgt_tokenizer = SimpleTokenizer(vocab_size=120)
    tgt_tokenizer.fit(tgt_texts)

    # 3) Split data
    train_size = int(0.8 * len(src_texts))
    train_src, valid_src = src_texts[:train_size],
    ↪   src_texts[train_size:]
    train_tgt, valid_tgt = tgt_texts[:train_size],
    ↪   tgt_texts[train_size:]

    # 4) Create datasets
    train_dataset = ParallelDataset(train_src, train_tgt,
    ↪   src_tokenizer, tgt_tokenizer)
    valid_dataset = ParallelDataset(valid_src, valid_tgt,
    ↪   src_tokenizer, tgt_tokenizer)

    # 5) Create dataloaders
    train_loader = DataLoader(train_dataset, batch_size=32,
    ↪   shuffle=True,
                              collate_fn=collate_fn)
    valid_loader = DataLoader(valid_dataset, batch_size=32,
    ↪   shuffle=False,
                              collate_fn=collate_fn)

    # 6) Initialize model
    device = torch.device("cuda" if torch.cuda.is_available() else
    ↪   "cpu")
    model = TransformerTranslator(
        src_vocab_size=len(src_tokenizer.stoi),
        tgt_vocab_size=len(tgt_tokenizer.stoi),
        embed_dim=64,
        num_heads=4,
        ff_dim=128,
        num_layers=2,
        dropout=0.1
    ).to(device)
```

38

```
# 7) Define loss, optimizer
criterion =
 ↪  nn.CrossEntropyLoss(ignore_index=src_tokenizer.stoi["[PAD]"])
optimizer = optim.AdamW(model.parameters(), lr=1e-3)

# 8) Training loop
num_epochs = 5
for epoch in range(num_epochs):
    train_loss = train_model(model, train_loader, optimizer,
 ↪      criterion, device)
    valid_loss = evaluate_model(model, valid_loader, criterion,
 ↪      device)

    print(f"Epoch {epoch+1}/{num_epochs}: Train
 ↪      Loss={train_loss:.4f}, "
          f"Val Loss={valid_loss:.4f}")

# 9) Test translation
test_sentences = [
    "i love transformers",
    "you play music",
    "we speak python and football"
]

print("\nSample translations:")
for s in test_sentences:
    translation = translate_sentence(model, s, src_tokenizer,
 ↪      tgt_tokenizer, device)
    print(f"Source: {s} -> Translation: {translation}")
```

Key Implementation Details:

- **Tokenizer**: The class `SimpleTokenizer` collects the most
  frequent tokens and uses special tokens for padding, start of
  sequence (`[SOS]`), and end of sequence (`[EOS]`). This ensures
  our synthetic parallel dataset can be encoded/decoded reli-
  ably.

- **Transformer Model**: The core architecture is
  `TransformerTranslator`, which uses PyTorch's built-in
  `nn.Transformer` to handle the encoder and decoder. The
  model is split into source and target embeddings, and a linear head (`output_fc`) to map the decoder's hidden states to
  vocabulary logits for the next-token prediction.

- **Encoder-Decoder Forward Pass**: The encoder reads the
  source embeddings; the decoder processes shifted target to-

39

kens and performs multi-head attention over the encoder output. A subsequent-mask ensures that the model never peeks at future tokens.

- **Teacher Forcing**: During training, we feed the target sequence offset by one position (`tgt_input` vs. `tgt_labels`) to train the network to predict the next token.

- **Greedy Decoding**: `translate_sentence` illustrates a simple greedy decoding approach. The next token is chosen by taking the `argmax` over output logits at each step, until [EOS] is encountered or a maximum length is reached.

- **End-to-End Pipeline**: The `if __name__ == "__main__"` block demonstrates data generation, tokenizer creation, dataset splitting, model training, and inference on sample sentences. This shows a complete workflow for building and evaluating a Transformer-based machine translation system.

Chapter 6

Named Entity Recognition (NER) with Transformers

Used for extracting entities like people, locations, or organizations from text, NER is essential in information extraction and content categorization. To build a Transformer-based NER model, gather a token-labeled dataset (e.g., CoNLL format) and tokenize the text using a subword tokenizer. Represent each subword with the Transformer embeddings (e.g., from BERT) and attach a token classification head that computes a probability distribution over entity classes (or the 'O' class for non-entities). During training, apply a sequence labeling loss (often cross-entropy) for each token position. Innovatively, you might combine attention-based entity linking, which maps recognized entities to knowledge bases, or incorporate domain-specific pre-training for specialized fields like biomedical NER. You can also explore conditional random fields (CRFs) on top of Transformer outputs to maintain label consistency.

Python Code Snippet

```
import torch
import torch.nn as nn
import torch.optim as optim
from torch.utils.data import Dataset, DataLoader
import numpy as np
```

41

```
import random
from transformers import BertTokenizerFast,
 ↪  BertForTokenClassification

# For reproducibility
torch.manual_seed(42)
random.seed(42)
np.random.seed(42)


# ------------------------------------------------------------
# 1) Define a Small Synthetic NER Dataset
# ------------------------------------------------------------
# Suppose we have a few simple sentences with labeled entities.
# This is purely demonstrative; real NER tasks use larger datasets.

SENTENCES = [
    ["John", "lives", "in", "Paris", "."],
    ["Maria", "is", "from", "Germany", "."],
    ["Alice", "and", "Bob", "visited", "London", "."],
    ["The", "President", "of", "USA", "spoke", "today", "."],
    ["Microsoft", "was", "founded", "by", "Bill", "Gates", "."]
]

# Labels correspond to each token. We'll mark:
#  - B-PER for beginning of person name
#  - I-PER for continuation of person name
#  - B-LOC for beginning of location
#  - B-ORG for beginning of organization
#  - O for tokens that are not entities
LABELS = [
    ["B-PER", "O", "O", "B-LOC", "O"],
    ["B-PER", "O", "O", "B-LOC", "O"],
    ["B-PER", "O", "B-PER", "O", "B-LOC", "O"],
    ["O", "O", "O", "B-LOC", "O", "O", "O"],
    ["B-ORG", "O", "O", "O", "B-PER", "I-PER", "O"]
]


# ------------------------------------------------------------
# 2) Label-to-ID Mapping
# ------------------------------------------------------------
label_to_id = {
    "O": 0,
    "B-PER": 1,
    "I-PER": 2,
    "B-LOC": 3,
    "B-ORG": 4
}
id_to_label = {v: k for k, v in label_to_id.items()}


# ------------------------------------------------------------
# 3) Tokenizer Initialization (BERT)
# ------------------------------------------------------------
tokenizer = BertTokenizerFast.from_pretrained("bert-base-uncased")
```

```python
# ---------------------------------------------------------------
# 4) Prepare a Custom PyTorch Dataset
# ---------------------------------------------------------------
class NERDataset(Dataset):
    """
    A simple dataset that encodes tokens using a pre-trained BERT
    ↪  tokenizer.
    For each token, we assign the corresponding label ID.

    During tokenization, subword tokens will be generated. We only
    ↪  mark
    the first subword of a token with the entity label, while
    ↪  subsequent
    subwords get a special label like -100 for ignoring in loss
    ↪  computation.
    """
    def __init__(self, sentences, labels, tokenizer, label_to_id,
    ↪  max_len=32):
        self.sentences = sentences
        self.labels = labels
        self.tokenizer = tokenizer
        self.label_to_id = label_to_id
        self.max_len = max_len

        self.encodings = []
        self.encoding_labels = []
        self._prepare_data()

    def _prepare_data(self):
        for words, ner_tags in zip(self.sentences, self.labels):
            # Tokenize words, keeping track of how tokens align with
            ↪  original words.
            tokenized = self.tokenizer(words,
                                       is_split_into_words=True,
                                       truncation=True,
                                       padding='max_length',
                                       max_length=self.max_len,
                                       return_offsets_mapping=True)

            offset_mapping = tokenized.pop("offset_mapping")
            # We will build label IDs for each subword
            subword_labels = np.ones(len(tokenized["input_ids"]),
            ↪  dtype=int) * -100

            word_ids = tokenized.word_ids()  # Map each subword to
            ↪  its original word index

            previous_word_idx = None
            for i, word_idx in enumerate(word_ids):
                if word_idx is None:
                    continue
                # Only label the first subword of each word
```

43

```python
            if word_idx != previous_word_idx:
                subword_labels[i] =
                ↪    self.label_to_id[ner_tags[word_idx]]
            previous_word_idx = word_idx

        self.encodings.append(tokenized)
        self.encoding_labels.append(subword_labels)

    def __len__(self):
        return len(self.encodings)

    def __getitem__(self, idx):
        item = {k: torch.tensor(v[idx]) for k, v in
        ↪    self._batchify().items() if k != "labels"}
        labels = torch.tensor(self.encoding_labels[idx])
        return item, labels

    def _batchify(self):
        """
        Gather all fields from self.encodings into a dictionary of
        ↪    lists,
        so PyTorch's DataLoader can batch them properly.
        """
        collated = {}
        for key in self.encodings[0].keys():
            collated[key] = [enc[key] for enc in self.encodings]
        # Convert each to stacked arrays
        for key in collated.keys():
            collated[key] = np.stack(collated[key], axis=0)
        return collated

# Build dataset
dataset = NERDataset(SENTENCES, LABELS, tokenizer, label_to_id,
↪    max_len=16)

# -------------------------------------------------------------
# 5) DataLoader
# -------------------------------------------------------------
# In this small example, we won't split into train/test for brevity.
# Typically, you'd split your dataset accordingly.
dataloader = DataLoader(dataset, batch_size=2, shuffle=True)

# -------------------------------------------------------------
# 6) Define the Transformer Model for Token Classification
# -------------------------------------------------------------
# We use BertForTokenClassification from Hugging Face, which has
# a classification head on top of BERT for token-level labels.
model = BertForTokenClassification.from_pretrained(
    "bert-base-uncased",
    num_labels=len(label_to_id)
)

# -------------------------------------------------------------
```

```python
# 7) Training Setup
# ---------------------------------------------------------------
device = torch.device("cuda" if torch.cuda.is_available() else
↪  "cpu")
model.to(device)
optimizer = optim.AdamW(model.parameters(), lr=5e-5)
epochs = 3


# ---------------------------------------------------------------
# 8) Training Loop
# ---------------------------------------------------------------
model.train()
for epoch in range(epochs):
    total_loss = 0.0
    for batch_idx, (inputs, labels) in enumerate(dataloader):
        # Move data to device
        inputs = {k: v.to(device) for k, v in inputs.items()}
        labels = labels.to(device)

        # Forward pass
        outputs = model(**inputs, labels=labels)
        loss = outputs.loss

        # Backward pass
        optimizer.zero_grad()
        loss.backward()
        optimizer.step()

        total_loss += loss.item()

    avg_loss = total_loss / len(dataloader)
    print(f"Epoch {epoch+1}/{epochs}, Loss: {avg_loss:.4f}")

# ---------------------------------------------------------------
# 9) Evaluation (Inference) - Demonstration
# ---------------------------------------------------------------
model.eval()

def predict_ner(sentence):
    """
    Given a raw sentence (list of tokens), predict NER labels using
    ↪  the trained model.
    """
    inputs = tokenizer(sentence, is_split_into_words=True,
    ↪  return_tensors="pt", truncation=True)
    inputs = {k: v.to(device) for k, v in inputs.items()}
    with torch.no_grad():
        outputs = model(**inputs)
    logits = outputs.logits  # [batch_size, seq_len, num_labels]
    predictions = torch.argmax(logits, dim=2).cpu().numpy()[0]  #
    ↪  shape: (seq_len,)
    # Convert IDs back to labels, ignoring special tokens (CLS, SEP)
```

45

```
tokens =
↪ tokenizer.convert_ids_to_tokens(inputs["input_ids"][0].cpu().numpy())
final_preds = []
for tk, pred_id in zip(tokens, predictions):
    if tk not in ["[CLS]", "[SEP]", "[PAD]"]:
        final_preds.append((tk, id_to_label[pred_id]))
return final_preds

# Test the inference on a new sentence
test_sentence = ["Bob", "works", "at", "Google", "in", "California",
↪ "."]
predictions = predict_ner(test_sentence)
print("Sentence:", test_sentence)
print("Predictions:", predictions)

print("Done. Model trained and sample inference complete.")
```

Key Implementation Details:

- **Subword Tokenization**: A pre-trained tokenizer
  (BertTokenizerFast) divides text into subwords, ensuring
  that entity labels are properly aligned with the first subword
  of each token.

- **Transformer Architecture**: The backbone
  (BertForTokenClassification) leverages BERT's multi-head
  self-attention. A token classification head computes a label
  distribution for each subword.

- **Sequence Labeling Loss**: By passing the labels to the
  model via labels=labels in the forward call, the standard
  cross-entropy for token classification is applied internally, ignoring subword positions marked with -100.

- **Explicit Label Alignment**: We track the original token-
  to-subword alignment so only the first subword inherits the
  entity tag, while subsequent subwords are marked -100 (ig-
  nored in loss).

- **Training and Optimization**: We employ the AdamW optimizer, iterating through a few epochs on a small synthetic
  dataset. In a real scenario, you'd train on a labeled corpus
  like CoNLL.

- **Inference Pipeline**: The predict_ner function demonstrates how to tokenize a new sentence, run it through the

46

model, decode label IDs, and recover predictions for each subword token.

Chapter 7

Dialogue Systems with Transformers

Used in chatbots and virtual assistants, dialogue systems rely on context-driven replies to user queries. Construct a Transformer-based dialogue system by pairing user queries and system responses in a supervised setting, or by using large conversational datasets (e.g., Reddit, customer support transcripts). An encoder-decoder model can effectively track conversational context, generating responses token-by-token. For multi-turn dialogues, you can concatenate the last N turns or maintain a context window, letting the model attend to previous user and system utterances. Advanced setups include blending retrieval with generation: retrieve candidate answers from a knowledge base, then condition the Transformer decoder on these candidates to produce a more accurate or contextual response. You can further refine the system by injecting persona or speaker embeddings to maintain consistent style or tone.

Python Code Snippet

```
import torch
import torch.nn as nn
import torch.optim as optim
from torch.utils.data import Dataset, DataLoader
import random

# For reproducibility
torch.manual_seed(42)
```

```python
random.seed(42)

# ---------------------------------------------------------------
# 1) Synthetic Data Generation & A Simple Tokenizer
# ---------------------------------------------------------------

class SimpleTokenizer:
    """
    A bare-bones tokenizer implemented for demonstration purposes.
    It splits on whitespace, collects top tokens for a limited
    ↪  vocab,
    and treats unknown words as [UNK].
    """
    def __init__(self, vocab_size=50):
        self.vocab_size = vocab_size
        self.token2id = {}
        self.id2token = {}

    def fit(self, text_pairs):
        """
        text_pairs: list of tuples (user_utterance, system_response)
        We collect unique tokens from both sides of the
        ↪  conversation.
        """
        all_tokens = {}
        for (user_text, system_text) in text_pairs:
            for token in user_text.split():
                all_tokens[token] = all_tokens.get(token, 0) + 1
            for token in system_text.split():
                all_tokens[token] = all_tokens.get(token, 0) + 1

        # Sort by frequency and keep top (vocab_size - special
        ↪  tokens)
        sorted_tokens = sorted(all_tokens.items(), key=lambda x:
        ↪  x[1], reverse=True)
        truncated = sorted_tokens[: self.vocab_size - 4]  # Reserve
        ↪  special tokens

        # Build token2id (with special tokens)
        self.token2id = {
            "[UNK]": 0,
            "[PAD]": 1,
            "[SOS]": 2,
            "[EOS]": 3,
        }
        idx = 4
        for token, _ in truncated:
            self.token2id[token] = idx
            idx += 1

        self.id2token = {v: k for k, v in self.token2id.items()}

    def encode(self, text, add_special_tokens=False):
```

49

```
        """
        Converts text to a list of token IDs. Optionally add [SOS]
        ↪   and [EOS].
        """
        tokens = text.split()
        encoded = []
        for t in tokens:
            if t in self.token2id:
                encoded.append(self.token2id[t])
            else:
                encoded.append(self.token2id["[UNK]"])
        if add_special_tokens:
            encoded = [self.token2id["[SOS]"]] + encoded +
            ↪   [self.token2id["[EOS]"]]
        return encoded

    def decode(self, token_ids):
        """
        Converts a list of token IDs back into a string
        ↪   (best-effort).
        """
        tokens = [self.id2token.get(i, "[UNK]") for i in token_ids]
        return " ".join(tokens)

    def pad_batch(self, batch, max_len):
        """
        Pads sequences to a fixed max_len using [PAD] token ID.
        """
        result = []
        for seq in batch:
            if len(seq) < max_len:
                seq = seq + [self.token2id["[PAD]"]] * (max_len -
                ↪   len(seq))
            else:
                seq = seq[:max_len]
            result.append(seq)
        return result

def generate_synthetic_conversations(num_samples=1000):
    """
    Generate random user -> system text pairs to mimic a basic
    ↪   conversation.
    User queries are short, system responses are slightly longer.
    """
    user_prompts = [
        "hello", "hi", "can you help me", "what time is it",
        "thanks very much", "tell me a joke", "goodbye"
    ]
    system_responses = [
        "hi how can i help you",
        "hello nice to meet you",
        "sure what do you need",
        "the time is irrelevant",
```

50

```
            "my pleasure",
            "here is a funny one",
            "goodbye see you soon"
        ]

        pairs = []
        for _ in range(num_samples):
            user_text = random.choice(user_prompts)
            system_text = random.choice(system_responses)
            pairs.append((user_text, system_text))
        return pairs

# ----------------------------------------------------------------
# 2) PyTorch Dataset and DataLoader
# ----------------------------------------------------------------

class DialogueDataset(Dataset):
    """
    Holds user -> system text pairs for training a Transformer-based
    ↪ dialogue system.
    """
    def __init__(self, text_pairs, tokenizer, max_len=20):
        self.text_pairs = text_pairs
        self.tokenizer = tokenizer
        self.max_len = max_len

    def __len__(self):
        return len(self.text_pairs)

    def __getitem__(self, idx):
        user_text, system_text = self.text_pairs[idx]
        # Encoder input doesn't need [SOS]/[EOS]; decoder input
        ↪ requires them
        enc_input = self.tokenizer.encode(user_text,
        ↪ add_special_tokens=False)
        dec_input = self.tokenizer.encode(system_text,
        ↪ add_special_tokens=True)
        # We also create a shifted version for the "teacher forcing"
        ↪ target
        # to align predictions with subsequent tokens
        target = dec_input[1:]  # everything after [SOS]
        return enc_input, dec_input[:-1], target  # dec_input
        ↪ excludes the last for alignment

def collate_fn_dialogue(batch):
    """
    Collates a batch of (enc_input, dec_input, target) while padding
    ↪ to uniform lengths.
    """
    enc_inputs, dec_inputs, targets = zip(*batch)

    # Find maximum lengths
    max_enc_len = max(len(seq) for seq in enc_inputs)
```

```
        max_dec_len = max(len(seq) for seq in dec_inputs)
        max_tgt_len = max(len(seq) for seq in targets)

        # For demonstration, limit max length. Real usage might let it
        ↪  grow or set to a known limit.
        max_enc_len = min(max_enc_len, 30)
        max_dec_len = min(max_dec_len, 30)
        max_tgt_len = min(max_tgt_len, 30)

        # Pad
        enc_padded = tokenizer.pad_batch(enc_inputs, max_enc_len)
        dec_padded = tokenizer.pad_batch(dec_inputs, max_dec_len)
        tgt_padded = tokenizer.pad_batch(targets, max_tgt_len)

        enc_tensor = torch.tensor(enc_padded, dtype=torch.long)
        dec_tensor = torch.tensor(dec_padded, dtype=torch.long)
        tgt_tensor = torch.tensor(tgt_padded, dtype=torch.long)

        return enc_tensor, dec_tensor, tgt_tensor

# -----------------------------------------------------------------
# 3) Building a Seq2Seq Transformer
# -----------------------------------------------------------------

class TransformerSeq2Seq(nn.Module):
    """
    A simple Seq2Seq Transformer with separate Encoder and Decoder
    ↪  stacks.
    """
    def __init__(
        self,
        vocab_size,
        d_model=32,
        nhead=2,
        num_encoder_layers=2,
        num_decoder_layers=2,
        dim_feedforward=64,
        dropout=0.1,
        pad_idx=1
    ):
        super(TransformerSeq2Seq, self).__init__()
        self.d_model = d_model
        self.pad_idx = pad_idx

        # Embeddings
        self.embedding_enc = nn.Embedding(vocab_size, d_model,
        ↪  padding_idx=pad_idx)
        self.embedding_dec = nn.Embedding(vocab_size, d_model,
        ↪  padding_idx=pad_idx)

        # Positional encodings can be added here if desired.

        # Encoder and Decoder
```

```python
        self.transformer = nn.Transformer(
            d_model=d_model,
            nhead=nhead,
            num_encoder_layers=num_encoder_layers,
            num_decoder_layers=num_decoder_layers,
            dim_feedforward=dim_feedforward,
            dropout=dropout
        )

        # Final linear layer maps decoder output to vocabulary
        self.fc_out = nn.Linear(d_model, vocab_size)

    def forward(self, enc_input, dec_input):
        """
        enc_input: [batch_size, enc_seq_len]
        dec_input: [batch_size, dec_seq_len]
        Returns: logits of shape [batch_size, dec_seq_len,
        ↪  vocab_size]
        """
        # Create masks
        enc_mask = self.make_src_mask(enc_input)
        dec_mask = self.make_tgt_mask(dec_input)
        # Transformer internally also might use cross-attention mask
        ↪  if needed,
        # but if we want to handle that, we can pass it as well.

        # Embed
        enc_embed = self.embedding_enc(enc_input)   # [bs,
        ↪  enc_seq_len, d_model]
        dec_embed = self.embedding_dec(dec_input)   # [bs,
        ↪  dec_seq_len, d_model]

        # Transformer requires shape [seq_len, batch_size, d_model]
        enc_embed = enc_embed.permute(1, 0, 2)
        dec_embed = dec_embed.permute(1, 0, 2)

        # Forward pass through Transformer
        outs = self.transformer(
            src=enc_embed,
            tgt=dec_embed,
            src_key_padding_mask=enc_mask,
            tgt_key_padding_mask=dec_mask
        )

        # outs => [dec_seq_len, bs, d_model]
        outs = outs.permute(1, 0, 2)  # => [bs, dec_seq_len,
        ↪  d_model]

        logits = self.fc_out(outs)     # => [bs, dec_seq_len,
        ↪  vocab_size]
        return logits

    def make_src_mask(self, src):
```

```
    """
    Mask out padding tokens in the source.
    src: [batch_size, src_seq_len]
    Return: mask shaped [batch_size, src_seq_len], with True for
    ↪  PAD
    """
    return (src == self.pad_idx)

def make_tgt_mask(self, tgt):
    """
    Mask out padding tokens in the target.
    tgt: [batch_size, tgt_seq_len]
    Return: mask shaped [batch_size, tgt_seq_len]
    """
    return (tgt == self.pad_idx)


# ------------------------------------------------------------
# 4) Training and Inference
# ------------------------------------------------------------

def train_one_epoch(model, dataloader, optimizer, criterion,
↪  device):
    model.train()
    total_loss = 0
    for enc_inp, dec_inp, tgt in dataloader:
        enc_inp, dec_inp, tgt = enc_inp.to(device),
        ↪  dec_inp.to(device), tgt.to(device)

        optimizer.zero_grad()
        logits = model(enc_inp, dec_inp)
        # We need logits of shape [bs, dec_seq_len, vocab_size]
        # and targets of shape [bs, dec_seq_len]
        # We'll flatten them for cross-entropy
        loss = criterion(logits.view(-1, logits.size(-1)),
        ↪  tgt.view(-1))
        loss.backward()
        optimizer.step()

        total_loss += loss.item()
    return total_loss / len(dataloader)

def evaluate(model, dataloader, criterion, device):
    model.eval()
    total_loss = 0
    with torch.no_grad():
        for enc_inp, dec_inp, tgt in dataloader:
            enc_inp, dec_inp, tgt = enc_inp.to(device),
            ↪  dec_inp.to(device), tgt.to(device)
            logits = model(enc_inp, dec_inp)
            loss = criterion(logits.view(-1, logits.size(-1)),
            ↪  tgt.view(-1))
            total_loss += loss.item()
    return total_loss / len(dataloader)
```

```python
def greedy_decode(model, enc_input, max_len=15, start_token=2,
↪   end_token=3, device="cpu"):
    """
    A simple greedy decoding function to generate responses.
    enc_input: [1, enc_seq_len] - single example (batch=1)
    """
    model.eval()
    # Start with <SOS> token in the decoder
    dec_input = torch.tensor([[start_token]], dtype=torch.long,
↪       device=device)

    for _ in range(max_len):
        logits = model(enc_input, dec_input)
        # Look at the last token's distribution
        next_token_logits = logits[:, -1, :]   # shape [1,
↪           vocab_size]
        next_token = torch.argmax(next_token_logits, dim=-1)

        if next_token.item() == end_token:
            break
        # Append token to dec_input
        dec_input = torch.cat([dec_input, next_token.unsqueeze(0)],
↪           dim=1)

    return dec_input.squeeze(0).tolist()

# -------------------------------------------------------------
# 5) Main Script
# -------------------------------------------------------------

if __name__ == "__main__":
    # 1) Generate synthetic conversation pairs
    pairs = generate_synthetic_conversations(num_samples=2000)

    # 2) Initialize and fit tokenizer
    tokenizer = SimpleTokenizer(vocab_size=100)
    tokenizer.fit(pairs)

    # 3) Split into train/test
    split_idx = int(len(pairs) * 0.8)
    train_pairs = pairs[:split_idx]
    test_pairs  = pairs[split_idx:]

    # 4) Create Datasets and DataLoaders
    train_dataset = DialogueDataset(train_pairs, tokenizer,
↪       max_len=20)
    test_dataset  = DialogueDataset(test_pairs, tokenizer,
↪       max_len=20)

    train_loader = DataLoader(train_dataset, batch_size=32,
↪       shuffle=True, collate_fn=collate_fn_dialogue)
```

```
test_loader  = DataLoader(test_dataset, batch_size=32,
↪  shuffle=False, collate_fn=collate_fn_dialogue)

# 5) Construct model
device = torch.device("cuda" if torch.cuda.is_available() else
↪  "cpu")
model = TransformerSeq2Seq(vocab_size=len(tokenizer.token2id),
↪  d_model=64, nhead=2,
                            num_encoder_layers=2,
                            ↪  num_decoder_layers=2,
                            ↪  dim_feedforward=128,
                            dropout=0.1,
                            ↪  pad_idx=tokenizer.token2id["[PAD]"])
model.to(device)

# 6) Set up optimizer and loss function
optimizer = optim.AdamW(model.parameters(), lr=1e-3)
criterion =
↪  nn.CrossEntropyLoss(ignore_index=tokenizer.token2id["[PAD]"])

# 7) Training loop
num_epochs = 5
for epoch in range(num_epochs):
    train_loss = train_one_epoch(model, train_loader, optimizer,
    ↪  criterion, device)
    val_loss = evaluate(model, test_loader, criterion, device)
    print(f"Epoch {epoch+1}/{num_epochs}, Train Loss:
    ↪  {train_loss:.4f}, Val Loss: {val_loss:.4f}")

# 8) Demonstration of Greedy Inference
example_user_inputs = ["hello", "tell me a joke", "what time is
↪  it"]
for user_text in example_user_inputs:
    # encode user input
    enc_input = tokenizer.encode(user_text,
    ↪  add_special_tokens=False)
    enc_input = torch.tensor([enc_input], dtype=torch.long,
    ↪  device=device)
    generated_ids = greedy_decode(model, enc_input,
    ↪  device=device)
    # decode
    response_text = tokenizer.decode(generated_ids)
    print(f"User: {user_text}\nSystem: {response_text}\n")
```

Key Implementation Details:

- **Data Preparation**: We create synthetic user-system text pairs and tokenize them with SimpleTokenizer.

- **Seq2Seq Transformer Architecture**: Our TransformerSeq2Seq model includes separate embedding layers for encoder and decoder, feeding into PyTorch's built-in Transformer modules.

- **Masking and Padding**: Functions `make_src_mask` and `make_tgt_mask` generate binary masks to ignore padded tokens.

- **Training Loop**: The `train_one_epoch` function performs teacher forcing by aligning decoder logits with shifted target tokens. We use `CrossEntropyLoss` to compute the loss.

- **Generation**: The `greedy_decode` function exemplifies a basic inference approach that uses the model's output to select tokens step by step, stopping at an end token.

- **Pipeline Flow**: We demonstrate the entire process from data generation to final system responses, showing how a Transformer-based dialogue system can be trained and used to produce conversational replies.

Chapter 8

Vision Transformers for Image Classification

Prevalent in image recognition tasks such as classifying product images, medical scans, or wildlife photos, Vision Transformers (ViT) treat images as sequences of patches. To implement ViT, first split the image into fixed-size patches (e.g., 16×16 pixels) and flatten each patch into a 1D vector. Then embed these patch vectors with linear projections and position embeddings. Feed the resulting sequence into a Transformer encoder, which applies multi-head self-attention and feedforward layers. Finally, use a classification head on the [CLS] token (or global average) for label prediction. Innovatively, you can introduce hierarchical variants (Swin Transformer) that process patches at multiple scales or incorporate convolution-like local attention blocks. For training, large-scale labeled image datasets are often used, with transfer learning helpful for specialized domains.

Python Code Snippet

```python
import torch
import torch.nn as nn
import torch.optim as optim
import torchvision.transforms as T
import random

from torch.utils.data import Dataset, DataLoader
```

```python
# For reproducibility
torch.manual_seed(42)
random.seed(42)


# ------------------------------------------------------------
# 1) Synthetic Data Generation
# ------------------------------------------------------------
class SyntheticImageDataset(Dataset):
    """
    Generate synthetic images (random noise) and assign random
    ↪ labels.
    Each image is channel-first, e.g., shape [3, H, W].
    """
    def __init__(self, num_samples=1000, image_size=64,
    ↪ num_classes=10):
        super().__init__()
        self.num_samples = num_samples
        self.image_size = image_size
        self.num_classes = num_classes
        self.data = torch.rand(num_samples, 3, image_size,
        ↪ image_size)
        self.labels = torch.randint(0, num_classes, (num_samples,))

        self.transform = T.Compose([
            T.Normalize(mean=[0.5, 0.5, 0.5],
                        std=[0.5, 0.5, 0.5])
        ])

    def __len__(self):
        return self.num_samples

    def __getitem__(self, idx):
        img = self.data[idx]
        label = self.labels[idx]
        # Apply normalization
        img = self.transform(img)
        return img, label


# ------------------------------------------------------------
# 2) Patch Embedding and Positional Encoding
# ------------------------------------------------------------
class PatchEmbedding(nn.Module):
    """
    Splits each image into patches, flattens them, and applies a
    ↪ linear projection.
    """
    def __init__(self, in_channels=3, patch_size=16, emb_size=256,
    ↪ img_size=64):
        super().__init__()
        self.patch_size = patch_size
        self.num_patches = (img_size // patch_size) * (img_size //
        ↪ patch_size)
        self.emb_size = emb_size
```

59

```
        # Flattened patch dimension = in_channels * patch_size *
        ↪    patch_size
        self.linear = nn.Linear(in_channels * patch_size *
        ↪    patch_size, emb_size)

    def forward(self, x):
        # x shape: [batch_size, in_channels, H, W]
        B, C, H, W = x.shape
        # Reshape into patches: patch_size x patch_size
        # => [B, (H/patch_size)*(W/patch_size),
        ↪    C*patch_size*patch_size]
        patches = x.unfold(2, self.patch_size, self.patch_size) \
                   .unfold(3, self.patch_size, self.patch_size)
        # patches shape: [B, C, num_patches_height,
        ↪    num_patches_width, patch_size, patch_size]
        patches = patches.contiguous().view(B, C, -1,
        ↪    self.patch_size, self.patch_size)
        patches = patches.permute(0, 2, 1, 3, 4)   # [B, #patches, C,
        ↪    pH, pW]
        patches = patches.flatten(2)               # flatten C, pH,
        ↪    pW => [B, #patches, C*pH*pW]

        # Linear projection
        embedded_patches = self.linear(patches)   # [B, num_patches,
        ↪    emb_size]
        return embedded_patches


class PositionalEncoding(nn.Module):
    """
    Classic learnable positional encoding for patch embeddings.
    """
    def __init__(self, num_patches, emb_size):
        super().__init__()
        self.pos_embed = nn.Parameter(torch.zeros(1, num_patches,
        ↪    emb_size))

    def forward(self, x):
        # x: [B, num_patches, emb_size]
        return x + self.pos_embed

# ---------------------------------------------------------------
# 3) Vision Transformer Model Definition
# ---------------------------------------------------------------
class VisionTransformer(nn.Module):
    """
    Implementation of a simplified Vision Transformer for image
    ↪    classification.
    """
    def __init__(self, img_size=64, patch_size=16, in_channels=3,
                 emb_size=256, num_heads=4, hidden_dim=512,
                 num_layers=4, num_classes=10, dropout=0.1):
```

60

```python
        super().__init__()

        self.patch_embedding = PatchEmbedding(
            in_channels=in_channels,
            patch_size=patch_size,
            emb_size=emb_size,
            img_size=img_size
        )
        self.num_patches = self.patch_embedding.num_patches

        self.pos_encoding = PositionalEncoding(
            num_patches=self.num_patches,
            emb_size=emb_size
        )

        self.cls_token = nn.Parameter(torch.zeros(1, 1, emb_size))

        encoder_layer = nn.TransformerEncoderLayer(
            d_model=emb_size,
            nhead=num_heads,
            dim_feedforward=hidden_dim,
            dropout=dropout,
            batch_first=True
        )
        self.transformer_encoder =
        ↪ nn.TransformerEncoder(encoder_layer, num_layers)

        self.mlp_head = nn.Sequential(
            nn.LayerNorm(emb_size),
            nn.Linear(emb_size, num_classes)
        )

        self._init_weights()

    def _init_weights(self):
        nn.init.normal_(self.cls_token, std=0.02)
        for name, param in self.named_parameters():
            if param.dim() > 1 and 'pos_embed' not in name:
                nn.init.xavier_uniform_(param)

    def forward(self, x):
        # x shape: [B, 3, H, W]
        B = x.size(0)

        # Patch embedding
        x = self.patch_embedding(x)  # [B, num_patches, emb_size]

        # Prepend cls_token
        cls_tokens = self.cls_token.repeat(B, 1, 1)  # [B, 1,
        ↪ emb_size]
        x = torch.cat([cls_tokens, x], dim=1)        # [B, 1 +
        ↪ num_patches, emb_size]
```

```python
        # Positional encoding (except for the [CLS] token, we can
        ↪   expand pos_embed or keep it uniform)
        # We'll incorporate the entire position embedding; the first
        ↪   position will be for CLS
        x[:, 1:] = self.pos_encoding(x[:, 1:])        # Only apply to
        ↪   the patch tokens
        # Alternatively, you could define a separate pos_enc for CLS
        ↪   token or include it in the same param

        # Transformer encoder
        x = self.transformer_encoder(x)   # [B, 1 + num_patches,
        ↪   emb_size]

        # Take the CLS token representation
        cls_rep = x[:, 0]  # [B, emb_size]

        # Final classification
        logits = self.mlp_head(cls_rep)
        return logits


# -----------------------------------------------------------------
# 4) Training and Evaluation
# -----------------------------------------------------------------
def texttt_train_model(model, dataloader, optimizer, criterion,
↪   device):
    model.train()
    total_loss = 0.0
    for images, labels in dataloader:
        images, labels = images.to(device), labels.to(device)

        optimizer.zero_grad()
        outputs = model(images)
        loss = criterion(outputs, labels)
        loss.backward()
        optimizer.step()

        total_loss += loss.item()
    return total_loss / len(dataloader)

def texttt_evaluate_model(model, dataloader, device):
    model.eval()
    correct = 0
    total = 0
    with torch.no_grad():
        for images, labels in dataloader:
            images, labels = images.to(device), labels.to(device)
            outputs = model(images)
            preds = torch.argmax(outputs, dim=1)
            correct += (preds == labels).sum().item()
            total += labels.size(0)
    return correct / total


# -----------------------------------------------------------------
```

```
# 5) Main Execution (Data Prep, Model Init, Training)
# ----------------------------------------------------------------
if __name__ == "__main__":
    # Basic configuration
    device = torch.device("cuda" if torch.cuda.is_available() else
    ↪  "cpu")

    # Create synthetic dataset
    dataset = SyntheticImageDataset(num_samples=1000, image_size=64,
    ↪  num_classes=5)
    test_size = 200
    train_size = len(dataset) - test_size

    # Split data
    train_dataset, test_dataset =
    ↪  torch.utils.data.random_split(dataset, [train_size,
    ↪  test_size])

    train_loader = DataLoader(train_dataset, batch_size=16,
    ↪  shuffle=True)
    test_loader = DataLoader(test_dataset, batch_size=16,
    ↪  shuffle=False)

    # Instantiate model
    model = VisionTransformer(
        img_size=64,
        patch_size=16,
        in_channels=3,
        emb_size=128,          # reduced for demonstration
        num_heads=4,
        hidden_dim=256,
        num_layers=4,
        num_classes=5,
        dropout=0.1
    )
    model.to(device)

    # Define loss and optimizer
    criterion = nn.CrossEntropyLoss()
    optimizer = optim.AdamW(model.parameters(), lr=1e-3)

    # Training
    num_epochs = 5
    for epoch in range(num_epochs):
        train_loss = texttt_train_model(model, train_loader,
        ↪  optimizer, criterion, device)
        accuracy = texttt_evaluate_model(model, test_loader, device)
        print(f"Epoch [{epoch+1}/{num_epochs}] - Loss:
        ↪  {train_loss:.4f}, Accuracy: {accuracy:.4f}")

    print("Training complete. Model is ready for inference.")
```

Key Implementation Details:

- **Patch Embedding**: The class `PatchEmbedding` splits each image into smaller patches and flattens them. Then a linear layer projects each patch to a fixed-dimensional embedding.

- **Positional Encoding**: The class `PositionalEncoding` adds positional embeddings to the patch embeddings to preserve spatial information.

- **Vision Transformer**: The `VisionTransformer` class defines the core architecture: patch embedding, positional encoding, a learnable [CLS] token, and an `nn.TransformerEncoder` stack. We then pool by selecting the [CLS] representation for classification.

- **Training Loop**: The `texttt_train_model` function updates the model weights using cross-entropy loss and the `AdamW` optimizer.

- **Evaluation**: The `texttt_evaluate_model` function computes accuracy by comparing predicted classes to the true labels on the test set.

- **Overall Pipeline**: A synthetic dataset is constructed, the model is trained for a specified number of epochs, and accuracy is measured. This end-to-end example demonstrates how to implement, train, and evaluate a simple ViT for image classification.

Chapter 9

Image Captioning with Multi-Modal Transformers

Common in accessibility tools and digital asset management, image captioning converts visual inputs into descriptive text. Construct a multi-modal Transformer by feeding image features (extracted via a CNN or a Vision Transformer) into a Transformer-based decoder that generates captions. The encoder might be a CNN like ResNet or a ViT that outputs feature embeddings for each image region or patch. These embeddings are then passed to the Decoder that uses cross-attention to align language tokens with image features. Fine-tune on datasets pairing images and captions (e.g., MS COCO). For innovative approaches, incorporate region-of-interest features or bounding boxes as input embeddings, allowing the Transformer to focus on salient objects. You can also apply self-critical sequence training, rewarding generated captions that better match ground truth references.

Python Code Snippet

```python
import torch
import torch.nn as nn
import torch.optim as optim
from torch.utils.data import Dataset, DataLoader
from torchvision import models, transforms
```

```python
import numpy as np
import random
import os

# For reproducibility
random.seed(42)
np.random.seed(42)
torch.manual_seed(42)

# ------------------------------------------
# 1) Synthetic Image-Caption Dataset
# ------------------------------------------
class SyntheticImageCaptionDataset(Dataset):
    """
    A basic synthetic dataset for demonstration of multi-modal
    ↪  captioning.
    Generates random 'images' (here, we'll just create random pixel
    ↪  data
    and transform it as if it's a real image), along with a random
    ↪  tokenized caption.
    """
    def __init__(self, vocab, transform=None, num_samples=1000,
    ↪  max_caption_len=8):
        super().__init__()
        self.vocab = vocab
        self.transform = transform
        self.num_samples = num_samples
        self.max_caption_len = max_caption_len

        # Generate random text data
        self.captions = []
        for _ in range(num_samples):
            length = random.randint(3, max_caption_len)
            words = [random.choice(list(vocab.keys())[2:]) for __ in
            ↪  range(length)]
            # We wrap each caption with <SOS> and <EOS>
            caption_ids = [vocab["<SOS>"]] + [vocab[w] for w in
            ↪  words] + [vocab["<EOS>"]]
            self.captions.append(caption_ids)

    def __len__(self):
        return self.num_samples

    def __getitem__(self, idx):
        # Fake image as random tensor. Shape: (3, 224, 224)
        image = torch.rand((3, 224, 224), dtype=torch.float32)
        if self.transform is not None:
            image = self.transform(image)
        caption = self.captions[idx]

        return image, caption

# ------------------------------------------
```

```python
# 2) Collate Function for Dataloader
# --------------------------------------------
def collate_fn(batch):
    """
    Pads captions to the same length within a batch,
    returning (images, padded_captions, lengths) for training.
    """
    imgs, caps = zip(*batch)

    # We can stack images into a single tensor
    imgs = torch.stack(imgs, dim=0)

    # Determine max length in this batch
    max_len = max([len(c) for c in caps])

    # Pad captions
    padded_caps = []
    lengths = []
    for c in caps:
        lengths.append(len(c))
        if len(c) < max_len:
            c = c + [vocab["<PAD>"]] * (max_len - len(c))
        padded_caps.append(c)

    padded_caps = torch.tensor(padded_caps, dtype=torch.long)

    return imgs, padded_caps, lengths


# --------------------------------------------
# 3) Simple Vocabulary
# --------------------------------------------
# We'll build a small vocab with special tokens
vocab = {
    "<PAD>": 0,
    "<SOS>": 1,
    "<EOS>": 2,
    "dog": 3,
    "cat": 4,
    "sleeps": 5,
    "runs": 6,
    "outside": 7,
    "chases": 8,
    "bird": 9,
    "on": 10,
    "grass": 11,
    "the": 12,
    "sunny": 13,
    "a": 14
}


# --------------------------------------------
# 4) Image Feature Extractor (Encoder)
# --------------------------------------------
```

67

```python
class ImageEncoder(nn.Module):
    """

    Extracts feature embeddings from images. Here, we use a
    ↪ pretrained
    ResNet without the final classification layer to obtain a
    ↪ feature vector.
    """

    def __init__(self, embed_size=256):
        super(ImageEncoder, self).__init__()
        # Use a pretrained ResNet-18 model
        resnet = models.resnet18(pretrained=False)
        # Remove the final layer
        modules = list(resnet.children())[:-1]
        self.resnet = nn.Sequential(*modules)
        self.linear = nn.Linear(resnet.fc.in_features, embed_size)
        self.bn = nn.BatchNorm1d(embed_size, momentum=0.01)


    def forward(self, images):
        """
        images: [batch_size, 3, H, W]
        Returns: [batch_size, embed_size]
        """
        with torch.no_grad():
            features = self.resnet(images)
            # features shape => [batch_size, 512, 1, 1]
        features = features.view(features.size(0), -1)
        features = self.linear(features)    # [batch_size,
        ↪ embed_size]
        features = self.bn(features)
        return features


# --------------------------------------------
# 5) Transformer Decoder for Captions
# --------------------------------------------
class CaptionDecoder(nn.Module):
    """
    A simplified Transformer-based decoder that uses cross-attention
    ↪ on
    the image embedding.
    """

    def __init__(self, embed_dim, vocab_size, num_heads=2,
    ↪ ffn_dim=512, num_layers=2, dropout=0.1):
        super(CaptionDecoder, self).__init__()
        self.embed_dim = embed_dim
        self.word_embedding = nn.Embedding(vocab_size, embed_dim,
        ↪ padding_idx=0)
        self.pos_embedding = nn.Embedding(100, embed_dim)    # Max
        ↪ positional length

        decoder_layer = nn.TransformerDecoderLayer(
            d_model=embed_dim,
            nhead=num_heads,
            dim_feedforward=ffn_dim,
```

68

```
        dropout=dropout
    )
    self.transformer_decoder =
    ↪   nn.TransformerDecoder(decoder_layer, num_layers)

    # Final linear to map decoder output to vocab
    self.fc_out = nn.Linear(embed_dim, vocab_size)

def forward(self, features, captions, teacher_forcing=True):
    """
    features: [batch_size, embed_dim] (encoded image features)
    captions: [batch_size, max_len]
    """
    batch_size, max_len = captions.shape

    # Prepare target embeddings for the decoder
    # We'll add positional embeddings as well
    positions = torch.arange(0,
    ↪   max_len).unsqueeze(0).repeat(batch_size,
    ↪   1).to(captions.device)
    word_embed = self.word_embedding(captions)  # [batch_size,
    ↪   max_len, embed_dim]
    pos_embed = self.pos_embedding(positions)
    tgt = word_embed + pos_embed            # [batch_size,
    ↪   max_len, embed_dim]

    # For cross-attention, we treat "features" as the memory.
    # The Transformer Decoder expects shape [sequence_len,
    ↪   batch_size, embed_dim].
    # Here, we have a single "feature token" per image. Let's
    ↪   unsqueeze dim=0:
    memory = features.unsqueeze(0)  # [1, batch_size, embed_dim]
    # The target also needs to be permuted: [max_len,
    ↪   batch_size, embed_dim]
    tgt = tgt.permute(1, 0, 2)

    # Generate a causal mask for decoding (subsequent tokens not
    ↪   visible):
    # shape => [max_len, max_len]
    subseq_mask =
    ↪   nn.Transformer.generate_square_subsequent_mask(
    max_len).to(captions.device)

    # Because we only have a single memory token, no need for
    ↪   memory mask
    outputs = self.transformer_decoder(tgt, memory,
    ↪   tgt_mask=subseq_mask)

    # outputs => [max_len, batch_size, embed_dim]
    outputs = outputs.permute(1, 0, 2)  # => [batch_size,
    ↪   max_len, embed_dim]
    logits = self.fc_out(outputs)       # => [batch_size,
    ↪   max_len, vocab_size]
```

69

```python
        return logits

# ----------------------------------------
# 6) Combined Image Captioning Model
# ----------------------------------------
class ImageCaptioningModel(nn.Module):
    """
    Full model that:
      - Encodes images to feature vectors
      - Decodes these with a Transformer-based decoder to generate
      ↪  captions.
    """
    def __init__(self, embed_size, vocab_size):
        super(ImageCaptioningModel, self).__init__()
        self.encoder = ImageEncoder(embed_size)
        self.decoder = CaptionDecoder(
            embed_dim=embed_size,
            vocab_size=vocab_size,
            num_heads=4,
            ffn_dim=512,
            num_layers=2,
            dropout=0.1
        )

    def forward(self, images, captions):
        features = self.encoder(images)
        outputs = self.decoder(features, captions)
        return outputs

# ----------------------------------------
# 7) Training Utilities
# ----------------------------------------
def train_one_epoch(model, dataloader, criterion, optimizer,
↪  device):
    model.train()
    total_loss = 0.0
    for images, captions, _ in dataloader:
        images, captions = images.to(device), captions.to(device)

        optimizer.zero_grad()
        # Forward
        outputs = model(images, captions[:, :-1])   # input all
        ↪  except last token
        # We compare outputs to the target shifted by one:
        ↪  captions[:, 1:]
        loss = criterion(outputs.reshape(-1, outputs.size(-1)),
        ↪  captions[:, 1:].reshape(-1))
        loss.backward()
        optimizer.step()

        total_loss += loss.item()
    return total_loss / len(dataloader)
```

70

```
def evaluate_model(model, dataloader, criterion, device):
    model.eval()
    total_loss = 0.0
    with torch.no_grad():
        for images, captions, _ in dataloader:
            images, captions = images.to(device),
            ↪ captions.to(device)
            outputs = model(images, captions[:, :-1])
            loss = criterion(outputs.reshape(-1, outputs.size(-1)),
            ↪ captions[:, 1:].reshape(-1))
            total_loss += loss.item()
    return total_loss / len(dataloader)

def generate_caption(model, image, vocab, max_length=15,
↪ device="cpu"):
    """
    Simple greedy decoding to generate a caption for one image.
    """
    model.eval()
    with torch.no_grad():
        img = image.unsqueeze(0).to(device)
        features = model.encoder(img)  # [1, embed_dim]

        # Start with <SOS>
        caption_tokens = [vocab["<SOS>"]]

        for _ in range(max_length):
            cap_tensor = torch.tensor([caption_tokens],
            ↪ dtype=torch.long).to(device)
            # Pass through decoder
            outputs = model.decoder(features, cap_tensor,
            ↪ teacher_forcing=False)
            # Take the last time-step
            next_token_logits = outputs[:, -1, :]
            _, next_token_id = torch.max(next_token_logits, dim=1)
            next_token_id = next_token_id.item()

            # Append and check termination
            caption_tokens.append(next_token_id)
            if next_token_id == vocab["<EOS>"]:
                break

    # Convert token IDs back to words
    inv_vocab = {v: k for k, v in vocab.items()}
    words = [inv_vocab[t] for t in caption_tokens]
    return " ".join(words)

# --------------------------------------------
# 8) Main Execution - Synthetic Demo
# --------------------------------------------
if __name__ == "__main__":
    # Hyperparams
```

71

```python
embed_size = 256
batch_size = 8
num_epochs = 3
learning_rate = 1e-3
device = torch.device("cuda" if torch.cuda.is_available() else
↪    "cpu")

# Transforms
# We'll just keep it minimal; typically you'd normalize by
↪    ImageNet stats
transform = transforms.Compose([
    transforms.Resize((224, 224)),   # If needed
])

# Create dataset and dataloader
train_dataset = SyntheticImageCaptionDataset(
    vocab=vocab, transform=transform, num_samples=200,
    ↪    max_caption_len=6
)
val_dataset = SyntheticImageCaptionDataset(
    vocab=vocab, transform=transform, num_samples=50,
    ↪    max_caption_len=6
)

train_loader = DataLoader(train_dataset, batch_size=batch_size,
                          shuffle=True, collate_fn=collate_fn)
val_loader = DataLoader(val_dataset, batch_size=batch_size,
                        shuffle=False, collate_fn=collate_fn)

# Init model
model = ImageCaptioningModel(embed_size=embed_size,
↪    vocab_size=len(vocab))
model = model.to(device)

# Use CrossEntropyLoss ignoring <PAD> index
criterion = nn.CrossEntropyLoss(ignore_index=vocab["<PAD>"])
optimizer = optim.Adam(model.parameters(), lr=learning_rate)

# Training Loop
for epoch in range(num_epochs):
    train_loss = train_one_epoch(model, train_loader, criterion,
    ↪    optimizer, device)
    val_loss = evaluate_model(model, val_loader, criterion,
    ↪    device)
    print(f"Epoch [{epoch+1}/{num_epochs}] - Train Loss:
    ↪    {train_loss:.4f}, Val Loss: {val_loss:.4f}")

# Demo: Generate caption
sample_img, _ = val_dataset[0]   # get one sample
predicted_caption = generate_caption(model, sample_img, vocab,
↪    device=device)
print("Predicted Caption:", predicted_caption)
```

Key Implementation Details:

- **Data Preparation**: A synthetic dataset (`SyntheticImageCaptionDataset`) simulates images by generating random pixel values and random token sequences representing captions.

- **Encoder (CNN)**: The `ImageEncoder` class uses a ResNet-18 backbone (with the last fully-connected layer removed) to produce feature embeddings. These embeddings serve as the "memory" for cross-attention in the decoder.

- **Transformer Decoder**: The core Transformer logic resides in the `CaptionDecoder` class. Cross-attention layers align textual tokens and the image feature embeddings. A causal mask is used to enforce autoregressive decoding.

- **Combined Model**: The `ImageCaptioningModel` integrates the encoder and Transformer-based decoder to form a fully trainable end-to-end architecture for image captioning.

- **Training Loop**: The `train_one_epoch` and `evaluate_model` functions illustrate how to optimize the model using cross-entropy loss, ignoring `<PAD>` tokens. Teacher forcing is achieved by shifting the input captions by one timestep.

- **Inference**: The `generate_caption` function performs greedy decoding, repeatedly passing the growing sequence back into the decoder until the end-of-sequence token is reached.

Chapter 10

Object Detection with Transformer Architectures

Essential for robotics, surveillance, and autonomous vehicles, object detection identifies bounding boxes and categories for objects within an image. DETR (**D**etection **TR**ansformer) introduced a sequence-to-sequence formulation for this task. To build it, encode images into feature maps via a CNN backbone or a Vision Transformer. Flatten these feature maps into a sequence and add positional encodings. Pass the sequence to a Transformer encoder, then use a Transformer decoder with a fixed set of object queries. Each decoder output corresponds to a potential object. Fully connected heads then predict bounding box coordinates and class probabilities. For more advanced designs, you can integrate hierarchical features or multi-scale attention (e.g., Deformable DETR). This approach eliminates the need for region proposals, simplifying the object detection pipeline and promoting end-to-end training.

Python Code Snippet

```
import torch
import torch.nn as nn
import torch.optim as optim
from torch.utils.data import Dataset, DataLoader
import random
```

```python
# ------------------------------------------------------------
# 1) Synthetic Dataset and Dataloader
# ------------------------------------------------------------
class RandomDetectionDataset(Dataset):
    """
    A random dataset to demonstrate the DETR-like object detection
    pipeline. Each sample is a synthetic image (random noise)
    and random bounding boxes with class labels.
    """
    def __init__(self, num_samples=100, image_size=(3, 128, 128),
                 num_boxes=5, num_classes=3):
        super().__init__()
        self.num_samples = num_samples
        self.image_size = image_size
        self.num_boxes = num_boxes
        self.num_classes = num_classes
        self.data = []
        for _ in range(num_samples):
            # Generate random image
            img = torch.rand(*image_size)
            # Generate random bounding boxes: [x_center, y_center,
            ↪  width, height],
            # and class labels
            boxes = torch.rand(num_boxes, 4)
            labels = torch.randint(low=0, high=num_classes,
            ↪  size=(num_boxes,))
            self.data.append((img, boxes, labels))

    def __len__(self):
        return self.num_samples

    def __getitem__(self, idx):
        return self.data[idx]


def collate_fn(batch):
    """
    Collate function to create mini-batches of images, boxes, and
    ↪  labels.
    We place images in a tensor [batch, channels, H, W] while boxes
    ↪  and
    labels remain in lists, as they can have variable shapes.
    """
    images = []
    all_boxes = []
    all_labels = []
    for img, boxes, labels in batch:
        images.append(img)
        all_boxes.append(boxes)
        all_labels.append(labels)
    images = torch.stack(images, dim=0)
    return images, all_boxes, all_labels
```

```python
# ------------------------------------------------------------
# 2) Positional Encoding
# ------------------------------------------------------------
class PositionalEncoding(nn.Module):
    """
    Standard sine/cosine positional encoding for 2D feature maps.
    We flatten the 2D spatial dimensions into a sequence; this
    class helps the model keep track of spatial positions.
    """
    def __init__(self, d_model=256, max_h=32, max_w=32):
        super().__init__()
        self.d_model = d_model
        # Create buffers for row and column encodings
        row_pos = torch.arange(max_h).unsqueeze(1)
        col_pos = torch.arange(max_w).unsqueeze(0)

        # Convert these to angles
        div_term = torch.exp(torch.arange(0, d_model, 2) *
                             (-torch.log(torch.tensor(10000.0)) /
                              ↪ d_model))

        pe = torch.zeros(max_h, max_w, d_model)
        # We fill even indices with sin, odd with cos
        pe[..., 0::2] = torch.sin(row_pos * div_term) +
        ↪ torch.sin(col_pos * div_term)
        pe[..., 1::2] = torch.cos(row_pos * div_term) +
        ↪ torch.cos(col_pos * div_term)

        # Flatten the 2D into shape [max_h * max_w, d_model]
        pe = pe.view(max_h * max_w, d_model)
        self.register_buffer('pe', pe)

    def forward(self, x):
        """
        x shape: [batch_size, seq_len, d_model]
        We assume seq_len == h*w for a flattened feature map.
        """
        seq_len = x.shape[1]
        return x + self.pe[:seq_len, :]


# ------------------------------------------------------------
# 3) Transformer-based DETR Model
# ------------------------------------------------------------
class DetrLikeModel(nn.Module):
    """
    A simplified DETR-like architecture including:
     - A simple CNN backbone (to produce feature maps).
     - Positional encodings.
     - Transformer encoder & decoder.
     - Prediction heads for bounding boxes and class labels.
    """
    def __init__(self, num_classes=3, hidden_dim=256,
                 nheads=4, num_encoder_layers=2,
```

```python
                num_decoder_layers=2, num_queries=5):
    super().__init__()
    self.backbone = nn.Sequential(
        nn.Conv2d(3, 64, kernel_size=4, stride=2, padding=1),
        nn.ReLU(),
        nn.Conv2d(64, hidden_dim, kernel_size=4, stride=2,
        ↪  padding=1),
        nn.ReLU(),
    )

    self.pos_enc = PositionalEncoding(d_model=hidden_dim,
    ↪  max_h=32, max_w=32)

    encoder_layer =
    ↪  nn.TransformerEncoderLayer(d_model=hidden_dim,
                        nhead=nheads,
                        dim_feedforward=hidden_dim*2)
    self.transformer_encoder =
    ↪  nn.TransformerEncoder(encoder_layer,
                        num_layers=num_encoder_layers)

    decoder_layer =
    ↪  nn.TransformerDecoderLayer(d_model=hidden_dim,
                        nhead=nheads,
                        dim_feedforward=hidden_dim*2)
    self.transformer_decoder =
    ↪  nn.TransformerDecoder(decoder_layer,
                        num_layers=num_decoder_layers)

    # Object queries
    self.query_embed = nn.Embedding(num_queries, hidden_dim)

    # Prediction heads (for each query)
    # Box prediction: 4 coordinates
    self.bbox_head = nn.Linear(hidden_dim, 4)
    # Class prediction
    self.class_head = nn.Linear(hidden_dim, num_classes)

def forward(self, x):
    """
    x: [batch_size, 3, H, W]
    Return: predicted boxes and classes
            shaped [batch_size, num_queries, 4] for boxes,
            [batch_size, num_queries, num_classes] for class
            ↪  logits
    """
    bsz = x.shape[0]
    # 1) Extract feature maps using the CNN backbone
    feat = self.backbone(x)    # shape [batch_size, hidden_dim,
    ↪  H', W']
    _, c, h, w = feat.shape

    # 2) Flatten the spatial dimensions
```

77

```
feat = feat.view(bsz, c, h*w).permute(0, 2, 1)    #
↪   [batch_size, seq_len, hidden_dim]

# 3) Add positional encoding
feat = self.pos_enc(feat)

# Transformer requires shape [seq_len, batch_size, d_model]
feat = feat.permute(1, 0, 2)    # [seq_len, batch_size,
↪   hidden_dim]

# 4) Pass through transformer encoder
memory = self.transformer_encoder(feat)    # [seq_len,
↪   batch_size, hidden_dim]

# 5) Prepare queries
queries = self.query_embed.weight    # [num_queries,
↪   hidden_dim]
# Expand queries for the batch dimension
queries = queries.unsqueeze(1).repeat(1, bsz, 1)

# 6) Decode
# The decoder outputs shape [num_queries, batch_size,
↪   hidden_dim]
decoded = self.transformer_decoder(tgt=queries,
↪   memory=memory)

# Permute back to shape [batch_size, num_queries,
↪   hidden_dim]
decoded = decoded.permute(1, 0, 2)

# 7) Predict bounding boxes and class logits
pred_boxes = self.bbox_head(decoded)        # [batch_size,
↪   num_queries, 4]
pred_classes = self.class_head(decoded)     # [batch_size,
↪   num_queries, num_classes]

return pred_boxes, pred_classes

# -----------------------------------------------------------
# 4) Training and Loss Functions
# -----------------------------------------------------------
def detr_loss(pred_boxes, pred_classes, target_boxes,
↪   target_labels):
    """
    A toy loss function approximating DETR training:
    We'll do L1 loss for box coords and CE loss for classes
    (with naive matching: correspond queries to target boxes
    by index in this demo).
    """
    bsz, num_queries, _ = pred_boxes.shape
    device = pred_boxes.device

    # Flatten predictions and targets
```

78

```python
        pred_boxes = pred_boxes.view(bsz * num_queries, 4)
        pred_classes = pred_classes.view(bsz * num_queries, -1)

        all_boxes = []
        all_labels = []
        for boxes, labels in zip(target_boxes, target_labels):
            # If there are fewer boxes than queries, we'll pad
            # If there are more, we'll truncate (toy approach)
            boxes = boxes[:num_queries]
            labels = labels[:num_queries]
            len_diff = num_queries - boxes.shape[0]
            if len_diff > 0:
                pad_boxes = torch.zeros(len_diff, 4, device=device)
                pad_labels = torch.zeros(len_diff, dtype=torch.long,
                ↪    device=device)
                boxes = torch.cat([boxes, pad_boxes], dim=0)
                labels = torch.cat([labels, pad_labels], dim=0)
            all_boxes.append(boxes)
            all_labels.append(labels)

        gt_boxes = torch.stack(all_boxes, dim=0)       # [batch_size,
        ↪    num_queries, 4]
        gt_labels = torch.stack(all_labels, dim=0)     # [batch_size,
        ↪    num_queries]

        gt_boxes = gt_boxes.view(bsz * num_queries, 4)
        gt_labels = gt_labels.view(bsz * num_queries,)

        l1_loss_fn = nn.L1Loss()
        ce_loss_fn = nn.CrossEntropyLoss()

        box_loss = l1_loss_fn(pred_boxes, gt_boxes)
        cls_loss = ce_loss_fn(pred_classes, gt_labels)

        return box_loss + cls_loss

    def train_one_epoch(model, dataloader, optimizer, device):
        model.train()
        total_loss = 0.0
        for images, target_boxes, target_labels in dataloader:
            images = images.to(device)

            optimizer.zero_grad()
            pred_boxes, pred_classes = model(images)
            loss = detr_loss(pred_boxes, pred_classes, target_boxes,
            ↪    target_labels)
            loss.backward()
            optimizer.step()

            total_loss += loss.item()
        return total_loss / len(dataloader)

    def evaluate(model, dataloader, device):
```

```
"""
A placeholder evaluation function that just checks
forward pass success on the test set. No real metrics
in this demo.
"""
model.eval()
total_loss = 0.0
with torch.no_grad():
    for images, target_boxes, target_labels in dataloader:
        images = images.to(device)
        pred_boxes, pred_classes = model(images)
        loss = detr_loss(pred_boxes, pred_classes, target_boxes,
        ↪  target_labels)
        total_loss += loss.item()
    return total_loss / len(dataloader)


# ---------------------------------------------------------------
# 5) Main Execution
# ---------------------------------------------------------------
if __name__ == "__main__":
    device = torch.device("cuda" if torch.cuda.is_available() else
    ↪  "cpu")

    # Create synthetic dataset
    train_dataset = RandomDetectionDataset(num_samples=200,
    ↪  image_size=(3, 64, 64),
                                            num_boxes=5,
                                            ↪  num_classes=3)
    test_dataset = RandomDetectionDataset(num_samples=50,
    ↪  image_size=(3, 64, 64),
                                           num_boxes=5,
                                           ↪  num_classes=3)

    train_loader = DataLoader(train_dataset, batch_size=8,
    ↪  shuffle=True,
                               collate_fn=collate_fn)
    test_loader = DataLoader(test_dataset, batch_size=8,
    ↪  shuffle=False,
                              collate_fn=collate_fn)

    # Initialize the DETR-like model
    model = DetrLikeModel(num_classes=3, hidden_dim=128,
                           nheads=4, num_encoder_layers=2,
                           num_decoder_layers=2, num_queries=5)
    model.to(device)

    optimizer = optim.AdamW(model.parameters(), lr=1e-4)

    # Train for a few epochs
    num_epochs = 5
    for epoch in range(num_epochs):
        train_loss = train_one_epoch(model, train_loader, optimizer,
        ↪  device)
```

```
test_loss = evaluate(model, test_loader, device)
print(f"Epoch [{epoch+1}/{num_epochs}]  Train Loss:
↪ {train_loss:.4f}, Test Loss: {test_loss:.4f}")

print("Training complete. Model is ready for inference.")
```

Key Implementation Details:

- **Positional Encoding**: The class `PositionalEncoding` uses sine-cosine patterns to help the Transformer attend to spatial positions in flattened feature maps.

- **Transformer Encoder & Decoder**: The `DetrLikeModel` core includes an encoder for feature processing and a decoder that uses learnable object queries.

- **Bounding Box & Class Prediction**: After decoding, each query predicts a bounding box and class distribution via fully connected heads (`bbox_head` and `class_head`).

- **Toy Loss Function**: `detr_loss` combines an L1 loss for bounding boxes and cross-entropy loss for class predictions, illustrating the overall training objective.

- **End-to-End Training**: The entire pipeline, from synthetic data generation to inference, is enclosed in the **main** block, demonstrating a minimal DETR-like training loop for object detection.

Chapter 11

Visual Question Answering (VQA) with Transformers

VQA systems can interpret images and answer corresponding queries, enabling support in educational tools or assistive technologies. To construct a VQA Transformer, combine image embeddings from a Vision Transformer or CNN with token embeddings of the question. The multi-modal Transformer merges these vectors, applying cross-attention to align text and image features. You then feed the output into a classification or decoding layer, depending on whether answers are discrete (like multiple choice) or open-ended. Advanced approaches incorporate bounding box features (region-based features) to target specific objects in the image. You can also use a textual question-and-answer Transformer (like T5) that receives object tags or region descriptions as part of the input, thus bridging the gap between purely visual input and language-based attention.

Python Code Snippet

```
import torch
import torch.nn as nn
import torch.optim as optim
from torch.utils.data import Dataset, DataLoader
import random
```

```python
import numpy as np

# For reproducibility
torch.manual_seed(42)
random.seed(42)
np.random.seed(42)

#
↪   --------------------------------------------------------------------
# 1) Synthetic Data Generation Function for VQA
#
↪   --------------------------------------------------------------------
def generate_synthetic_vqa_data(num_samples=1000,
↪   question_vocab_size=50,
                                num_possible_answers=4,
                                ↪  feature_dim=128):
    """
    Generate random 'image' features, textual questions, and labels
    ↪   for a
    simplified VQA dataset.
    - image_features: randomly sampled from a normal distribution,
    ↪   shape [feature_dim]
    - question_text: random tokens from a finite vocabulary
    - label: integer from 0 to num_possible_answers-1 representing
    ↪   the 'answer'
    """
    # Create a small pool of 'question words' for synthetic
    ↪   questions
    question_word_pool = [f"word{i}" for i in
    ↪   range(question_vocab_size)]

    image_features_list = []
    questions_list = []
    labels_list = []

    for _ in range(num_samples):
        # Random image features (simulate features extracted by a
        ↪   backbone)
        img_feat = np.random.randn(feature_dim).astype(np.float32)

        # Random question
        q_length = random.randint(3, 8)
        q_tokens = [random.choice(question_word_pool) for __ in
        ↪   range(q_length)]
        question_text = " ".join(q_tokens)

        # Random label from a set of possible answers
        label = random.randint(0, num_possible_answers - 1)

        image_features_list.append(img_feat)
        questions_list.append(question_text)
        labels_list.append(label)
```

83

```
        return image_features_list, questions_list, labels_list


#
↪   --------------------------------------------------------------------------
# 2) Simple Text Tokenizer
#
↪   --------------------------------------------------------------------------
class SimpleTextTokenizer:
    """
    Basic whitespace tokenizer with a limited vocabulary.
    Unknown tokens are mapped to [UNK], padding is [PAD].
    """
    def __init__(self, vocab_size=50):
        self.vocab_size = vocab_size
        self.token2id = {}
        self.id2token = {}

    def fit(self, texts):
        # Collect frequency of tokens
        freq = {}
        for txt in texts:
            for token in txt.split():
                freq[token] = freq.get(token, 0) + 1

        # Sort by frequency
        sorted_tokens = sorted(freq.items(), key=lambda x: x[1],
        ↪   reverse=True)
        # Reserve 2 slots for [UNK], [PAD]
        truncated_tokens = sorted_tokens[:(self.vocab_size - 2)]

        # Build token2id
        self.token2id = {"[UNK]": 0, "[PAD]": 1}
        idx = 2
        for token, _ in truncated_tokens:
            self.token2id[token] = idx
            idx += 1

        # Build id2token
        self.id2token = {v: k for k, v in self.token2id.items()}

    def encode(self, text):
        tokens = text.split()
        encoded = [self.token2id.get(t, 0) for t in tokens]   # map
        ↪   to [UNK] if not found
        return encoded

    def decode(self, token_ids):
        return " ".join([self.id2token.get(tid, "[UNK]") for tid in
        ↪   token_ids])

    def pad_batch(self, list_of_encoded, max_len=10):
        """
```

```
    Pad or truncate each sequence in list_of_encoded to max_len
    ↪   tokens.
    """

    output = []
    for seq in list_of_encoded:
        if len(seq) < max_len:
            seq = seq + [1] * (max_len - len(seq))   # 1 is
            ↪   [PAD]
        else:
            seq = seq[:max_len]
        output.append(seq)
    return output


#
↪   --------------------------------------------------------------------
# 3) Custom Dataset for VQA
#
↪   --------------------------------------------------------------------
class VQADataset(Dataset):
    """
    Each sample contains:
      - image_features (already extracted, so we treat them as
      ↪   vectors)
      - question encoded as integer IDs
      - label (the chosen index of the answer)
    """
    def __init__(self, image_features_list, questions_list,
    ↪   labels_list,
                 tokenizer, max_len=10):
        self.image_features_list = image_features_list
        self.questions_list = questions_list
        self.labels_list = labels_list
        self.tokenizer = tokenizer
        self.max_len = max_len

        # Pre-encode questions for efficiency
        self.encoded_questions = [self.tokenizer.encode(q) for q in
        ↪   self.questions_list]

    def __len__(self):
        return len(self.labels_list)

    def __getitem__(self, idx):
        img_feat = self.image_features_list[idx]
        enc_q = self.encoded_questions[idx]
        label = self.labels_list[idx]
        return img_feat, enc_q, label

def vqa_collate_fn(batch):
    """
    Collate function to batch image features and question tokens,
    ↪   ensuring
    proper padding and conversion to tensors.
```

```
    """
    img_feats, encoded_qs, labels = zip(*batch)
    # Determine the max length for padding or use a default
    # We'll use the dataset's max_len as an upper bound
    max_len = max(len(seq) for seq in encoded_qs)
    max_len = min(max_len, 10)  # forcibly set a limit
    padded_qs = tokenizer.pad_batch(encoded_qs, max_len=max_len)

    img_feats_tensor = torch.tensor(img_feats, dtype=torch.float32)
    qs_tensor = torch.tensor(padded_qs, dtype=torch.long)
    labels_tensor = torch.tensor(labels, dtype=torch.long)

    return img_feats_tensor, qs_tensor, labels_tensor

#
↪   -------------------------------------------------------------------
# 4) Multi-Modal Transformer Model
#
↪   -------------------------------------------------------------------
class MultiModalTransformer(nn.Module):
    """
    Combines image features and question embeddings into a single
    ↪   sequence
    for a multi-head attention mechanism. Followed by a
    ↪   classification head
    to predict the answer.
    """
    def __init__(self,
                 question_vocab_size,
                 question_embed_dim=64,
                 img_feature_dim=128,
                 transformer_embed_dim=64,
                 n_heads=2,
                 ff_dim=128,
                 n_layers=2,
                 num_answers=4,
                 dropout=0.1):
        super(MultiModalTransformer, self).__init__()

        # Text embedding
        self.question_embedding = nn.Embedding(question_vocab_size,
        ↪   question_embed_dim, padding_idx=1)

        # Linear to convert image features to same dimension as
        ↪   question embeddings
        self.image_projection = nn.Linear(img_feature_dim,
        ↪   transformer_embed_dim)

        # Positional embeddings for tokens (both image token +
        ↪   question tokens)
        # We'll allow maximum length of 1 (image-as-token) + 10
        ↪   question tokens = 11
        self.max_seq_len = 11
```

86

```python
        self.pos_embedding = nn.Embedding(self.max_seq_len,
        ↪   transformer_embed_dim)

        # Transformer Encoder
        encoder_layer = nn.TransformerEncoderLayer(
            d_model=transformer_embed_dim,
            nhead=n_heads,
            dim_feedforward=ff_dim,
            dropout=dropout
        )
        self.transformer_encoder =
        ↪   nn.TransformerEncoder(encoder_layer,
        ↪   num_layers=n_layers)

        # Classification head
        self.classifier = nn.Linear(transformer_embed_dim,
        ↪   num_answers)

    def forward(self, image_feats, question_ids):
        """
        image_feats: [batch_size, img_feature_dim]
        question_ids: [batch_size, seq_len_q]
        Returns logits: [batch_size, num_answers]
        """
        batch_size, seq_len_q = question_ids.shape

        # Project image features to match the transformer's hidden
        ↪   size
        projected_img = self.image_projection(image_feats)  #
        ↪   [batch_size, transformer_embed_dim]
        projected_img = projected_img.unsqueeze(1)              # =>
        ↪   [batch_size, 1, transformer_embed_dim]

        # Embed question tokens => [batch_size, seq_len_q,
        ↪   question_embed_dim]
        embedded_q = self.question_embedding(question_ids)

        # Concatenate image token + question embeddings =>
        ↪   total_seq_len = 1 + seq_len_q
        multimodal_seq = torch.cat([projected_img, embedded_q],
        ↪   dim=1)
        # shape => [batch_size, 1 + seq_len_q,
        ↪   transformer_embed_dim]

        # Add positional embeddings
        positions = torch.arange(0, self.max_seq_len,
        ↪   device=multimodal_seq.device).unsqueeze(0)
        # We'll slice positions to match actual used length
        used_seq_len = 1 + seq_len_q  # e.g. up to 11
        pos_embeds = self.pos_embedding(positions[:, :used_seq_len])
        # => [1, used_seq_len, transformer_embed_dim]
        pos_embeds = pos_embeds.repeat(batch_size, 1, 1)
```

87

```python
        # Sum input embeddings and positional embeddings
        multimodal_seq = multimodal_seq + pos_embeds

        # Transformer expects shape [seq_len, batch_size, embed_dim]
        multimodal_seq = multimodal_seq.permute(1, 0, 2)

        # Pass through transformer encoder
        encoded = self.transformer_encoder(multimodal_seq)
        # => [sequence_len, batch_size, transformer_embed_dim]

        # We can pool the final hidden state of the 'image token'
        # for classification. The 'image token' is at index=0
        image_token_encoding = encoded[0, :, :]   # => [batch_size,
        ↪    transformer_embed_dim]

        # Classification
        logits = self.classifier(image_token_encoding)   # =>
        ↪    [batch_size, num_answers]
        return logits


# ---------------------------------------------------------------------------
↪
# 5) Training and Evaluation Functions
# ---------------------------------------------------------------------------
↪
def train_one_epoch(model, dataloader, optimizer, criterion,
↪    device):
    model.train()
    running_loss = 0.0
    for img_feats, qs, labels in dataloader:
        img_feats, qs, labels = img_feats.to(device), qs.to(device),
        ↪    labels.to(device)

        optimizer.zero_grad()
        logits = model(img_feats, qs)
        loss = criterion(logits, labels)
        loss.backward()
        optimizer.step()

        running_loss += loss.item()
    return running_loss / len(dataloader)

def evaluate_model(model, dataloader, device):
    model.eval()
    correct = 0
    total = 0
    with torch.no_grad():
        for img_feats, qs, labels in dataloader:
            img_feats, qs, labels = img_feats.to(device),
            ↪    qs.to(device), labels.to(device)
            logits = model(img_feats, qs)
            preds = torch.argmax(logits, dim=1)
            correct += (preds == labels).sum().item()
```

```python
            total += labels.size(0)
    return correct / total


# -----------------------------------------------------------------
↪
# 6) Main Execution (Synthetic Data, Model Setup, Training)
# -----------------------------------------------------------------
↪
if __name__ == "__main__":
    # Generate synthetic VQA data
    img_features, questions, labels = generate_synthetic_vqa_data(
        num_samples=2000,
        question_vocab_size=50,
        num_possible_answers=4,
        feature_dim=128
    )

    # Build tokenizer
    tokenizer = SimpleTextTokenizer(vocab_size=50)
    tokenizer.fit(questions)

    # Train/test split
    train_size = int(0.8 * len(img_features))
    train_img = img_features[:train_size]
    train_q   = questions[:train_size]
    train_lbl = labels[:train_size]

    test_img  = img_features[train_size:]
    test_q    = questions[train_size:]
    test_lbl  = labels[train_size:]

    # Create Datasets
    train_dataset = VQADataset(train_img, train_q, train_lbl,
    ↪ tokenizer)
    test_dataset  = VQADataset(test_img, test_q, test_lbl,
    ↪ tokenizer)

    # Create Dataloaders
    train_loader = DataLoader(train_dataset, batch_size=32,
    ↪ shuffle=True, collate_fn=vqa_collate_fn)
    test_loader  = DataLoader(test_dataset, batch_size=32,
    ↪ shuffle=False, collate_fn=vqa_collate_fn)

    # Initialize model
    device = torch.device("cuda" if torch.cuda.is_available() else
    ↪ "cpu")
    model = MultiModalTransformer(
        question_vocab_size=len(tokenizer.token2id),
        question_embed_dim=64,
        img_feature_dim=128,
        transformer_embed_dim=64,
        n_heads=2,
        ff_dim=128,
```

89

```
        n_layers=2,
        num_answers=4,
        dropout=0.1
    ).to(device)

    optimizer = optim.AdamW(model.parameters(), lr=1e-3)
    criterion = nn.CrossEntropyLoss()

    # Training
    epochs = 5
    for epoch in range(epochs):
        train_loss = train_one_epoch(model, train_loader, optimizer,
        ↪   criterion, device)
        accuracy = evaluate_model(model, test_loader, device)
        print(f"Epoch {epoch+1}/{epochs} - Loss: {train_loss:.4f} -
        ↪   Accuracy: {accuracy:.4f}")

    print("Training complete. Model ready for VQA inference.")
```

Key Implementation Details:

- **Data Generation**: We employ `generate_synthetic_vqa_data` to create random image feature vectors, textual questions, and corresponding labels.

- **Tokenizer**: A simple whitespace-based tokenizer, `SimpleTextTokenizer`, builds a minimal vocabulary and encodes questions into integer IDs.

- **Dataset and Collate Function**: `VQADataset` stores the image features, question text, and labels. The `vqa_collate_fn` handles padding of question token sequences and arranges data into batches.

- **MultiModalTransformer Model**: This core module projects image features and question embeddings into a common embedding dimension and combines them in a single sequence for transformer-based multi-head attention. The classification head (`self.classifier`) outputs the final predicted answer.

- **Training and Evaluation**: The `train_one_epoch` function updates model parameters using cross-entropy loss, while `evaluate_model` calculates classification accuracy. We optimize with `AdamW`.

90

- **End-to-End Pipeline**: All components (data creation, tokenizer fitting, model instantiation, training loop, and testing) are demonstrated in the `__main__` block, providing a straightforward reference for building a Transformer-based VQA system.

Chapter 12

Time-Series Forecasting with Transformers

Applications include predicting stock prices, weather patterns, or sales figures. The Transformer's self-attention can capture long-term dependencies in time-series data. Start by segmenting the time-series into input windows with associated targets. Encode each time step with a positional or temporal embedding, then feed the sequence into a Transformer encoder. For forecasting multiple steps, either use an encoder-decoder approach, or train the encoder to predict future values based on masked input tokens (e.g., using a masked language modeling strategy). To handle irregular intervals or multiple covariates (like weather data), embed additional features alongside the primary series. For novel methods, investigate combining seasonal-trend decomposition or specialized attention mechanisms that adapt to periodicity. This helps the model focus on cyclical patterns common in time-series tasks.

Python Code Snippet

```python
import torch
import torch.nn as nn
import torch.optim as optim
import numpy as np
import random
```

```
from torch.utils.data import Dataset, DataLoader

# For reproducibility
torch.manual_seed(42)
random.seed(42)
np.random.seed(42)

# ------------------------------------------------------------
# 1) Synthetic Time-Series Data Generation
# ------------------------------------------------------------
def generate_synthetic_time_series(seq_length=1000, freq=0.04,
↪   noise_level=0.05):
    """
    Generate a synthetic sine wave with optional noise for
    ↪   demonstration.
    """
    x = np.arange(seq_length)
    y = np.sin(2 * np.pi * freq * x) + noise_level *
    ↪   np.random.randn(seq_length)
    return y.astype(np.float32)

# ------------------------------------------------------------
# 2) Dataset & DataLoader for Time-Series
# ------------------------------------------------------------
class TimeSeriesDataset(Dataset):
    """
    Creates windows of length 'input_window' and the subsequent
    ↪   time-step as the target.
    If forecasting multiple steps, modify 'target_window'
    ↪   accordingly.
    """
    def __init__(self, series, input_window=24):
        self.series = series
        self.input_window = input_window

    def __len__(self):
        return len(self.series) - self.input_window

    def __getitem__(self, idx):
        x = self.series[idx : idx + self.input_window]
        y = self.series[idx + self.input_window]  # Next step as
        ↪   target
        return x, y

def collate_fn(batch_data):
    """
    Convert the list of (x,y) tuples into properly shaped tensors.
    """
    xs, ys = zip(*batch_data)
    xs_tensor = torch.tensor(xs, dtype=torch.float32)
    ys_tensor = torch.tensor(ys, dtype=torch.float32)
    # Reshape for model input: [batch_size, seq_len] -> we'll add a
    ↪   feature dim
```

```
    xs_tensor = xs_tensor.unsqueeze(-1)  # shape: [batch_size,
    ↪  seq_len, 1]
    return xs_tensor, ys_tensor

# ------------------------------------------------------------
# 3) Transformer Model Definition
# ------------------------------------------------------------
class TimeSeriesTransformer(nn.Module):
    """
    A simple Transformer model for time-series forecasting.
    We encode each time step with an embedding layer, then apply
    TransformerEncoder layers. Finally, we use an MLP to predict
    the next value.
    """
    def __init__(self, d_model=32, nhead=2, num_layers=2,
    ↪  dim_feedforward=64, dropout=0.1):
        super(TimeSeriesTransformer, self).__init__()

        # We'll handle input embedding with a linear projection
        ↪  (data dimension -> d_model)
        self.input_dim = 1  # single feature, can be changed
        self.d_model = d_model

        self.embedding = nn.Linear(self.input_dim, d_model)

        # Positional encoding (basic version: using sine/cosine or
        ↪  learnable)
        self.pos_encoding = PositionalEncoding(d_model=d_model,
        ↪  dropout=dropout)

        encoder_layer = nn.TransformerEncoderLayer(
            d_model=d_model,
            nhead=nhead,
            dim_feedforward=dim_feedforward,
            dropout=dropout,
            batch_first=True  # PyTorch >= 1.10
        )
        self.transformer_encoder =
        ↪  nn.TransformerEncoder(encoder_layer,
        ↪  num_layers=num_layers)

        # Prediction head: for single-step forecast, we reduce the
        ↪  final hidden state
        self.fc_out = nn.Linear(d_model, 1)

    def forward(self, x):
        """
        x shape: [batch_size, seq_len, 1]
        Returns single-step forecast per sample in the batch.
        """
        # Map input to d_model dimension
        x_emb = self.embedding(x)  # [batch_size, seq_len, d_model]
```

94

```python
        # Apply positional encoding
        x_emb = self.pos_encoding(x_emb)  # [batch_size, seq_len,
        ↪    d_model]

        # Pass through the Transformer encoder
        encoded_output = self.transformer_encoder(x_emb)  #
        ↪    [batch_size, seq_len, d_model]

        # We will take the last time step's encoded vector for
        ↪    prediction
        last_step = encoded_output[:, -1, :]  # shape: [batch_size,
        ↪    d_model]

        # Pass through output head
        out = self.fc_out(last_step)  # shape: [batch_size, 1]
        return out.squeeze(-1)  # shape: [batch_size]

class PositionalEncoding(nn.Module):
    """
    Basic positional encoding for time-series.
    By default, uses sine/cosine frequency approach.
    """
    def __init__(self, d_model, dropout=0.1, max_len=5000):
        super(PositionalEncoding, self).__init__()
        self.dropout = nn.Dropout(p=dropout)

        # Create a long enough PEs
        pe = torch.zeros(max_len, d_model)
        position = torch.arange(0, max_len,
        ↪    dtype=torch.float).unsqueeze(1)
        div_term = torch.exp(torch.arange(0, d_model, 2).float() *
        ↪    -(np.log(10000.0) / d_model))

        pe[:, 0::2] = torch.sin(position * div_term)
        pe[:, 1::2] = torch.cos(position * div_term)

        # Add batch dimension
        pe = pe.unsqueeze(0)  # shape: [1, max_len, d_model]

        self.register_buffer('pe', pe)

    def forward(self, x):
        """
        x shape: [batch_size, seq_len, d_model]
        """
        seq_len = x.size(1)
        x = x + self.pe[:, :seq_len, :]
        return self.dropout(x)

# ----------------------------------------------------------------
# 4) Training and Evaluation Functions
# ----------------------------------------------------------------
def train_model(model, dataloader, criterion, optimizer, device):
```

```
        model.train()
        total_loss = 0
        for batch_x, batch_y in dataloader:
            batch_x, batch_y = batch_x.to(device), batch_y.to(device)

            optimizer.zero_grad()
            output = model(batch_x)   # shape: [batch_size]
            loss = criterion(output, batch_y)
            loss.backward()
            optimizer.step()

            total_loss += loss.item()
        return total_loss / len(dataloader)

def evaluate_model(model, dataloader, device):
    model.eval()
    total_loss = 0
    criterion = nn.MSELoss()
    with torch.no_grad():
        for batch_x, batch_y in dataloader:
            batch_x, batch_y = batch_x.to(device),
            ↪   batch_y.to(device)
            output = model(batch_x)
            loss = criterion(output, batch_y)
            total_loss += loss.item()
        return total_loss / len(dataloader)

# -------------------------------------------------------------
# 5) Main Execution
# -------------------------------------------------------------
if __name__ == "__main__":
    # Generate synthetic data
    data = generate_synthetic_time_series(seq_length=1200,
    ↪   freq=0.03, noise_level=0.1)

    # Hyperparameters
    input_window = 24
    batch_size = 32
    epochs = 5
    d_model = 32
    nhead = 2
    num_layers = 2
    dim_feedforward = 64
    dropout = 0.1

    # Split data into train and test
    train_size = int(0.8 * len(data))
    train_data = data[:train_size]
    test_data = data[train_size:]

    # Create datasets
    train_dataset = TimeSeriesDataset(train_data,
    ↪   input_window=input_window)
```

```
test_dataset = TimeSeriesDataset(test_data,
↪   input_window=input_window)

# Create dataloaders
train_loader = DataLoader(train_dataset, batch_size=batch_size,
↪   shuffle=True,
                          collate_fn=collate_fn)
test_loader = DataLoader(test_dataset, batch_size=batch_size,
↪   shuffle=False,
                          collate_fn=collate_fn)

# Model, loss, optimizer
device = torch.device("cuda" if torch.cuda.is_available() else
↪   "cpu")
model = TimeSeriesTransformer(d_model=d_model, nhead=nhead,
↪   num_layers=num_layers,
                              dim_feedforward=dim_feedforward,
                              ↪   dropout=dropout)
model.to(device)

criterion = nn.MSELoss()
optimizer = optim.AdamW(model.parameters(), lr=1e-3)

# Training loop
for epoch in range(epochs):
    train_loss = train_model(model, train_loader, criterion,
    ↪   optimizer, device)
    val_loss = evaluate_model(model, test_loader, device)
    print(f"Epoch [{epoch+1}/{epochs}] | Train Loss:
    ↪   {train_loss:.4f} | Test Loss: {val_loss:.4f}")

print("Training completed. Model is ready for inference.")
```

Key Implementation Details:

- **Synthetic Time-Series Data**: A sine wave with noise is generated by the function `generate_synthetic_time_series`, yielding a floating-point array.

- **Dataset Handling**: The class `TimeSeriesDataset` segments data into windows of length `input_window` and the subsequent time step as the target.

- **Transformer Architecture**: In `TimeSeriesTransformer`, inputs are projected into a higher-dimensional space by `self.embedding`, and positional encoding is applied with the class `PositionalEncoding`. The encoded sequence is then passed

97

through
`nn.TransformerEncoder` layers.

- **Prediction Head**: The final forecast is obtained from the last time step's encoder output, fed into a linear layer (`fc_out`).

- **Training & Evaluation**: The functions `train_model` and `evaluate_model` optimize and measure performance (MSE) respectively. An `AdamW` optimizer with `MSELoss` is used by default in this example.

- **End-to-End Pipeline**: The `main` block handles data splitting, loader creation, training, and testing, demonstrating an end-to-end time-series forecasting workflow in PyTorch using a Transformer.

Chapter 13

Reinforcement Learning with Transformer-based Agents

Used in strategy games or robotics, reinforcement learning (RL) benefits from Transformers' ability to handle sequential decision-making. To build a Transformer-based RL agent, maintain an episodic buffer of states, actions, and rewards. Represent each state (image frames or numerical vectors) with an embedding or a Vision Transformer feature. Concatenate states, actions, and rewards as a sequence of tokens, then feed them into a causal Transformer. For training, you can use policy gradient methods or Q-learning variants by predicting future distribution of returns. Innovative methods utilize offline RL, where the agent learns from fixed datasets of past experience by predicting optimal actions that yield high returns. Another advanced strategy is to incorporate memory layers that track longer horizons or to use multi-modal embeddings for state input.

Python Code Snippet

```
import torch
import torch.nn as nn
```

```python
import torch.optim as optim
import numpy as np
import random
from collections import deque

# -------------------------------------------------------------
# 1) Simple 1D Environment (LineWorld)
# -------------------------------------------------------------
class LineWorldEnv:
    """
    A simple 1D grid environment:
    - The agent starts at position 2 in a 5-cell line (positions:
    ↪  0..4).
    - The goal is to reach position 4, receiving a reward of +1.
    - The agent can move left or right (+action is +1 step, -action
    ↪  is -1 step).
    - Stepping outside the range 0..4 yields a penalty of -1 and
    ↪  terminates.
    """
    def __init__(self):
        self.state_space = 5
        self.action_space = 2  # 0: move left, 1: move right
        self.reset()

    def reset(self):
        self.agent_pos = 2
        return self._get_state()

    def step(self, action):
        # Convert discrete action to movement
        move = -1 if action == 0 else 1
        old_pos = self.agent_pos
        self.agent_pos += move

        if self.agent_pos < 0 or self.agent_pos >= self.state_space:
            # Out of bounds -> negative reward, end episode
            return self._get_state(), -1.0, True
        elif self.agent_pos == 4:
            # Goal reached
            return self._get_state(), +1.0, True
        else:
            # Normal step
            return self._get_state(), 0.0, False

    def _get_state(self):
        # Represent state as a one-hot vector of length 5
        state_vec = np.zeros(self.state_space, dtype=np.float32)
        state_vec[self.agent_pos] = 1.0
        return state_vec


# -------------------------------------------------------------
# 2) Replay Buffer for Storing Trajectories
```

```python
# --------------------------------------------------------------
class ReplayBuffer:
    """
    Stores experiences (state, action, reward, next_state, done) to
    train a Transformer-based agent with offline or online updates.
    """
    def __init__(self, capacity=10000):
        self.buffer = deque(maxlen=capacity)

    def push(self, state, action, reward, next_state, done):
        self.buffer.append((state, action, reward, next_state,
        ↪   done))

    def sample_all(self):
        # We return all experiences for policy gradient updates
        return list(self.buffer)

    def __len__(self):
        return len(self.buffer)


# --------------------------------------------------------------
# 3) Transformer-based Policy Network
# --------------------------------------------------------------
class TransformerPolicy(nn.Module):
    """
    A causal Transformer for sequential state-action embedding:
    Each step in the trajectory is turned into a 'token':
    - Combined embedding of [state, previous_action, reward].
    The model outputs a distribution over possible next actions.
    """
    def __init__(self, state_dim=5, action_dim=2, embed_dim=16,
    ↪   nhead=2,
                 num_layers=2, dim_feedforward=32, max_len=50):
        super(TransformerPolicy, self).__init__()
        self.state_dim = state_dim
        self.action_dim = action_dim
        self.embed_dim = embed_dim
        self.max_len = max_len

        # Linear embeddings for state, action, reward
        # We will combine them into a single embedding
        self.state_emb = nn.Linear(state_dim, embed_dim)
        self.action_emb = nn.Embedding(action_dim, embed_dim)
        self.reward_emb = nn.Linear(1, embed_dim)

        # Positional encoding for sequence steps
        self.pos_embedding = nn.Embedding(max_len, embed_dim)

        # Transformer layers
        encoder_layer =
        ↪   nn.TransformerEncoderLayer(d_model=embed_dim,
                        nhead=nhead,
```

```python
                    dim_feedforward=dim_feedforward,
                    dropout=0.1)
        self.transformer_encoder =
        ↪  nn.TransformerEncoder(encoder_layer,
                            num_layers=num_layers)

        # Output: distribution over actions
        self.action_head = nn.Linear(embed_dim, action_dim)

    def forward(self, state_seq, action_seq, reward_seq):
        """
        state_seq:  [batch_size, seq_len, state_dim]
        action_seq: [batch_size, seq_len] (discrete act indices)
        reward_seq: [batch_size, seq_len, 1]
        Returns:
            A tensor of shape [batch_size, seq_len, action_dim]
            representing the action logits.
        """
        batch_size, seq_len, _ = state_seq.shape

        # Embeddings for state, action, reward
        state_emb = self.state_emb(state_seq)              # [B,
        ↪  seq_len, embed_dim]
        act_emb = self.action_emb(action_seq)              # [B,
        ↪  seq_len, embed_dim]
        rew_emb = self.reward_emb(reward_seq)              # [B,
        ↪  seq_len, embed_dim]

        # Combine them (for simplicity, we sum up these embeddings)
        combined = state_emb + act_emb + rew_emb           # [B,
        ↪  seq_len, embed_dim]

        # Add positional embeddings
        positions = torch.arange(seq_len,
        ↪  device=combined.device).unsqueeze(0).expand(batch_size,
        ↪  seq_len)
        pos_emb = self.pos_embedding(positions)            # [B,
        ↪  seq_len, embed_dim]
        combined = combined + pos_emb

        # Transformer expects [seq_len, batch_size, embed_dim]
        combined = combined.permute(1, 0, 2)

        # Pass through transformer encoder
        encoded = self.transformer_encoder(combined)       #
        ↪  [seq_len, B, embed_dim]

        # Output logits: [seq_len, B, action_dim] -> re-permute ->
        ↪  [B, seq_len, action_dim]
        logits = self.action_head(encoded).permute(1, 0, 2)
        return logits
```

102

```python
# ----------------------------------------------------------------
# 4) REINFORCE Training with Transformer Policy
# ----------------------------------------------------------------
def select_action(policy_model, state, previous_action, reward,
↪  device):
    """
    Given the current step's state, previous action, and reward,
    produce an action. For simplicity, we assume sequence length=1
    ↪  at inference step.
    """
    state_tensor =
    ↪  torch.FloatTensor(state).unsqueeze(0).unsqueeze(0).to(device)
    action_tensor =
    ↪  torch.LongTensor([previous_action]).unsqueeze(0).to(device)
    reward_tensor =
    ↪  torch.FloatTensor([reward]).unsqueeze(0).unsqueeze(0).to(device)

    with torch.no_grad():
        logits = policy_model(state_tensor, action_tensor,
        ↪  reward_tensor)[0, 0]
    probs = torch.softmax(logits, dim=-1)
    action = torch.multinomial(probs, 1).item()
    return action

def generate_trajectory(env, policy_model, device, max_steps=20):
    """
    Run one episode in the environment using the current policy.
    Store (state, action, reward) for each step.
    """
    states = []
    actions = []
    rewards = []

    state = env.reset()
    done = False
    step_count = 0

    # We need a placeholder for 'previous_action' and 'reward'
    prev_action = 0  # Let's define 0 as default
    prev_reward = 0.0

    while not done and step_count < max_steps:
        action = select_action(policy_model, state, prev_action,
        ↪  prev_reward, device)
        next_state, reward, done = env.step(action)

        states.append(state)
        actions.append(action)
        rewards.append(reward)

        state = next_state
        prev_action = action
        prev_reward = reward
```

103

```
        step_count += 1

    return states, actions, rewards

def compute_returns(rewards, gamma=0.99):
    """
    Given a list of immediate rewards, compute discounted returns
    for each time step in an episode.
    """
    returns = []
    running_return = 0.0
    for r in reversed(rewards):
        running_return = r + gamma * running_return
        returns.insert(0, running_return)
    return returns

def reinforce_update(policy_model, optimizer, states, actions,
↪   rewards, device, gamma=0.99):
    """
    Compute REINFORCE update. The sequence length is the length of
    ↪   the episode.
    We feed the entire sequence into the model in one go.
    """
    # Convert data to Tensors
    seq_len = len(states)
    state_seq = torch.FloatTensor(states).unsqueeze(0).to(device)
    ↪   # [1, seq_len, state_dim]
    action_seq = torch.LongTensor(actions).unsqueeze(0).to(device)
    ↪   # [1, seq_len]
    rewards_seq =
    ↪   torch.FloatTensor(rewards).unsqueeze(-1).unsqueeze(0).to(device)
    ↪   # [1, seq_len, 1]

    # Forward pass
    logits = policy_model(state_seq, action_seq, rewards_seq)
    ↪   # [1, seq_len, action_dim]
    log_probs = torch.log_softmax(logits, dim=-1)
    ↪   # [1, seq_len, action_dim]

    # Gather log-prob for the action taken
    chosen_log_probs = log_probs[0, torch.arange(seq_len),
    ↪   action_seq[0]]   # [seq_len]

    # Discounted returns
    G = compute_returns(rewards, gamma)
    G = torch.FloatTensor(G).to(device)

    # Loss = sum(-log_prob * return)
    loss = -torch.sum(chosen_log_probs * G)

    optimizer.zero_grad()
    loss.backward()
    optimizer.step()
```

```
    return loss.item()


# ---------------------------------------------------------------
# 5) Main Training Loop
# ---------------------------------------------------------------
if __name__ == "__main__":
    # Reproducibility
    random.seed(42)
    np.random.seed(42)
    torch.manual_seed(42)

    device = torch.device("cuda" if torch.cuda.is_available() else
    ↪  "cpu")

    # Environment
    env = LineWorldEnv()

    # Policy Model
    policy_model = TransformerPolicy().to(device)

    # Optimizer
    optimizer = optim.Adam(policy_model.parameters(), lr=1e-3)

    # Training config
    num_episodes = 200
    max_steps = 20
    gamma = 0.99

    for episode in range(num_episodes):
        states, actions, rewards = generate_trajectory(env,
        ↪  policy_model, device, max_steps)
        ep_loss = reinforce_update(policy_model, optimizer, states,
        ↪  actions, rewards, device, gamma)

        # Evaluate progress: average reward in this episode
        total_reward = sum(rewards)
        print(f"Episode {episode+1}/{num_episodes}, Loss:
        ↪  {ep_loss:.4f}, Reward: {total_reward:.2f}")

    print("Training complete. The Transformer-based RL agent is
    ↪  ready.")
```

Key Implementation Details:

- **1D Environment**: A simple environment `LineWorldEnv`
  places the agent on a 1D line of 5 cells. The agent moves

105

left or right attempting to reach the goal.

- **Transformer Policy**: In `TransformerPolicy`, we embed the current state, previous action, and reward. A causal Transformer encoder (i.e., `nn.TransformerEncoder`) processes these sequential embeddings to produce action logits at each timestep.

- **Replay Buffer**: Demonstrated by `ReplayBuffer`, though in this example we train from full episodes immediately. For larger tasks, a replay buffer can store more extensive experiences for offline RL.

- **REINFORCE Training**: We combine the log-probabilities of each action with the discounted returns (computed in `compute_returns`) to form the policy gradient update. The function `reinforce_update` executes this procedure.

- **Generate Trajectories**: The function `generate_trajectory` runs an episode within the environment, applying the current policy to gather states, actions, and rewards.

- **Main Loop**: The entire RL pipeline is orchestrated in the `__main__` block, iterating through the environment episodes, generating trajectories, and performing gradient updates until training converges or hits a specified number of episodes.

Chapter 14

Graph Transformers for Node Classification

Many real-world data structures (e.g., social networks, chemical molecules) can be represented as graphs. Graph Transformers adapt self-attention to handle nodes and their relationships. To construct such a model, embed each node and incorporate edge information through adjacency matrices or edge encodings. Instead of sequential tokens, treat node embeddings as a set. Self-attention is computed across all node pairs, using positional or structural encodings to represent graph connectivity. After multiple Transformer layers, classify each node via a final linear layer. This allows capturing global interactions, unlike graph convolution networks which rely on local neighborhoods. Innovative algorithms introduce hierarchical pooling or patching, segmenting large graphs into subgraphs for more efficient processing. Additional techniques might combine multi-head attention with random walk features to capture complex graph structures.

Python Code Snippet

```
import torch
import torch.nn as nn
import torch.optim as optim
import random
from torch.utils.data import Dataset, DataLoader

# For reproducibility
```

```python
torch.manual_seed(42)
random.seed(42)

# ------------------------------------------------------------
# 1) Synthetic Graph Dataset Generation
# ------------------------------------------------------------
class SyntheticGraphDataset(Dataset):
    """
    Generates random graphs where each sample corresponds to one
    ↪  graph,
    and the task is node classification (each node in the graph has
    ↪  a label).

    For simplicity, we'll assume:
    - A fixed number of nodes per graph
    - A random adjacency matrix
    - Random node features
    - Node labels are assigned from a finite set of classes
    """
    def __init__(self, num_graphs=100, num_nodes=10, feature_dim=8,
    ↪  num_classes=3):
        self.num_graphs = num_graphs
        self.num_nodes = num_nodes
        self.feature_dim = feature_dim
        self.num_classes = num_classes

        # Each item in the dataset will store:
        #   - adjacency_matrix (num_nodes x num_nodes)
        #   - node_features (num_nodes x feature_dim)
        #   - node_labels (num_nodes)
        self.data = []
        for _ in range(num_graphs):
            # Create a random adjacency matrix
            adj_matrix = (torch.rand(num_nodes, num_nodes) >
            ↪  0.7).float()
            # Symmetrize it to represent an undirected graph
            adj_matrix = ((adj_matrix + adj_matrix.t()) > 0).float()
            # Zero out the diagonal (no self-loops for simplicity)
            adj_matrix.fill_diagonal_(0)

            # Create random node features
            features = torch.randn(num_nodes, feature_dim)

            # Create random labels for each node
            labels = torch.randint(low=0, high=num_classes,
            ↪  size=(num_nodes,))

            self.data.append((adj_matrix, features, labels))

    def __len__(self):
        return self.num_graphs

    def __getitem__(self, idx):
```

```
            return self.data[idx]

    def collate_fn(batch):
        """
        Custom collate function to group multiple graphs into a batch.
        We'll keep them as individual items in a list for each field
        ↪ because
        the graph sizes are consistent in this synthetic example.
        """
        adj_matrices = []
        features = []
        labels = []
        for adj, feat, lab in batch:
            adj_matrices.append(adj)
            features.append(feat)
            labels.append(lab)

        # Stack them on a new dimension
        adj_matrices = torch.stack(adj_matrices, dim=0)      # [B, N, N]
        features = torch.stack(features, dim=0)              # [B, N, F]
        labels = torch.stack(labels, dim=0)                  # [B, N]

        return adj_matrices, features, labels

# ----------------------------------------------------------------
# 2) Graph Positional Encoding (Optional)
# ----------------------------------------------------------------
class GraphPositionalEncoding(nn.Module):
    """
    A placeholder for a variety of graph positional or structural
    ↪ encodings
    that can be added to the node features. For demonstration, we
    ↪ will
    encode the node index as a vector via an embedding layer.
    """
    def __init__(self, num_nodes, embed_dim):
        super(GraphPositionalEncoding, self).__init__()
        self.node_embedding = nn.Embedding(num_nodes, embed_dim)

    def forward(self, node_features):
        """
        node_features: [B, N, F]
        We'll assume N is constant across the dataset for
        ↪ simplicity.
        We'll generate a range [0..N-1], embed it, and add it to
        ↪ node_features.
        """
        B, N, F = node_features.shape
        indices = torch.arange(N).unsqueeze(0).expand(B,
        ↪ N).to(node_features.device)
        positional_emb = self.node_embedding(indices)   # [B, N, F]

        return node_features + positional_emb
```

109

```python
# -----------------------------------------------------------
# 3) Graph Transformer Model
# -----------------------------------------------------------
class GraphTransformer(nn.Module):
    """
    A simple Graph Transformer for node classification that:
    - Embeds node features
    - (Optionally) adds positional encoding
    - Applies multi-head self-attention across all nodes
    - Outputs logits for each node
    """
    def __init__(self, feature_dim, embed_dim, num_heads,
    ↪  ff_hidden_dim,
                 num_classes, num_layers=2, dropout=0.1,
                     ↪  max_nodes=10):
        super(GraphTransformer, self).__init__()

        # Embedding projection to match transformer's d_model
        self.input_proj = nn.Linear(feature_dim, embed_dim)

        # Optional positional (structural) encoding
        self.pos_encoder =
        ↪  GraphPositionalEncoding(num_nodes=max_nodes,

                                   ↪  embed_dim=embed_dim)

        # We'll implement adjacency-aware attention by applying a
        ↪  mask
        # that zeroes out attention on non-edges (except for
        ↪  demonstration
        # we'll just rely on adjacency gating).

        # Transformer Encoder
        encoder_layer =
        ↪  nn.TransformerEncoderLayer(d_model=embed_dim,
                    nhead=num_heads,
                    dim_feedforward=ff_hidden_dim,
                    dropout=dropout,
                    batch_first=False)
        self.transformer_encoder =
        ↪  nn.TransformerEncoder(encoder_layer,
                    num_layers=num_layers)

        # Final classification layer for node-level output
        self.classifier = nn.Linear(embed_dim, num_classes)

    def forward(self, adj_matrix, node_features):
        """
        adj_matrix: [B, N, N]
        node_features: [B, N, feature_dim]
        """
        B, N, _ = node_features.size()
```

```python
# Project input features to embed_dim
h = self.input_proj(node_features)  # [B, N, embed_dim]

# Add positional/structural encoding
h = self.pos_encoder(h)             # [B, N, embed_dim]

# Reshape for PyTorch's Transformer: [N, B, embed_dim]
h = h.permute(1, 0, 2)

# We'll create an attention mask from the adjacency:
# The transformer expects a float mask with shape [N, N] or
↪   [B, N, N].
# If a position is masked, we want it to be True (or 1).
# Here, adjacency=1 means "connected," so no mask there.
# We'll keep zeros for connections, 1 for no connection.

# In order to block attention for positions that are not
↪   connected,
# we invert the adjacency (plus identity to allow
↪   self-attention on the node itself if needed).
# However, typically you'd incorporate adjacency in the
↪   attention weighting directly,
# or do advanced adjustments. For demonstration, let's
↪   produce a mask that
# sets True where adjacency=0 (no connection).

# Expand adjacency for transformer if needed. We'll produce
↪   shape [B, N, N].
# We also want shape [B, N, N], but the transformer's
↪   attn_mask is typically [N, N] or [B, n_heads, N, N].
# For simplicity, let's just create a single mask. We'll not
↪   incorporate batch dimension for demonstration.
# Instead, we could pass None or a single adjacency pattern
↪   if everything is same-sized.

# We can pass None to let the transformer attend to all
↪   pairs.
# In a real scenario, we'd adopt a more advanced approach or
↪   a custom attention layer.
# So for clarity, let's omit the adjacency mask usage in the
↪   built-in API here.

# Encode
encoded = self.transformer_encoder(h, mask=None)  # [N, B,
↪   embed_dim]

# Re-permute back
encoded = encoded.permute(1, 0, 2)  # [B, N, embed_dim]

# Classify each node
logits = self.classifier(encoded)   # [B, N, num_classes]
return logits
```

111

```
# ----------------------------------------------------------------
# 4) Training and Evaluation Routines
# ----------------------------------------------------------------
def train_epoch(model, dataloader, optimizer, criterion, device):
    model.train()
    total_loss = 0.0
    for adj, feat, lab in dataloader:
        adj, feat, lab = adj.to(device), feat.to(device),
        ↪  lab.to(device)

        optimizer.zero_grad()
        logits = model(adj, feat)    # [B, N, num_classes]

        # Flatten out for computation
        # We'll treat node classification as [B*N] vs. [B*N]
        B, N, C = logits.shape
        loss = criterion(logits.view(B*N, C), lab.view(B*N))
        loss.backward()
        optimizer.step()

        total_loss += loss.item()
    return total_loss / len(dataloader)

def evaluate_model(model, dataloader, device):
    model.eval()
    correct = 0
    total = 0
    with torch.no_grad():
        for adj, feat, lab in dataloader:
            adj, feat, lab = adj.to(device), feat.to(device),
            ↪  lab.to(device)
            logits = model(adj, feat)    # [B, N, num_classes]
            B, N, C = logits.shape
            preds = torch.argmax(logits, dim=2)    # [B, N]
            correct += (preds == lab).sum().item()
            total += B * N
    return correct / total


# ----------------------------------------------------------------
# 5) Main Execution
# ----------------------------------------------------------------
if __name__ == "__main__":
    # Hyperparameters
    num_graphs = 200
    num_nodes = 12
    feature_dim = 16
    num_classes = 4
    embed_dim = 32
    num_heads = 2
    ff_hidden_dim = 64
    num_layers = 2
    dropout = 0.1
```

```python
batch_size = 8
lr = 1e-3
num_epochs = 5

device = torch.device("cuda" if torch.cuda.is_available() else
↪    "cpu")

# Create dataset and dataloader
dataset = SyntheticGraphDataset(num_graphs=num_graphs,
                                num_nodes=num_nodes,
                                feature_dim=feature_dim,
                                num_classes=num_classes)
train_size = int(0.8 * len(dataset))
test_size = len(dataset) - train_size
train_dataset, test_dataset =
↪    torch.utils.data.random_split(dataset, [train_size,
↪    test_size])

train_loader = DataLoader(train_dataset, batch_size=batch_size,
↪    shuffle=True,
                          collate_fn=collate_fn)
test_loader = DataLoader(test_dataset, batch_size=batch_size,
↪    shuffle=False,
                         collate_fn=collate_fn)

# Initialize model
model = GraphTransformer(feature_dim=feature_dim,
                         embed_dim=embed_dim,
                         num_heads=num_heads,
                         ff_hidden_dim=ff_hidden_dim,
                         num_classes=num_classes,
                         num_layers=num_layers,
                         dropout=dropout,
                         max_nodes=num_nodes).to(device)

# Optimizer and loss
optimizer = optim.AdamW(model.parameters(), lr=lr)
criterion = nn.CrossEntropyLoss()

# Training loop
for epoch in range(num_epochs):
    train_loss = train_epoch(model, train_loader, optimizer,
    ↪    criterion, device)
    acc = evaluate_model(model, test_loader, device)
    print(f"Epoch {epoch+1}/{num_epochs}, Loss:
    ↪    {train_loss:.4f}, Test Accuracy: {acc:.4f}")

print("Training completed. Model ready for inference.")
```

Key Implementation Details:

- **Synthetic Graph Generation**: The class `SyntheticGraphDataset` creates random graphs, including adjacency matrices, node features, and node labels.

- **Graph Positional Encoding**: In `GraphPositionalEncoding`, each node index is encoded via an embedding and added to the node features to capture positional information.

- **Graph Transformer**: The core model is `GraphTransformer`, which projects node features to a Transformer-compatible embedding, applies multi-head self-attention through `nn.TransformerEncoder`, and then classifies each node via `self.classifier`.

- **Training Procedure**: The function `train_epoch` computes cross-entropy loss for node classification and backpropagates through the graph transformer's parameters using the `AdamW` optimizer.

- **Evaluation**: The function `evaluate_model` measures the overall accuracy by comparing predicted labels for all nodes against the ground-truth labels in the test set.

- **Execution Flow**: The `main` block puts it all together: splits data, builds and trains the model, and prints the test accuracy after each epoch.

Chapter 15

Protein Structure Modeling with Transformers

Transformers excel at processing amino acid sequences to predict protein structure or function, crucial in drug discovery. Begin by representing protein sequences as tokens (individual amino acids). A specialized Transformer (e.g., AlphaFold's Transformer blocks or ProtBert) is then trained to predict 3D coordinates or secondary structure. Positional embeddings capture sequence order, while attention weights reveal inter-residue relationships. For advanced structural modeling, incorporate evolutionary data from multiple sequence alignments, letting the model leverage homologous proteins. You can also add geometric constraints: predicted distance maps or rotation angles. The final output might be pairwise residue distances plus angles that define the protein's shape. This approach dramatically accelerates structural predictions and can be further refined by post-processing steps, such as energy minimization or template-based alignment.

Python Code Snippet

```
import torch
import torch.nn as nn
import torch.optim as optim
import random
```

```python
from torch.utils.data import Dataset, DataLoader

# For reproducibility
torch.manual_seed(42)
random.seed(42)

# ----------------------------------------------------------------
# 1) Synthetic Data Generation
# ----------------------------------------------------------------
AMINO_ACIDS = [
    'A', 'R', 'N', 'D', 'C',
    'E', 'Q', 'G', 'H', 'I',
    'L', 'K', 'M', 'F', 'P',
    'S', 'T', 'W', 'Y', 'V'
]
MAX_SEQ_LEN = 8  # For demonstration, we keep sequences short

def random_protein_sequence(seq_len=MAX_SEQ_LEN):
    """
    Generates a random protein sequence of fixed length
    using standard amino acids.
    """
    return ''.join(random.choice(AMINO_ACIDS) for _ in
    ↪ range(seq_len))

def random_distance_matrix(seq_len=MAX_SEQ_LEN):
    """
    Generates a random NxN distance matrix for demonstration.
    We'll produce values between 0 and 20 (angstroms, e.g.).
    """
    mat = [[random.uniform(0.0, 20.0) for _ in range(seq_len)]
            for __ in range(seq_len)]
    return mat

def generate_synthetic_protein_data(num_samples=200):
    """
    Create synthetic protein data: each sample has a random
    protein sequence and an NxN distance matrix we aim to predict.
    """
    sequences = []
    distance_matrices = []
    for _ in range(num_samples):
        seq = random_protein_sequence()
        dist_mat = random_distance_matrix()
        sequences.append(seq)
        distance_matrices.append(dist_mat)
    return sequences, distance_matrices

# ----------------------------------------------------------------
# 2) Mapping Amino Acids to Indices
# ----------------------------------------------------------------
aa_to_idx = {aa: i+2 for i, aa in enumerate(AMINO_ACIDS)}
# We'll reserve index 0 for [PAD], 1 for [UNK], then 2.. cover A..V
```

116

```python
idx_to_aa = {v: k for k, v in aa_to_idx.items()}

def encode_sequence(seq):
    """
    Convert amino acid characters in seq to their corresponding IDs.
    If an amino acid is somehow missing from AMINO_ACIDS, map to
    ↪    [UNK].
    """
    encoded = []
    for aa in seq:
        if aa in aa_to_idx:
            encoded.append(aa_to_idx[aa])
        else:
            encoded.append(1)  # [UNK]
    return encoded

def decode_sequence(encoded):
    """
    For debugging: convert IDs to amino acid characters.
    """
    return ''.join(idx_to_aa.get(x, '?') for x in encoded)

# -------------------------------------------------------------
# 3) Custom Dataset & Collate Func
# -------------------------------------------------------------
class ProteinDataset(Dataset):
    """
    A PyTorch dataset that holds protein sequences and
    their distance matrices.
    """
    def __init__(self, sequences, distance_matrices):
        self.sequences = sequences
        self.distance_matrices = distance_matrices
        # We'll encode each sequence into IDs
        self.encoded_sequences = [encode_sequence(seq) for seq in
        ↪    sequences]

        # Flatten the distance matrices so we treat them as a vector
        ↪    (seq_len~2).
        # This is purely for demonstration; in a real scenario, you
        ↪    might
        # handle them as a matrix or use a more advanced approach.
        self.flattened_distances = []
        for mat in distance_matrices:
            flat = []
            for row in mat:
                flat.extend(row)
            self.flattened_distances.append(flat)

    def __len__(self):
        return len(self.sequences)

    def __getitem__(self, idx):
```

117

```python
        return self.encoded_sequences[idx],
        ↪    self.flattened_distances[idx]

def collate_fn(batch_data):
    """
    Collate function to handle padding or truncation of
    ↪    variable-length sequences.
    Here, we keep the sequence length fixed to MAX_SEQ_LEN for
    ↪    clarity.
    """
    # Extract sequences and distance vectors from the batch
    encoded_lists, dist_vectors = zip(*batch_data)

    # Each sequence is already length = MAX_SEQ_LEN, so no further
    ↪    padding needed
    batch_x = torch.tensor(encoded_lists, dtype=torch.long)

    # Convert distance vectors into tensors (each is length
    ↪    MAX_SEQ_LEN^2)
    batch_y = torch.tensor(dist_vectors, dtype=torch.float)

    return batch_x, batch_y

# ----------------------------------------------------------------
# 4) Transformer Model for Distance Prediction
# ----------------------------------------------------------------
class ProteinTransformerModel(nn.Module):
    """
    This model embeds a protein sequence, processes it through
    a Transformer encoder, then outputs a flattened NxN distance map
    for the sequence.
    """
    def __init__(self, vocab_size, embed_dim=32, num_heads=2,
                 hidden_dim=64, num_layers=2, dropout=0.1):
        super(ProteinTransformerModel, self).__init__()
        self.embed_dim = embed_dim
        # We'll reserve 0 for [PAD] index
        self.embedding = nn.Embedding(vocab_size, embed_dim,
        ↪    padding_idx=0)

        # Transformer encoder
        encoder_layer = nn.TransformerEncoderLayer(
            d_model=embed_dim,
            nhead=num_heads,
            dim_feedforward=hidden_dim,
            dropout=dropout
        )
        self.transformer_encoder =
        ↪    nn.TransformerEncoder(encoder_layer, num_layers)

        # For a sequence of length L=MAX_SEQ_LEN, we want to output
        ↪    L*L distances
```

118

```python
        # We'll do a simple feed-forward from the pooled
        ↪   representation to
        # L*L outputs. As an alternative, you could apply more
        ↪   sophisticated
        # row/column attention or per-token predictions.
        self.output_dim = MAX_SEQ_LEN * MAX_SEQ_LEN

        self.fc = nn.Linear(embed_dim, self.output_dim)

    def forward(self, x):
        """
        x: [batch_size, seq_len]
        We'll permute to [seq_len, batch_size, embed_dim] for the
        ↪   transformer.
        """
        # Embedded => [batch_size, seq_len, embed_dim]
        embedded = self.embedding(x)

        # Permute => [seq_len, batch_size, embed_dim]
        embedded = embedded.permute(1, 0, 2)

        # Transformer Encoder
        encoded = self.transformer_encoder(embedded)

        # We'll do mean pooling across seq_len dimension =>
        ↪   [batch_size, embed_dim]
        mean_pool = torch.mean(encoded, dim=0)

        # Output feed-forward: produce a flattened distance map
        # [batch_size, L^2]
        out = self.fc(mean_pool)
        return out

# ----------------------------------------------------------------
# 5) Training & Evaluation
# ----------------------------------------------------------------
def train_model(model, dataloader, optimizer, criterion, device):
    """
    Training loop for one epoch. The model attempts to predict
    flattened distance matrices (regression) from amino acid
    ↪   sequences.
    """
    model.train()
    total_loss = 0.0

    for batch_x, batch_y in dataloader:
        batch_x = batch_x.to(device)
        batch_y = batch_y.to(device)

        optimizer.zero_grad()
        preds = model(batch_x)   # [batch_size, L^2]
        loss = criterion(preds, batch_y)
        loss.backward()
```

119

```python
        optimizer.step()

        total_loss += loss.item()

    return total_loss / len(dataloader)

def evaluate_model(model, dataloader, criterion, device):
    """
    Evaluation loop that calculates the average loss on the test
    ↪   set.
    """
    model.eval()
    total_loss = 0.0

    with torch.no_grad():
        for batch_x, batch_y in dataloader:
            batch_x = batch_x.to(device)
            batch_y = batch_y.to(device)

            preds = model(batch_x)
            loss = criterion(preds, batch_y)
            total_loss += loss.item()

    return total_loss / len(dataloader)

# ---------------------------------------------------------------
# 6) Main Execution Block
# ---------------------------------------------------------------
if __name__ == "__main__":
    # Generate synthetic dataset
    sequences, dist_matrices =
    ↪   generate_synthetic_protein_data(num_samples=500)

    # Split into train/test
    train_size = int(0.8 * len(sequences))
    train_seqs = sequences[:train_size]
    train_mats = dist_matrices[:train_size]
    test_seqs = sequences[train_size:]
    test_mats = dist_matrices[train_size:]

    # Create datasets
    train_dataset = ProteinDataset(train_seqs, train_mats)
    test_dataset  = ProteinDataset(test_seqs, test_mats)

    # Dataloaders
    train_loader = DataLoader(train_dataset, batch_size=16,
    ↪   shuffle=True, collate_fn=collate_fn)
    test_loader  = DataLoader(test_dataset, batch_size=16,
    ↪   shuffle=False, collate_fn=collate_fn)

    # Model instantiation
    # +2 for [PAD] and [UNK]
    vocab_size = len(AMINO_ACIDS) + 2
```

```
device = torch.device('cuda' if torch.cuda.is_available() else
↪   'cpu')
model =
↪   ProteinTransformerModel(vocab_size=vocab_size).to(device)

# Optimizer & Loss
optimizer = optim.AdamW(model.parameters(), lr=1e-3)
criterion = nn.MSELoss()   # A simple regression objective for
↪   distance maps

# Train the model
num_epochs = 5
for epoch in range(num_epochs):
    train_loss = train_model(model, train_loader, optimizer,
    ↪   criterion, device)
    val_loss = evaluate_model(model, test_loader, criterion,
    ↪   device)
    print(f"Epoch {epoch+1}/{num_epochs}, Train Loss:
    ↪   {train_loss:.4f}, Test Loss: {val_loss:.4f}")

print("Training complete. Model is ready for inference or
↪   further refinement.")
```

Key Implementation Details:

- **Data Generation**: The function `random_protein_sequence` creates synthetic protein sequences at a fixed length, and `random_distance_matrix` provides random NxN values for distances.

- **Dataset and Collation**: The class `ProteinDataset` pairs each protein sequence with a flattened distance matrix, and `collate_fn` organizes them into batches for training.

- **Transformer Architecture**: The core of the model is in `ProteinTransformerModel`, which uses an embedding layer plus `nn.TransformerEncoder` to transform amino acid inputs into latent representations, then outputs predicted distance maps.

- **Training Loop**: The functions `train_model` and `evaluate_model` illustrate how to optimize a regression loss (`nn.MSELoss`) and monitor performance on a validation set.

- **Usage**: The `if __name__ == "__main__"` block demonstrates a complete workflow for generating synthetic data, splitting

121

into train/test sets, and iteratively refining the transformer-based distance predictor.

Chapter 16

Speech Recognition with Transformers

Used in virtual assistants and automated transcription, speech recognition converts audio into text. First, process raw audio into spectrograms or mel-frequency cepstral coefficients (MFCCs). Then, treat each time slice as a 'token' and feed it into a Transformer encoder that captures time-based relationships. In an encoder-decoder setup (e.g., Speech Transformer), the decoder predicts text tokens, leveraging cross-attention over the encoded audio features. Transfer learning can be done via large speech datasets (e.g., LibriSpeech) to initialize the model. For innovative approaches, incorporate convolutional front-ends to downsample the audio features or use alignment-free training strategies. As an alternative, direct audio-to-text models (like wav2vec2) use self-supervised pre-training on raw waveforms before fine-tuning on labeled transcripts, improving recognition accuracy and robustness in noisy environments.

Python Code Snippet

```
import torch
import torch.nn as nn
import torch.optim as optim
from torch.utils.data import Dataset, DataLoader
import random

# For reproducibility
```

```python
random.seed(42)
torch.manual_seed(42)

# -----------------------------------------------------------------
# 1) Tokenizer for Output Text
# -----------------------------------------------------------------
class SimpleCharTokenizer:
    '''
    Tokenizer for text output.
    Converts characters to indices and vice versa.
    Here we use a simplistic approach (a handful of characters),
    but in practice you'd expand to all relevant characters.
    '''
    def __init__(self, vocab=None):
        if vocab is None:
            # Some typical characters, plus special tokens
            self.vocab = ['<pad>', '<sos>', '<eos>', '<unk>',
                          'a','b','c','d','e','f','g','h','i','j',
                          'k','l','m','n','o','p','q','r','s','t',
                          'u','v','w','x','y','z',' ']
        else:
            self.vocab = vocab

        self.char2id = {ch: idx for idx, ch in
            enumerate(self.vocab)}
        self.id2char = {idx: ch for idx, ch in
            enumerate(self.vocab)}

    def encode(self, text):
        # Convert characters to IDs, with <sos> at start and <eos>
        # at end
        encoded = [self.char2id['<sos>']]
        for ch in text:
            if ch in self.char2id:
                encoded.append(self.char2id[ch])
            else:
                encoded.append(self.char2id['<unk>'])
        encoded.append(self.char2id['<eos>'])
        return encoded

    def decode(self, ids):
        # Convert IDs to characters, stopping at <eos> if
        # encountered
        result = []
        for _id in ids:
            ch = self.id2char.get(_id, '<unk>')
            if ch == '<eos>':
                break
            if ch not in ['<sos>', '<pad>', '<eos>']:
                result.append(ch)
        return "".join(result)

    def pad_sequence(self, sequences, max_len):
```

```python
        # Pad sequences to fixed length with <pad>
        padded = []
        for seq in sequences:
            if len(seq) < max_len:
                seq = seq + [self.char2id['<pad>']] * (max_len -
                ↪  len(seq))
            else:
                seq = seq[:max_len]
            padded.append(seq)
        return padded

    @property
    def pad_id(self):
        return self.char2id['<pad>']


# ----------------------------------------------------------------
# 2) Synthetic Speech Dataset
# ----------------------------------------------------------------
class SyntheticSpeechDataset(Dataset):
    '''
    Generates random spectrograms and random text transcripts for
    ↪  demonstration.
    Each spectrogram is a 2D tensor (time, freq) of random floats.
    Each transcript is a random string of letters, turned into token
    ↪  IDs.
    '''
    def __init__(self, num_samples=1000, max_time=50, freq_bins=40,
    ↪  max_text_len=10, tokenizer=None):
        super().__init__()
        self.num_samples = num_samples
        self.max_time = max_time
        self.freq_bins = freq_bins
        self.max_text_len = max_text_len

        if tokenizer is None:
            self.tokenizer = SimpleCharTokenizer()
        else:
            self.tokenizer = tokenizer

        # Create random data
        self.spectrograms = [torch.rand(self.max_time,
        ↪  self.freq_bins) for _ in range(self.num_samples)]
        # Create random text
        letters = [ch for ch in "abcdefghijklmnopqrstuvwxyz "]
        self.transcripts = []
        for _ in range(self.num_samples):
            length = random.randint(3, self.max_text_len)  # random
            ↪  text length
            text = "".join(random.choice(letters) for __ in
            ↪  range(length))
            self.transcripts.append(text)
```

125

```python
    def __len__(self):
        return self.num_samples

    def __getitem__(self, idx):
        spec = self.spectrograms[idx]
        txt = self.transcripts[idx]
        txt_encoded = self.tokenizer.encode(txt)
        return spec, torch.tensor(txt_encoded, dtype=torch.long)


def collate_fn(batch_data):
    '''
    Collate function for DataLoader:
    1) Stack the spectrograms (zero padding not strictly required
    ↪  here).
    2) Pad the text sequences.
    '''
    specs, txts = zip(*batch_data)
    # specs is a tuple of [time, freq] Tensors
    # We can stack them into shape [batch_size, max_time, freq_bins]
    specs_tensor = torch.stack(specs, dim=0)  # [batch_size, time,
    ↪  freq_bins]

    # Pad text sequences
    max_len = max(len(t) for t in txts)
    padded_txts = dataset.tokenizer.pad_sequence([t.tolist() for t
    ↪  in txts], max_len)
    txts_tensor = torch.tensor(padded_txts, dtype=torch.long)

    return specs_tensor, txts_tensor


# ---------------------------------------------------------------
# 3) Transformer Model (Encoder-Decoder)
# ---------------------------------------------------------------
class SpeechTransformer(nn.Module):
    '''
    Encoder-Decoder Transformer for speech recognition:
      - Encoder takes spectrogram frames as 'tokens'.
      - Decoder takes text tokens, cross-attending to the encoder
      ↪  output.
    '''
    def __init__(self, freq_bins=40, d_model=64, nhead=4,
    ↪  num_encoder_layers=3,
                 num_decoder_layers=3, dim_feedforward=128,
                 ↪  vocab_size=30,
                 dropout=0.1, pad_id=0):
        super(SpeechTransformer, self).__init__()

        # We'll project spectrogram frames into d_model dimension
        self.input_linear = nn.Linear(freq_bins, d_model)

        # Positional encodings for the input spectrogram
```

126

```python
        self.encoder_pos_encoding = PositionalEncoding(d_model,
        ↪ dropout)

        # Encoder
        encoder_layer = nn.TransformerEncoderLayer(
            d_model=d_model,
            nhead=nhead,
            dim_feedforward=dim_feedforward,
            dropout=dropout
        )
        self.encoder = nn.TransformerEncoder(encoder_layer,
        ↪ num_layers=num_encoder_layers)

        # Embedding for text tokens
        self.text_embedding = nn.Embedding(vocab_size, d_model,
        ↪ padding_idx=pad_id)
        self.decoder_pos_encoding = PositionalEncoding(d_model,
        ↪ dropout)

        # Decoder
        decoder_layer = nn.TransformerDecoderLayer(
            d_model=d_model,
            nhead=nhead,
            dim_feedforward=dim_feedforward,
            dropout=dropout
        )
        self.decoder = nn.TransformerDecoder(decoder_layer,
        ↪ num_layers=num_decoder_layers)

        # Final classifier to predict next character
        self.output_fc = nn.Linear(d_model, vocab_size)

    def generate_square_subsequent_mask(self, sz):
        '''
        Generates an upper-triangular mask of -inf, used in the
        ↪ decoder
        to ensure each position can only attend to previous
        ↪ positions.
        '''
        mask = (torch.triu(torch.ones(sz, sz)) == 1).transpose(0, 1)
        mask = mask.float().masked_fill(mask == 1, float('-inf'))
        return mask

    def forward(self, specs, text_inp):
        '''
        specs: [batch_size, time, freq_bins]
        text_inp: [batch_size, text_seq_len]

        Return: logits over the vocabulary for each time step in the
        ↪ text sequence
        '''
        batch_size, time, freq = specs.size()
        text_seq_len = text_inp.size(1)
```

127

```python
    # Encoder
    # Project freq_bins -> d_model
    encoder_inp = self.input_linear(specs)  # [batch_size, time,
    ↪   d_model]

    # [time, batch_size, d_model] for transformer
    encoder_inp = encoder_inp.permute(1, 0, 2)
    encoder_inp = self.encoder_pos_encoding(encoder_inp)
    memory = self.encoder(encoder_inp)  # [time, batch_size,
    ↪   d_model]

    # Decoder
    # text_emb => [batch_size, text_seq_len, d_model]
    text_emb = self.text_embedding(text_inp)
    text_emb = text_emb.permute(1, 0, 2)  # [text_seq_len,
    ↪   batch_size, d_model]
    text_emb = self.decoder_pos_encoding(text_emb)

    # Generate causal mask for the decoder
    tgt_mask = self.generate_square_subsequent_mask(
    text_seq_len).to(text_inp.device)

    # The cross-attention uses 'memory' from encoder
    out = self.decoder(text_emb, memory, tgt_mask=tgt_mask)

    # out => [text_seq_len, batch_size, d_model]
    out = out.permute(1, 0, 2)  # [batch_size, text_seq_len,
    ↪   d_model]

    logits = self.output_fc(out)  # [batch_size, text_seq_len,
    ↪   vocab_size]
    return logits


class PositionalEncoding(nn.Module):
    '''
    Standard positional encoding for Transformer (sine/cosine).
    '''
    def __init__(self, d_model, dropout=0.1, max_len=5000):
        super(PositionalEncoding, self).__init__()
        self.dropout = nn.Dropout(p=dropout)

        pe = torch.zeros(max_len, d_model)
        position = torch.arange(0, max_len,
        ↪   dtype=torch.float).unsqueeze(1)
        div_term = torch.exp(torch.arange(0, d_model, 2).float()
                            * (-torch.log(torch.tensor(10000.0)) /
        ↪   d_model))
        pe[:, 0::2] = torch.sin(position * div_term)
        pe[:, 1::2] = torch.cos(position * div_term)
        pe = pe.unsqueeze(1)  # [max_len, 1, d_model]
```

```python
        self.register_buffer('pe', pe)

    def forward(self, x):
        '''
        x: [seq_len, batch_size, d_model]
        '''
        seq_len = x.size(0)
        x = x + self.pe[:seq_len, :]
        return self.dropout(x)


# ------------------------------------------------------------
# 4) Training and Evaluation
# ------------------------------------------------------------
def train_model(model, dataloader, optimizer, criterion, device):
    model.train()
    total_loss = 0.0
    for specs, texts in dataloader:
        specs, texts = specs.to(device), texts.to(device)

        # Shift the decoder input by 1 (teacher forcing)
        # We want the model to predict the next token, given the
        ↪   previous tokens.
        # text_inp is everything except last token
        # text_target is everything except first token
        text_inp = texts[:, :-1]
        text_target = texts[:, 1:]

        optimizer.zero_grad()
        logits = model(specs, text_inp)

        # Flatten the logits and targets for cross entropy
        # logits => [batch_size, seq_len-1, vocab_size]
        # text_target => [batch_size, seq_len-1]
        logits_2d = logits.reshape(-1, logits.size(-1))
        target_2d = text_target.reshape(-1)

        loss = criterion(logits_2d, target_2d)
        loss.backward()
        optimizer.step()

        total_loss += loss.item()
    return total_loss / len(dataloader)


def evaluate_model(model, dataloader, device):
    model.eval()
    total_loss = 0.0
    total_samples = 0
    with torch.no_grad():
        for specs, texts in dataloader:
            specs, texts = specs.to(device), texts.to(device)
```

```
            text_inp = texts[:, :-1]
            text_target = texts[:, 1:]

            logits = model(specs, text_inp)

            logits_2d = logits.reshape(-1, logits.size(-1))
            target_2d = text_target.reshape(-1)

            loss = nn.functional.cross_entropy(logits_2d, target_2d,
            ↪  reduction='sum')
            total_loss += loss.item()
            total_samples += target_2d.numel()
    return total_loss / total_samples


# ------------------------------------------------------------
# 5) Main Execution (Data Prep, Model Init, Training)
# ------------------------------------------------------------
if __name__ == "__main__":
    # Instantiating dataset
    dataset = SyntheticSpeechDataset(num_samples=200, max_time=30,
    ↪  freq_bins=20, max_text_len=8)

    # Create DataLoader
    train_size = int(0.8 * len(dataset))
    test_size = len(dataset) - train_size
    train_dataset, test_dataset =
    ↪  torch.utils.data.random_split(dataset, [train_size,
    ↪  test_size])

    train_loader = DataLoader(train_dataset, batch_size=4,
    ↪  shuffle=True, collate_fn=collate_fn)
    test_loader = DataLoader(test_dataset, batch_size=4,
    ↪  shuffle=False, collate_fn=collate_fn)

    # Model, optimizer, loss
    device = torch.device("cuda" if torch.cuda.is_available() else
    ↪  "cpu")

    # Get vocab size from dataset tokenizer
    vocab_size = len(dataset.tokenizer.vocab)
    model = SpeechTransformer(
        freq_bins=20,
        d_model=64,
        nhead=2,
        num_encoder_layers=2,
        num_decoder_layers=2,
        dim_feedforward=128,
        vocab_size=vocab_size,
        pad_id=dataset.tokenizer.pad_id
    ).to(device)

    optimizer = optim.AdamW(model.parameters(), lr=1e-3)
```

```python
criterion =
↪  nn.CrossEntropyLoss(ignore_index=dataset.tokenizer.pad_id)

# Training
num_epochs = 5
for epoch in range(num_epochs):
    train_loss = train_model(model, train_loader, optimizer,
    ↪  criterion, device)
    val_loss = evaluate_model(model, test_loader, device)
    print(f"Epoch {epoch+1}/{num_epochs}, Train Loss:
    ↪  {train_loss:.4f}, Val Loss: {val_loss:.4f}")

print("Training complete. Model is ready for inference.")

# Quick demonstration of inference with a random sample
sample_specs, sample_text_ids = dataset[0]
sample_specs = sample_specs.unsqueeze(0).to(device)   # [1, time,
↪  freq_bins]

# Let's run a small greedy decoding loop
max_decode_len = 20
model.eval()
generated_tokens = [dataset.tokenizer.char2id['<sos>']]

with torch.no_grad():
    for _ in range(max_decode_len):
        inp = torch.tensor(generated_tokens,
        ↪  dtype=torch.long).unsqueeze(0).to(device)
        logits = model(sample_specs, inp)
        # Get the last step predictions
        next_token_logits = logits[0, -1, :]
        next_token = torch.argmax(next_token_logits)
        next_token_id = next_token.item()
        generated_tokens.append(next_token_id)

        if next_token_id == dataset.tokenizer.char2id['<eos>']:
            break

decoded_text = dataset.tokenizer.decode(generated_tokens)
print(f"Predicted transcript: {decoded_text}")
```

Key Implementation Details:

- **Synthetic Speech Dataset**: Demonstrates how random spectrograms (2D float tensors) can be paired with random text transcripts. In practice, you would load real audio data, convert it into spectrogram or MFCC features, and label with actual transcripts.

- **Speech Transformer Model**: Implemented by
  `SpeechTransformer`, an encoder-decoder architecture. The
  encoder handles spectrogram frames, while the decoder generates text tokens, using cross-attention over the encoder's
  outputs.

- **Positional Encodings**: Both spectrogram frames and text
  tokens are enriched with `PositionalEncoding` to map sequential positions to sine/cosine embeddings.

- **Training Loop**: The `train_model` function applies teacher
  forcing by cutting the target text into shifted input (without
  the last token) and the prediction target (without the first
  token).

- **Evaluation**: The `evaluate_model` function computes loss
  on the validation set with cross-entropy, ignoring pads.

- **Inference**: A small greedy loop demonstrates generating
  text predictions one token at a time, halting upon reaching
  the end-of-sequence token.

Chapter 17

Text Generation with Transformers (GPT-style)

Widely used in creative writing, chat applications, and automated text completion, Transformer-based generative models predict the next token given prior context. To build such a system, train a GPT-like model on large corpora for language modeling, optimizing the likelihood of each token in a phrase. Use a unidirectional Transformer: each token attends to previous tokens only, maintaining a causal structure. The model is fine-tuned for specific tasks (such as story completion) by providing domain-specific text and continuing the next-token prediction. Novel advancements include applying parallel decoding strategies or controlling generation with custom tokens that guide style, sentiment, or topic. Another technique is to use top-k or nucleus sampling to generate diverse yet coherent text while avoiding repetitive or nonsensical outputs.

Python Code Snippet

```
import torch
import torch.nn as nn
import torch.optim as optim
from torch.utils.data import Dataset, DataLoader
import random
import math
```

```
torch.manual_seed(42)
random.seed(42)

# ----------------------------------------------------------
# 1) Simple Subword Tokenizer (for demonstration purposes)
# ----------------------------------------------------------
class SimpleSubwordTokenizer:
    '''
    Minimal subword tokenizer for demonstration. Splits text
    by whitespace, collects tokens, and truncates by frequency.
    '''
    def __init__(self, vocab_size=100):
        self.vocab_size = vocab_size
        self.token2id = {}
        self.id2token = {}

    def fit(self, texts):
        # Count frequencies
        freq_dict = {}
        for txt in texts:
            for token in txt.split():
                freq_dict[token] = freq_dict.get(token, 0) + 1

        # Sort and keep top (vocab_size - special tokens)
        sorted_by_freq = sorted(freq_dict.items(),
                                key=lambda x: x[1],
                                reverse=True)
        truncated = sorted_by_freq[: self.vocab_size - 3]

        # Reserve special tokens
        self.token2id = {
            "<PAD>": 0,
            "<UNK>": 1,
            "<BOS>": 2  # We'll use <BOS> to denote beginning for
            ↪ generation
        }

        idx = 3
        for token, _ in truncated:
            self.token2id[token] = idx
            idx += 1

        # Inverse mapping
        self.id2token = {v: k for k, v in self.token2id.items()}

    def encode(self, text):
        # Basic whitespace splitting
        tokens = text.split()
        ids = []
        for tok in tokens:
            if tok in self.token2id:
                ids.append(self.token2id[tok])
```

```python
            else:
                ids.append(self.token2id["<UNK>"])
        return ids

    def decode(self, ids):
        # Convert IDs back to tokens
        return " ".join([self.id2token.get(i, "<UNK>") for i in
        ↪ ids])

    def pad_sequences(self, batch_sequences, max_len):
        padded = []
        for seq in batch_sequences:
            if len(seq) < max_len:
                seq += [self.token2id["<PAD>"]] * (max_len -
                ↪ len(seq))
            else:
                seq = seq[:max_len]
            padded.append(seq)
        return padded

# ----------------------------------------------------------
# 2) Synthetic Dataset for Next-Token Prediction
# ----------------------------------------------------------
def generate_synthetic_data(num_samples=2000):
    '''
    Create synthetic text data, each sample is a short sequence
    from a simple vocabulary. We'll pretend these are meaningful.
    '''
    vocab_pool = [
        "transformer", "gpt", "language", "model", "deep",
        "learning", "hello", "world", "generated", "text",
        "sample", "python", "token", "prediction", "chatbot"
    ]
    texts = []
    for _ in range(num_samples):
        length = random.randint(4, 10)
        tokens = [random.choice(vocab_pool) for __ in range(length)]
        texts.append(" ".join(tokens))
    return texts

class NextTokenDataset(Dataset):
    '''
    Dataset for language modeling: each item is (input_ids,
    ↪ target_ids).
    Target is the input sequence shifted by one token.
    '''
    def __init__(self, texts, tokenizer, seq_len=12):
        self.texts = texts
        self.tokenizer = tokenizer
        self.seq_len = seq_len

        self.encoded_texts = []
        for txt in texts:
```

```python
        encoded = tokenizer.encode(txt)
        # We'll add <BOS> in front so model learns to generate
        ↪  from it
        # For unconditional generation, we can feed <BOS> and
        ↪  let it produce next tokens.
        encoded = [tokenizer.token2id["<BOS>"]] + encoded
        self.encoded_texts.append(encoded)

    def __len__(self):
        return len(self.texts)

    def __getitem__(self, idx):
        seq = self.encoded_texts[idx]
        # Input is seq[:-1], target is seq[1:]
        # But we need them to be the same length. We'll handle
        ↪  padding/cutting in collate_fn
        return seq

def collate_fn(batch):
    # Pad or truncate
    max_len = max(len(seq) for seq in batch)
    max_len = min(max_len, 12)  # we'll restrict to 12 tokens for
    ↪  demonstration
    padded = tokenizer.pad_sequences(batch, max_len)

    # Input: all but last token, Target: all but first token
    # For causal LM, we typically predict the next token given the
    ↪  previous tokens
    input_batch = [seq[:-1] for seq in padded]
    target_batch = [seq[1:] for seq in padded]

    return (
        torch.tensor(input_batch, dtype=torch.long),
        torch.tensor(target_batch, dtype=torch.long)
    )


# ------------------------------------------------------------
# 3) Causal Transformer Model (GPT-style)
# ------------------------------------------------------------
class GPTStyleLanguageModel(nn.Module):
    '''
    A unidirectional transformer that predicts
    the next token from previous context.
    '''

    def __init__(self, vocab_size, d_model=64, num_heads=2,
                 num_layers=2, dim_feedforward=128, dropout=0.1):
        super().__init__()
        self.d_model = d_model
        self.embedding = nn.Embedding(vocab_size, d_model)

        # Positional encoding helps with position awareness
        self.positional_encoding = PositionalEncoding(d_model,
        ↪  dropout)
```

136

```python
    decoder_layer = nn.TransformerDecoderLayer(
        d_model=d_model,
        nhead=num_heads,
        dim_feedforward=dim_feedforward,
        dropout=dropout
    )
    self.transformer_decoder =
    ↪   nn.TransformerDecoder(decoder_layer,
                              num_layers=num_layers)
    self.fc_out = nn.Linear(d_model, vocab_size)

def forward(self, x):
    '''
    x shape: [batch_size, seq_len]
    We'll produce x_emb: [seq_len, batch_size, d_model]
    Because PyTorch's Transformer expects [T, B, E]
    '''
    batch_size, seq_len = x.shape
    x_emb = self.embedding(x) * math.sqrt(self.d_model)
    x_emb = self.positional_encoding(x_emb)
    # We feed a zero 'memory' to the decoder in this simplistic
    ↪   approach
    # because in GPT-like models, we only have a 'decoder'
    ↪   stack.
    # We'll define a causal mask so tokens can't attend to
    ↪   future tokens.
    x_emb = x_emb.permute(1, 0, 2)  # [seq_len, batch_size,
    ↪   d_model]
    causal_mask = generate_causal_mask(seq_len).to(x.device)

    # memory is None or zero in a standard GPT approach. We'll
    ↪   pass
    # an empty context for demonstration.
    memory = torch.zeros(0, dtype=torch.float, device=x.device)

    decoded = self.transformer_decoder(x_emb, memory,
    ↪   tgt_mask=causal_mask)
    # decoded shape: [seq_len, batch_size, d_model]
    logits = self.fc_out(decoded)  # [seq_len, batch_size,
    ↪   vocab_size]
    # Return in shape [batch_size, seq_len, vocab_size]
    return logits.permute(1, 0, 2)

class PositionalEncoding(nn.Module):
    '''
    Standard sine-cosine positional encoding.
    '''
    def __init__(self, d_model, dropout=0.1, max_len=5000):
        super().__init__()
        self.dropout = nn.Dropout(p=dropout)

        # Compute the positional encodings once in log space.
```

137

```python
        pe = torch.zeros(max_len, d_model)
        position = torch.arange(0, max_len,
        ↪   dtype=torch.float).unsqueeze(1)
        div_term = torch.exp(
            torch.arange(0, d_model, 2).float() *
            ↪   (-math.log(10000.0) / d_model)
        )
        pe[:, 0::2] = torch.sin(position * div_term)
        pe[:, 1::2] = torch.cos(position * div_term)

        pe = pe.unsqueeze(1)   # [max_len, 1, d_model]
        self.register_buffer("pe", pe)

    def forward(self, x):
        '''
        x shape: [seq_len, batch_size, d_model]
        '''
        seq_len = x.size(0)
        x = x + self.pe[:seq_len, :]
        return self.dropout(x)

def generate_causal_mask(size):
    '''
    Generate an upper-triangular matrix of -inf, with zeros on diag.
    This ensures each token only sees previous tokens.
    '''
    mask = torch.triu(torch.ones(size, size), diagonal=1).bool()
    return mask.masked_fill(mask, float('-inf'))

# ------------------------------------------------------------
# 4) Training & Generating
# ------------------------------------------------------------
def train_epoch(model, dataloader, optimizer, criterion, device):
    model.train()
    total_loss = 0
    for batch_x, batch_y in dataloader:
        batch_x, batch_y = batch_x.to(device), batch_y.to(device)

        optimizer.zero_grad()
        logits = model(batch_x)
        # logits: [batch_size, seq_len, vocab_size]
        # batch_y: [batch_size, seq_len]
        loss = criterion(logits.view(-1, logits.size(-1)),
        ↪   batch_y.view(-1))
        loss.backward()
        optimizer.step()

        total_loss += loss.item()
    return total_loss / len(dataloader)

def evaluate_model(model, dataloader, criterion, device):
    model.eval()
    total_loss = 0
```

```python
with torch.no_grad():
    for batch_x, batch_y in dataloader:
        batch_x, batch_y = batch_x.to(device),
        ↪ batch_y.to(device)
        logits = model(batch_x)
        loss = criterion(logits.view(-1, logits.size(-1)),
        ↪ batch_y.view(-1))
        total_loss += loss.item()
    return total_loss / len(dataloader)

def generate_text(model, tokenizer, start_text="<BOS>",
                  max_tokens=20, top_k=5, device="cpu"):
    '''
    Generate text using top-k sampling.
    '''
    model.eval()
    tokens = tokenizer.encode(start_text)
    # We place them on device
    input_ids = torch.tensor(tokens, dtype=torch.long,
    ↪ device=device).unsqueeze(0)
    # shape: [1, length_so_far]

    for _ in range(max_tokens):
        # forward pass
        logits = model(input_ids)
        # logits is [1, seq_len, vocab_size]
        next_token_logits = logits[0, -1, :]  # take last step
        # apply top-k
        topk_vals, topk_inds = torch.topk(next_token_logits,
        ↪ k=top_k)
        # pick one
        chosen_idx = random.choice(topk_inds).item()
        # append
        input_ids = torch.cat([input_ids,
        ↪ torch.tensor([[chosen_idx]], device=device)], dim=1)

    gen_ids = input_ids[0].tolist()
    return tokenizer.decode(gen_ids)

# ----------------------------------------------------------
# 5) Main - Putting It All Together
# ----------------------------------------------------------
if __name__ == "__main__":
    # 1) Generate synthetic texts
    texts = generate_synthetic_data(num_samples=2000)

    # 2) Build tokenizer and fit
    tokenizer = SimpleSubwordTokenizer(vocab_size=100)
    tokenizer.fit(texts)

    # 3) Split into training and validation
    split_idx = int(0.8 * len(texts))
    train_texts, valid_texts = texts[:split_idx], texts[split_idx:]
```

139

```
# 4) Create dataset & dataloader
train_dataset = NextTokenDataset(train_texts, tokenizer,
↪  seq_len=12)
valid_dataset = NextTokenDataset(valid_texts, tokenizer,
↪  seq_len=12)

train_loader = DataLoader(train_dataset, batch_size=32,
↪  shuffle=True, collate_fn=collate_fn)
valid_loader = DataLoader(valid_dataset, batch_size=32,
↪  shuffle=False, collate_fn=collate_fn)

# 5) Initialize model
vocab_size = len(tokenizer.token2id)
model = GPTStyleLanguageModel(vocab_size=vocab_size, d_model=64,
↪  num_heads=2,
                             num_layers=2, dim_feedforward=128,
                             ↪  dropout=0.1)
device = torch.device("cuda" if torch.cuda.is_available() else
↪  "cpu")
model.to(device)

# 6) Training setup
optimizer = optim.AdamW(model.parameters(), lr=1e-3)
criterion = nn.CrossEntropyLoss()
epochs = 5

# 7) Train loop
for epoch in range(epochs):
    train_l = train_epoch(model, train_loader, optimizer,
    ↪  criterion, device)
    val_l = evaluate_model(model, valid_loader, criterion,
    ↪  device)

    print(f"Epoch [{epoch+1}/{epochs}] Train Loss:
    ↪  {train_l:.4f} Valid Loss: {val_l:.4f}")

# 8) Generate sample text
print("\nSample Generation:")
sample_output = generate_text(model, tokenizer,
↪  start_text="<BOS> deep learning")
print("Generated text:", sample_output)
```

Key Implementation Details:

- **Unidirectional Transformer Decoder**: The core of the GPT-like network is the unidirectional decoder stack (nn.TransformerDecoder), which applies a causal mask so each token only attends to prior tokens.

140

- **Next-Token Prediction**: We train by shifting the input sequence right (i.e., predicting the next token given all previous tokens). The loss is computed via cross-entropy over each predicted token.

- **Positional Encoding**: As in standard GPT models, we inject positional signals into the embeddings so the model can differentiate token positions in the sequence.

- **Top-K Sampling**: In `generate_text`, we demonstrate a simple top-k sampling approach for creative text generation. Higher values of `k` produce more diverse outputs.

- **Synthetic Data Pipeline**: For demonstration, we create a small synthetic dataset of random tokens, tokenize them, and feed them into the decoder-only transformer to illustrate the entire workflow.

Chapter 18

Code Generation with Transformers

Automated code generation is invaluable for speeding up software development. Begin by collecting large code repositories, paired with text descriptions (e.g., function docstrings). Tokenize code (respecting programming language syntax) and feed it into a Transformer-based encoder-decoder setup, or a causal model (like GPT) specialized in code. During training, the model learns to generate code outputs from textual prompts or partial code snippets. Fine-tuning can focus on a particular language or domain, such as Python data analysis scripts or front-end web development. Innovative adaptations include using abstract syntax trees (ASTs) as structured inputs or outputs, ensuring syntactic correctness. Another approach employs a dual-model setup, where one model generates code and another performs static analysis or type checking to refine the results before final output.

Python Code Snippet

```
import torch
import torch.nn as nn
import torch.optim as optim
from torch.utils.data import Dataset, DataLoader
import random
import string

# --------------------------------------------------------------
```

```python
# 1) Tokenizer for Docstrings and Code
# ----------------------------------------------------------------
class SimpleCharTokenizer:
    '''
    This tokenizer performs a purely character-level encoding.
    It reserves indices for [PAD], [BOS], [EOS], and builds a
    small vocab from all characters found in the dataset.
    '''
    def __init__(self):
        self.pad_token = '[PAD]'
        self.bos_token = '[BOS]'
        self.eos_token = '[EOS]'
        self.pad_idx = 0
        self.bos_idx = 1
        self.eos_idx = 2
        self.char2idx = {}
        self.idx2char = {}
        self.vocab_size = 0

    def fit(self, text_list):
        # Collect all characters in the dataset
        unique_chars = set()
        for txt in text_list:
            for ch in txt:
                unique_chars.add(ch)

        # Sort for consistent ordering
        sorted_chars = sorted(list(unique_chars))

        # Initialize char2idx with reserved tokens
        self.char2idx = {
            self.pad_token: self.pad_idx,
            self.bos_token: self.bos_idx,
            self.eos_token: self.eos_idx
        }

        # Fill in the rest
        idx = 3
        for ch in sorted_chars:
            if ch not in self.char2idx:
                self.char2idx[ch] = idx
                idx += 1

        # Build idx2char
        self.idx2char = {v: k for k, v in self.char2idx.items()}

        self.vocab_size = len(self.char2idx)

    def encode(self, text, add_bos_eos=False):
        # Convert each character to an index
        # Optional: add [BOS] at start and [EOS] at end
        tokens = []
        if add_bos_eos:
```

```python
        tokens.append(self.bos_idx)
    for ch in text:
        tokens.append(self.char2idx.get(ch, self.eos_idx))  #
        ↪  fallback to [EOS] if not found
    if add_bos_eos:
        tokens.append(self.eos_idx)
    return tokens

def decode(self, token_ids, skip_special=True):
    # Convert list of token IDs back to characters
    chars = []
    for tid in token_ids:
        if skip_special and tid in [self.pad_idx, self.bos_idx,
        ↪  self.eos_idx]:
            continue
        chars.append(self.idx2char.get(tid, ' '))
    return "".join(chars)

def pad_batch(self, sequences, max_len):
    # Pad or truncate sequences to a fixed max length
    out = []
    for seq in sequences:
        if len(seq) < max_len:
            seq = seq + [self.pad_idx] * (max_len - len(seq))
        else:
            seq = seq[:max_len]
        out.append(seq)
    return out


# ---------------------------------------------------------------
# 2) Synthetic Dataset: Docstring -> Code
# ---------------------------------------------------------------
class Docstring2CodeDataset(Dataset):
    '''
    Toy dataset that pairs a simple docstring with its corresponding
    Python function code.
    '''
    def __init__(self, docstrings, codes, tokenizer, max_len=50):
        self.docstrings = docstrings
        self.codes = codes
        self.tokenizer = tokenizer
        self.max_len = max_len

        self.encoded_docstrings = [tokenizer.encode(d,
        ↪  add_bos_eos=True)
                                    for d in docstrings]
        self.encoded_codes     = [tokenizer.encode(c,
        ↪  add_bos_eos=True)
                                    for c in codes]

    def __len__(self):
        return len(self.docstrings)
```

144

```python
    def __getitem__(self, idx):
        return self.encoded_docstrings[idx], self.encoded_codes[idx]

def collate_fn(batch):
    '''
    Collate function to handle variable-length docstrings and code.
    We pad them to the maximum sequence length found in the batch.
    '''
    doc_enc, code_enc = zip(*batch)
    max_doc_len = max(len(d) for d in doc_enc)
    max_code_len = max(len(c) for c in code_enc)
    # We'll keep a limit:
    max_doc_len = min(max_doc_len, 50)
    max_code_len = min(max_code_len, 50)

    padded_docs  = tokenizer.pad_batch(doc_enc, max_doc_len)
    padded_codes = tokenizer.pad_batch(code_enc, max_code_len)

    docs_tensor  = torch.tensor(padded_docs, dtype=torch.long)
    code_tensor  = torch.tensor(padded_codes, dtype=torch.long)

    return docs_tensor, code_tensor

# ---------------------------------------------------------------
#  3) Transformer Model (Encoder-Decoder)
# ---------------------------------------------------------------
class CodeGenTransformer(nn.Module):
    '''
    A standard Transformer-based sequence-to-sequence model.
    This uses PyTorch's nn.Transformer, which requires carefully
    shaped inputs (S, N, E).
    '''
    def __init__(self, vocab_size, d_model=128, nhead=4,
    ↪ num_layers=2, dim_feedforward=256, dropout=0.1):
        super(CodeGenTransformer, self).__init__()
        self.d_model = d_model

        # Embedding layers for docstring (encoder) and code
        ↪ (decoder)
        self.encoder_embedding = nn.Embedding(vocab_size, d_model)
        self.decoder_embedding = nn.Embedding(vocab_size, d_model)

        # Positional encodings (simple learnable approach)
        self.pos_encoder = nn.Embedding(512, d_model)
        self.pos_decoder = nn.Embedding(512, d_model)

        encoder_layer = nn.TransformerEncoderLayer(d_model, nhead,
        ↪ dim_feedforward, dropout, batch_first=False)
        self.transformer_encoder =
        ↪ nn.TransformerEncoder(encoder_layer, num_layers)

        decoder_layer = nn.TransformerDecoderLayer(d_model, nhead,
        ↪ dim_feedforward, dropout, batch_first=False)
```

145

```python
        self.transformer_decoder =
        ↳  nn.TransformerDecoder(decoder_layer, num_layers)

        # Final linear layer to map decoder outputs to vocab
        self.fc_out = nn.Linear(d_model, vocab_size)

    def forward(self, src, tgt):
        '''
        src: [batch_size, src_len]
        tgt: [batch_size, tgt_len]

        We return logits of shape [batch_size, tgt_len, vocab_size].
        '''
        batch_size, src_len = src.shape
        batch_size_t, tgt_len = tgt.shape
        assert batch_size == batch_size_t, "Source and target batch
        ↳  size must match"

        # Create position indices
        src_positions = (torch.arange(0,
        ↳  src_len).unsqueeze(0).repeat(batch_size,
        ↳  1)).to(src.device)
        tgt_positions = (torch.arange(0,
        ↳  tgt_len).unsqueeze(0).repeat(batch_size,
        ↳  1)).to(tgt.device)

        # Embed
        src_embed = self.encoder_embedding(src) +
        ↳  self.pos_encoder(src_positions)
        tgt_embed = self.decoder_embedding(tgt) +
        ↳  self.pos_decoder(tgt_positions)

        # Reshape to [src_len, batch_size, d_model]
        src_embed = src_embed.permute(1, 0, 2)
        tgt_embed = tgt_embed.permute(1, 0, 2)

        # Generate source mask / target masks
        # Usually we create a causal mask for the target to prevent
        ↳  it from "seeing" future tokens
        tgt_mask = self.generate_square_subsequent_mask(tgt_len,
        ↳  tgt.device)

        # Pad masks if needed
        # (Here we omit detailed pad masking for brevity, focusing
        ↳  on the main Transformer's logic)

        # Encoder forward
        memory = self.transformer_encoder(src_embed)   # [src_len,
        ↳  batch_size, d_model]

        # Decoder forward (with causal mask for tgt_embed)
        out = self.transformer_decoder(tgt_embed, memory,
        ↳  tgt_mask=tgt_mask)
```

146

```python
        out = out.permute(1, 0, 2)  # [batch_size, tgt_len, d_model]

        logits = self.fc_out(out)
        return logits

    def generate_square_subsequent_mask(self, size, device):
        '''
        Generates an upper-triangular matrix of -inf, with zeros on
        ↳  diag.
        This is used for target tokens so that predictions for
        ↳  position i
        can only depend on positions < i.
        '''
        mask = torch.triu(torch.ones(size, size),
        ↳  diagonal=1).bool().to(device)
        return mask

# --------------------------------------------------------------
#  4) Training Function
# --------------------------------------------------------------
def train_model(model, dataloader, optimizer, criterion, device):
    model.train()
    total_loss = 0.0

    for doc_batch, code_batch in dataloader:
        doc_batch  = doc_batch.to(device)
        code_batch = code_batch.to(device)

        # Shift decoder input by 1 for teacher forcing
        # Let's define input to the decoder as all but the last
        ↳  token
        # and the target as all but the first token
        decoder_input = code_batch[:, :-1]
        decoder_target = code_batch[:, 1:]

        optimizer.zero_grad()
        logits = model(doc_batch, decoder_input)

        # Flatten everything for cross entropy
        # logits shape: [batch_size, seq_len, vocab_size]
        # decoder_target shape: [batch_size, seq_len]
        loss = criterion(logits.reshape(-1, logits.size(-1)),
        ↳  decoder_target.reshape(-1))
        loss.backward()
        optimizer.step()

        total_loss += loss.item()

    return total_loss / len(dataloader)

# --------------------------------------------------------------
#  5) Evaluation / Inference
# --------------------------------------------------------------
```

147

```python
def generate_code(model, docstring, max_len=50, device='cpu'):
    '''
    Greedy decoding: we feed tokens one by one and pick the argmax
    ↪    next token.
    docstring: a list of token IDs including [BOS] at the start,
    ↪    [EOS] at the end.
    '''
    model.eval()
    doc_tensor = torch.tensor([docstring]).to(device)

    # We start with [BOS] for the generated code
    ys = torch.tensor([[tokenizer.bos_idx]]).to(device)

    with torch.no_grad():
        for _ in range(max_len):
            logits = model(doc_tensor, ys)
            # logits shape: [batch_size=1, cur_len, vocab_size]
            next_token_logits = logits[0, -1, :]   # last timestep
            next_token = torch.argmax(next_token_logits)
            next_token_id = next_token.item()

            ys = torch.cat([ys, next_token.unsqueeze(0)], dim=1)
            if next_token_id == tokenizer.eos_idx:
                break

    return ys[0].cpu().numpy()

def evaluate_example(model, docstring_text, device='cpu'):
    # Encode with BOS/EOS
    encoded_doc = tokenizer.encode(docstring_text, add_bos_eos=True)
    generated_tokens = generate_code(model, encoded_doc,
    ↪    device=device)
    code_str = tokenizer.decode(generated_tokens, skip_special=True)
    return code_str

# --------------------------------------------------------------
#  6) Main Execution
# --------------------------------------------------------------
if __name__ == "__main__":
    # Toy data: docstrings -> code
    # In reality, you'd load large datasets of real functions and
    ↪    docstrings.

    docstrings = [
        "This function adds two numbers.",
        "Function that returns the factorial of n.",
        "Compute the square of x.",
        "Reverse the given string."
    ]

    codes = [
        "def add(a, b): return a + b",
        "def factorial(n): return 1 if n<=1 else n*factorial(n-1)",
```

```
        "def square(x): return x*x",
        "def reverse_str(s): return s[::-1]"
]

# Duplicate them a bit to have more training samples
docstrings = docstrings * 10
codes = codes * 10

# Build tokenizer over both docstrings and codes
all_texts = docstrings + codes
tokenizer = SimpleCharTokenizer()
tokenizer.fit(all_texts)

# Create dataset
train_dataset = Docstring2CodeDataset(docstrings, codes,
↪   tokenizer, max_len=50)
train_loader = DataLoader(train_dataset, batch_size=4,
↪   shuffle=True, collate_fn=collate_fn)

# Model init
device = torch.device("cuda" if torch.cuda.is_available() else
↪   "cpu")
model = CodeGenTransformer(vocab_size=tokenizer.vocab_size,
↪   d_model=128,
                        nhead=4, num_layers=2,
                        ↪   dim_feedforward=256,
                        ↪   dropout=0.1).to(device)

# Optimizer / Loss
optimizer = optim.AdamW(model.parameters(), lr=1e-3)
criterion = nn.CrossEntropyLoss(ignore_index=tokenizer.pad_idx)

# Train
epochs = 5
for epoch in range(epochs):
    avg_loss = train_model(model, train_loader, optimizer,
    ↪   criterion, device)
    print(f"Epoch [{epoch+1}/{epochs}], Loss: {avg_loss:.4f}")

# Perform inference on an example
test_doc = "This function adds two numbers."
generated_code_str = evaluate_example(model, test_doc, device)
print("Docstring:", test_doc)
print("Generated Code:", generated_code_str)
```

Key Implementation Details:

- **Character-Level Tokenization**: We demonstrate how to encode and decode text (both docstrings and code snippets) at the character level using SimpleCharTokenizer. This is

149

for illustration; in practice, more advanced subword or AST-based tokenizers are often used.

- **Transformer Architecture**: Most of the complexity lies in the `CodeGenTransformer` class, which defines both encoder and decoder using PyTorch's built-in `nn.Transformer`. Positional embeddings are introduced via learnable embeddings to inform token positions.

- **Training Procedure**: The `train_model` function applies a teacher-forcing scheme: the decoder input is shifted by one position relative to the target. The loss function (`nn.CrossEntropyLoss`) exhaustively trains the network to predict the next token in the sequence.

- **Inference / Code Generation**: We use `generate_code` to perform greedy decoding, adding one token at a time. The process stops upon encountering `[EOS]` (end-of-sequence) or when the maximum length is reached.

- **Docstring to Code Flow**: The sample docstrings and corresponding code snippets form a toy dataset. In practice, you would collect large-scale docstrings paired with full function implementations for realistic code generation tasks.

Chapter 19

Speech Synthesis with Transformers

Text-to-speech (TTS) systems convert text into audible speech, useful for accessibility and virtual assistants. By adopting a Transformer-based approach, we can implement a sequence-to-sequence model that ingests text tokens (potentially including phoneme representations) and outputs intermediate acoustic features such as mel spectrogram frames. The process typically involves three main steps: (1) a Transformer encoder that captures linguistic context from text embeddings, (2) a Transformer decoder that autoregressively predicts the spectrogram frames, and (3) a separate vocoder (e.g., WaveGlow, HiFi-GAN) that synthesizes raw waveforms from the predicted spectrogram. Variations include non-autoregressive models (FastSpeech) for faster inference, as well as speaker embeddings for multi-speaker TTS. Training hinges on paired text-audio datasets, and post-processing can refine audio output with volume normalization and noise reduction.

Python Code Snippet

```
import torch
import torch.nn as nn
import torch.optim as optim
from torch.utils.data import Dataset, DataLoader
import random

# ---------------------------------------------------------------
```

```
# 1) Simple Subword Tokenizer
# ----------------------------------------------------------------
class SimpleSubwordTokenizer:
    '''
    A basic tokenizer that splits text by whitespace and truncates
    to build a simple vocabulary. In practice, you'd use a more
    sophisticated phoneme or text-based tokenizer for TTS.
    '''
    def __init__(self, vocab_size=50):
        self.vocab_size = vocab_size
        self.token2id = {}
        self.id2token = {}

    def fit(self, texts):
        all_tokens = {}
        for txt in texts:
            for token in txt.split():
                all_tokens[token] = all_tokens.get(token, 0) + 1

        sorted_tokens = sorted(all_tokens.items(), key=lambda x:
        ↪  x[1], reverse=True)
        truncated_tokens = sorted_tokens[:self.vocab_size - 2]  #
        ↪  Reserve [UNK], [PAD]

        self.token2id = {"[UNK]": 0, "[PAD]": 1}
        idx = 2
        for token, _ in truncated_tokens:
            self.token2id[token] = idx
            idx += 1

        self.id2token = {v: k for k, v in self.token2id.items()}

    def encode(self, text):
        tokens = text.split()
        return [self.token2id.get(t, 0) for t in tokens]

    def decode(self, token_ids):
        return " ".join([self.id2token.get(i, "[UNK]") for i in
        ↪  token_ids])

    def pad(self, encoded_batch, max_len):
        padded_batch = []
        for seq in encoded_batch:
            if len(seq) < max_len:
                seq = seq + [self.token2id["[PAD]"]] * (max_len -
                ↪  len(seq))
            else:
                seq = seq[:max_len]
            padded_batch.append(seq)
        return padded_batch

# ----------------------------------------------------------------
# 2) Synthetic Dataset for Text-to-Spectrogram
```

152

```python
# ------------------------------------------------------------
class SyntheticTTSDataset(Dataset):
    '''
    For demonstration:
    - Generates random text from a small vocabulary.
    - Associates it with a synthetic mel spectrogram
      (random float values).
    '''
    def __init__(self, texts, tokenizer, max_mel_len=30,
    ↪ mel_bins=80):
        self.texts = texts
        self.tokenizer = tokenizer
        self.max_mel_len = max_mel_len
        self.mel_bins = mel_bins
        self.encoded_texts = [tokenizer.encode(t) for t in texts]

    def __len__(self):
        return len(self.texts)

    def __getitem__(self, idx):
        encoded_text = self.encoded_texts[idx]
        # Randomly generate synthetic mel spectrogram
        mel_len = random.randint(10, self.max_mel_len)
        # shape: [mel_len, mel_bins]
        spectrogram = torch.randn(mel_len, self.mel_bins)
        return encoded_text, spectrogram

def collate_fn_tts(batch_data):
    '''
    Collate function to handle padding for text tokens
    and spectrogram frames.
    Text shape: [batch_size, max_text_len]
    Spectrogram shape: [batch_size, max_mel_time, mel_bins]
    '''
    encoded_texts, spectrograms = zip(*batch_data)

    # Pad text
    max_text_len = max(len(seq) for seq in encoded_texts)
    max_text_len = min(max_text_len, 20)  # cap for demonstration
    padded_texts = tokenizer.pad(encoded_texts, max_text_len)

    # Pad spectrogram
    max_mel_time = max(spec.shape[0] for spec in spectrograms)
    max_mel_time = min(max_mel_time, 30)

    padded_spectrograms = []
    for spec in spectrograms:
        # spec: [time, mel_bins]
        if spec.shape[0] < max_mel_time:
            pad_len = max_mel_time - spec.shape[0]
            pad_tensor = torch.zeros(pad_len, spec.shape[1])
            padded_spec = torch.cat([spec, pad_tensor], dim=0)
        else:
```

153

```
        padded_spec = spec[:max_mel_time]
        padded_spectrograms.append(padded_spec)

    text_tensor = torch.tensor(padded_texts, dtype=torch.long)
    spec_tensor = torch.stack(padded_spectrograms, dim=0)   # [B, T,
    ↪  mel_bins]

    return text_tensor, spec_tensor


# -------------------------------------------------------------
# 3) Transformer-Based TTS Model
# -------------------------------------------------------------
class TransformerTTS(nn.Module):
    ''' 
    A simplified Transformer TTS model. It uses the built-in
    PyTorch nn.Transformer with separate embeddings for text
    (encoder input) and spectrogram frames (decoder input).
    The model predicts mel spectrogram frames in an autoregressive
    manner, using teacher forcing during training.
    '''
    def __init__(self, vocab_size, d_model=32, nhead=2,
    ↪  num_encoder_layers=2,
                 num_decoder_layers=2, dim_feedforward=64,
                 ↪  mel_bins=80, dropout=0.1):
        super(TransformerTTS, self).__init__()

        self.d_model = d_model
        self.text_embedding = nn.Embedding(vocab_size, d_model,
        ↪  padding_idx=1)
        # We'll embed each mel frame (mel_bins) into d_model
        self.mel_embedding = nn.Linear(mel_bins, d_model)

        self.transformer = nn.Transformer(
            d_model=d_model,
            nhead=nhead,
            num_encoder_layers=num_encoder_layers,
            num_decoder_layers=num_decoder_layers,
            dim_feedforward=dim_feedforward,
            dropout=dropout
        )
        # Predict mel_bins values from d_model
        self.fc_out = nn.Linear(d_model, mel_bins)

    def forward(self, text_input, spec_input):
        ''' 
        text_input: [batch_size, text_seq_len]
        spec_input: [batch_size, spec_seq_len, mel_bins] (teacher
        ↪  forcing)
        Returns predicted spectrogram: [batch_size, spec_seq_len,
        ↪  mel_bins]
        '''
        # Embedding for text
        # shape => [batch_size, text_seq_len, d_model]
```

```python
        text_emb = self.text_embedding(text_input)

        # Embedding for spectrogram frames
        # shape => [batch_size, spec_seq_len, d_model]
        spec_emb = self.mel_embedding(spec_input)

        # nn.Transformer expects [sequence, batch, d_model]
        text_emb = text_emb.permute(1, 0, 2)
        spec_emb = spec_emb.permute(1, 0, 2)

        # Create masks (for simplicity, not applying advanced
        ↪   masking here)
        # Usually for autoregressive decoding, we'd use
        # a causal mask on the target. We'll rely on PyTorch's
        # generate_square_subsequent_mask if needed.
        # For demonstration, we'll skip it.

        # Encode
        memory = self.transformer.encoder(text_emb)

        # Decode
        # shape => [spec_seq_len, batch_size, d_model]
        out = self.transformer.decoder(spec_emb, memory)

        # Convert to mel_bins
        out = self.fc_out(out)  # => [spec_seq_len, batch_size,
        ↪   mel_bins]
        # Permute back
        out = out.permute(1, 0, 2)  # => [batch_size, spec_seq_len,
        ↪   mel_bins]
        return out


# -----------------------------------------------------------------
# 4) Training & Evaluation Loops
# -----------------------------------------------------------------
def train_one_epoch(model, dataloader, optimizer, criterion,
↪   device):
    model.train()
    total_loss = 0.0
    for batch_text, batch_spec in dataloader:
        batch_text = batch_text.to(device)
        batch_spec = batch_spec.to(device)

        # Shift spectrogram by one step for teacher-forcing
        # We'll feed batch_spec[:, :-1, :] as decoder input
        # and compare predictions to batch_spec[:, 1:, :]
        if batch_spec.size(1) < 2:
            # If too short, skip (rare in random data, but handle
            ↪   it)
            continue
        spec_in = batch_spec[:, :-1, :]    # teacher forcing input
        spec_target = batch_spec[:, 1:, :]  # prediction target
```

155

```
        optimizer.zero_grad()
        spec_pred = model(batch_text, spec_in)
        # spec_pred => [batch_size, spec_seq_len-1, mel_bins]
        # spec_target => [batch_size, spec_seq_len-1, mel_bins]

        # MSE or L1
        loss = criterion(spec_pred, spec_target)
        loss.backward()
        optimizer.step()

        total_loss += loss.item()

    return total_loss / len(dataloader)

def evaluate(model, dataloader, criterion, device):
    model.eval()
    total_loss = 0.0
    with torch.no_grad():
        for batch_text, batch_spec in dataloader:
            batch_text = batch_text.to(device)
            batch_spec = batch_spec.to(device)

            if batch_spec.size(1) < 2:
                continue
            spec_in = batch_spec[:, :-1, :]
            spec_target = batch_spec[:, 1:, :]

            spec_pred = model(batch_text, spec_in)
            loss = criterion(spec_pred, spec_target)
            total_loss += loss.item()
    return total_loss / len(dataloader)

# ------------------------------------------------------------------
# 5) Main Execution (Demonstration of TTS Training)
# ------------------------------------------------------------------
if __name__ == "__main__":
    # Generate random text data
    random_texts = []
    vocab_words = ["hello", "world", "transformer", "voice",
                   "synthesis", "test", "speech", "data",
                   "mel", "token", "phoneme", "timbre"]

    for _ in range(500):
        length = random.randint(3, 7)
        sentence = " ".join(random.choice(vocab_words) for __ in
          ↪ range(length))
        random_texts.append(sentence)

    # Build tokenizer
    tokenizer = SimpleSubwordTokenizer(vocab_size=30)
    tokenizer.fit(random_texts)

    # Split train/test
```

156

```
train_size = int(0.8 * len(random_texts))
train_texts = random_texts[:train_size]
test_texts = random_texts[train_size:]

# Create dataset
train_dataset = SyntheticTTSDataset(train_texts, tokenizer)
test_dataset = SyntheticTTSDataset(test_texts, tokenizer)

train_loader = DataLoader(train_dataset, batch_size=8,
↪   shuffle=True,
                          collate_fn=collate_fn_tts)
test_loader = DataLoader(test_dataset, batch_size=8,
↪   shuffle=False,
                          collate_fn=collate_fn_tts)

# Initialize model
device = torch.device("cuda" if torch.cuda.is_available() else
↪   "cpu")
model = TransformerTTS(
    vocab_size=len(tokenizer.token2id),
    d_model=32,
    nhead=2,
    num_encoder_layers=2,
    num_decoder_layers=2,
    dim_feedforward=64,
    mel_bins=80
).to(device)

# Optimizer & Loss
optimizer = optim.Adam(model.parameters(), lr=1e-3)
criterion = nn.MSELoss()

# Training loop
epochs = 5
for epoch in range(epochs):
    train_loss = train_one_epoch(model, train_loader, optimizer,
↪   criterion, device)
    val_loss = evaluate(model, test_loader, criterion, device)
    print(f"Epoch [{epoch+1}/{epochs}] | Train Loss:
↪   {train_loss:.4f} | Val Loss: {val_loss:.4f}")

print("Training complete. The model now predicts mel spectrogram
↪   frames from text input.")
```

Key Implementation Details:

- **Text Tokenization**: Implemented by SimpleSubwordTokenizer, which maps words to integer IDs. In a production TTS system, you would typically use a phoneme-based tokenizer or a

157

more sophisticated subword method.

- **Encoder-Decoder Transformer**: The `TransformerTTS` class uses separate embeddings for text tokens and spectrogram frames, followed by the PyTorch `nn.Transformer` module with multiple encoder and decoder layers.

- **Mel Spectrogram Generation**: For demonstration, random spectrogram tensors are used. A real-world system would rely on actual audio-data pairs, converting audio into mel spectrograms via signal processing.

- **Teacher Forcing**: During training, ground-truth spectrogram frames are fed to the decoder (shifted by one step), and the model learns to predict the next frame.

- **Loss Function**: We employ a mean squared error (`MSELoss`) between the predicted spectrogram and the ground truth. In practice, L1 or more sophisticated spectral reconstruction losses may be used.

- **Vocoder Integration**: Post-training, an external vocoder like WaveGlow or HiFi-GAN would convert predictioned spectrograms into raw audio waveforms for playback.

Chapter 20

Image Generation with Transformer-based Models

Generative Transformers for images can automate tasks like concept art creation. To implement such a model, you can treat each image as a sequence of pixels or tokens (e.g., compressed via a VQ-VAE). A causal Transformer or encoder-decoder can learn to predict the next pixel (or token) given the previous context. During inference, the model iteratively samples tokens until the entire image is generated. For advanced methods, you might incorporate diffusion processes or masked token prediction (as used in DALL · E and image BERT variants). Conditioning the generation on text or labels enables text-to-image synthesis. You may also explore multi-resolution approaches, where the model first generates a low-resolution version and then refines details. This hierarchical generation strategy allows for faster and more detailed outputs.

Python Code Snippet

```
import torch
import torch.nn as nn
import torch.optim as optim
from torch.utils.data import Dataset, DataLoader
import random
import numpy as np
```

```python
# For reproducibility
torch.manual_seed(42)
random.seed(42)
np.random.seed(42)

# -------------------------------------------------------------
# 1) Synthetic Image Generation & Dataset
# -------------------------------------------------------------
class SyntheticImageDataset(Dataset):
    '''
    Generates random 'images' of size img_size x img_size with pixel
    ↪   values
    in [0..num_tokens-1]. Each flattened image is treated as a
    ↪   sequence of tokens.
    '''
    def __init__(self, num_samples=1000, img_size=4, num_tokens=16):
        super().__init__()
        self.img_size = img_size
        self.num_tokens = num_tokens
        self.data = []

        for _ in range(num_samples):
            # Create a random image of shape (img_size, img_size)
            # with discrete pixel values in [0..num_tokens-1]
            img = np.random.randint(0, num_tokens, (img_size,
            ↪   img_size))
            self.data.append(img.astype(np.int64))

    def __len__(self):
        return len(self.data)

    def __getitem__(self, idx):
        # Flatten the image to a sequence
        # e.g., a 4x4 image -> sequence length of 16
        img = self.data[idx].reshape(-1)
        return img

def image_collate_fn(batch_data):
    '''
    Collate function to fuse multiple sequences into a batch tensor.
    Each image in batch_data is a flattened tensor of length
    ↪   (img_size x img_size).
    We'll also create a shifted version for autoregressive training:
        x  => [pixel_1, pixel_2, ..., pixel_(N-1)]
        y  => [pixel_2, pixel_3, ..., pixel_N]
    '''
    sequences = torch.stack(batch_data, dim=0)  # [batch_size,
    ↪   seq_len]
    x = sequences[:, :-1]
    y = sequences[:, 1:]
    return x, y
```

160

```
# ----------------------------------------------------------------
# 2) Transformer Model for Autoregressive Image Generation
# ----------------------------------------------------------------
class ImageTransformer(nn.Module):
    '''
    A GPT-style Transformer:
      - Embedding layer converts discrete tokens (pixels) to dense
      ↪ vectors
      - Positional embeddings encode token positions
      - Stacked Transformer decoder layers (causal masking)
      - Output layer predicts the next pixel token
    '''
    def __init__(self, num_tokens=16, embed_dim=64, num_heads=4,
                 hidden_dim=128, num_layers=2, max_seq_len=16,
                 ↪ dropout=0.1):
        super().__init__()
        self.num_tokens = num_tokens
        self.embed_dim = embed_dim
        self.max_seq_len = max_seq_len

        # Token embedding
        self.token_embed = nn.Embedding(num_tokens, embed_dim)
        # Positional embedding
        self.pos_embed = nn.Embedding(max_seq_len, embed_dim)

        # Transformer decoder layers
        decoder_layer = nn.TransformerDecoderLayer(
            d_model=embed_dim,
            nhead=num_heads,
            dim_feedforward=hidden_dim,
            dropout=dropout
        )
        self.transformer_decoder =
        ↪ nn.TransformerDecoder(decoder_layer, num_layers)

        # Final linear layer to predict next token
        self.fc_out = nn.Linear(embed_dim, num_tokens)

    def forward(self, x):
        '''
        x shape: [batch_size, seq_len] (integer tokens)
        We create a target mask for causal attention.
        '''
        batch_size, seq_len = x.shape

        # Token + Positional embedding
        token_embeddings = self.token_embed(x)  # [batch_size,
        ↪ seq_len, embed_dim]
        positions = torch.arange(0, seq_len,
        ↪ device=x.device).unsqueeze(0)
        pos_embeddings = self.pos_embed(positions)  # [1, seq_len,
        ↪ embed_dim]
```

161

```python
embeddings = token_embeddings + pos_embeddings  #
↪ [batch_size, seq_len, embed_dim]

# Transformer expects shape [seq_len, batch_size, embed_dim]
embeddings = embeddings.permute(1, 0, 2)

# Causal mask to prevent attending to future tokens
tgt_mask = self.generate_square_subsequent_mask(seq_len,
↪ x.device)

# For a GPT-like approach, we treat embeddings as "target"
↪ for the decoder,
# with no explicit encoder input. We can pass embeddings as
↪ both 'tgt' and 'memory'.
decoded = self.transformer_decoder(
    tgt=embeddings,
    memory=embeddings,
    tgt_mask=tgt_mask
)  # [seq_len, batch_size, embed_dim]

# Output layer
decoded = decoded.permute(1, 0, 2)  # [batch_size, seq_len,
↪ embed_dim]
logits = self.fc_out(decoded)        # [batch_size, seq_len,
↪ num_tokens]
return logits

@staticmethod
def generate_square_subsequent_mask(sz, device):
    '''
    Generates an upper-triangular matrix of -inf, with zeros on
    ↪ diag.
    The negative infinity values mask future tokens in a causal
    ↪ manner.
    '''
    mask = (torch.triu(torch.ones(sz, sz, device=device)) ==
    ↪ 1).transpose(0, 1)
    mask = mask.float().masked_fill(mask == 0,
    ↪ float('-inf')).masked_fill(mask == 1, 0.0)
    return mask

# ------------------------------------------------------------
# 3) Training &Evaluation Functions
# ------------------------------------------------------------
def train_epoch(model, dataloader, optimizer, criterion, device):
    model.train()
    total_loss = 0
    for x, y in dataloader:
        x, y = x.to(device), y.to(device)
        optimizer.zero_grad()
        logits = model(x)
        # logits: [batch_size, seq_len, num_tokens]
        # y: [batch_size, seq_len]
```

162

```
        loss = criterion(logits.view(-1, logits.size(-1)),
        ↪  y.view(-1))
        loss.backward()
        optimizer.step()
        total_loss += loss.item()
    return total_loss / len(dataloader)

def evaluate_model(model, dataloader, criterion, device):
    model.eval()
    total_loss = 0
    with torch.no_grad():
        for x, y in dataloader:
            x, y = x.to(device), y.to(device)
            logits = model(x)
            loss = criterion(logits.view(-1, logits.size(-1)),
            ↪  y.view(-1))
            total_loss += loss.item()
    return total_loss / len(dataloader)


# ---------------------------------------------------------------
# 4) Inference / Sampling
# ---------------------------------------------------------------
def sample_image(model, start_token=0, seq_len=16, device='cpu'):
    '''
    Start from a single token. Iteratively predict next token.
    Returns a list of predicted tokens of length `seq_len`.
    '''
    model.eval()
    generated = [start_token]
    with torch.no_grad():
        for _ in range(seq_len - 1):
            x = torch.tensor([generated], dtype=torch.long,
            ↪  device=device)
            logits = model(x)   # [1, current_len, num_tokens]
            next_token_logits = logits[0, -1, :]   # last step's
            ↪  logits
            predicted_token = torch.argmax(next_token_logits,
            ↪  dim=-1).item()
            generated.append(predicted_token)
    return generated


# ---------------------------------------------------------------
# 5) Main Execution
# ---------------------------------------------------------------
if __name__ == "__main__":
    # Hyperparameters
    num_tokens = 16      # vocabulary size, e.g. discrete pixel values
    ↪  0..15
    img_size   = 4       # we'll do 4x4 image for demonstration
    seq_length = img_size * img_size
    batch_size = 32
    lr         = 1e-3
    epochs     = 5
```

```python
# Create dataset
dataset = SyntheticImageDataset(num_samples=2000,
↪   img_size=img_size, num_tokens=num_tokens)
train_size = int(len(dataset) * 0.8)
test_size  = len(dataset) - train_size
train_data, test_data = torch.utils.data.random_split(dataset,
↪   [train_size, test_size])

# DataLoaders
train_loader = DataLoader(train_data, batch_size=batch_size,
↪   shuffle=True, collate_fn=image_collate_fn)
test_loader  = DataLoader(test_data, batch_size=batch_size,
↪   shuffle=False, collate_fn=image_collate_fn)

# Device
device = torch.device("cuda" if torch.cuda.is_available() else
↪   "cpu")

# Model
model = ImageTransformer(
    num_tokens=num_tokens,
    embed_dim=64,
    num_heads=4,
    hidden_dim=128,
    num_layers=2,
    max_seq_len=seq_length,
    dropout=0.1
).to(device)

# Optimizer and Criterion
optimizer = optim.AdamW(model.parameters(), lr=lr)
criterion = nn.CrossEntropyLoss()

# Training Loop
for epoch in range(epochs):
    train_loss = train_epoch(model, train_loader, optimizer,
↪   criterion, device)
    val_loss = evaluate_model(model, test_loader, criterion,
↪   device)
    print(f"Epoch {epoch+1}/{epochs} | Train Loss:
↪   {train_loss:.4f} | Valid Loss: {val_loss:.4f}")

# Sampling demonstration
print("\nSampling a random image sequence from the model:")
generated_seq = sample_image(model, start_token=0,
↪   seq_len=seq_length, device=device)
print("Generated sequence of tokens:", generated_seq)

print("\nDone. Model can now generate simple synthetic images
↪   (token sequences).")
```

Key Implementation Details:

- **Synthetic Image Dataset**: The class `SyntheticImageDataset` creates a random grid of small "images," each flattened into a sequence of discrete tokens.

- **Transformer Architecture**: The `ImageTransformer` module demonstrates an autoregressive GPT-style model with an embedding layer, positional embeddings, and a stack of transformer decoder layers for next-token prediction.

- **Causal Masking**: In `generate_square_subsequent_mask`, we apply a strict upper-triangular mask to enforce the condition that each position only attends to tokens up to its own index, preserving autoregression.

- **Training Loop**: The function `train_epoch` calculates the cross-entropy loss over predicted tokens vs. ground-truth tokens, and optimizes the model's parameters.

- **Inference/Sampling**: The `sample_image` function starts from a single token and iteratively predicts subsequent tokens until a full image (sequence) is generated. This process demonstrates how the transformer "imagines" new image data.

Chapter 21

Music Composition with Transformers

Transformers can generate melodies, chord progressions, or entire compositions. Start by tokenizing musical notes, durations, or instruments, often using MIDI-based representations. Train a Transformer in a causal fashion to predict the next note or event, given the previous sequence. Positional embeddings are crucial, as timing defines musical structure. Fine-tune on a particular music genre for style-specific generation (e.g., jazz, classical). In more advanced implementations, an encoder-decoder model can convert a chord progression (encoder input) to a melody (decoder output). Additionally, multi-track architectures can handle drums, bass, and melody lines simultaneously. You could also combine music Transformer outputs with rule-based constraints, ensuring rhythmic coherence or adherence to music theory. The result is a controllable yet creative system for automated music composition.

Python Code Snippet

```
import torch
import torch.nn as nn
import torch.optim as optim
from torch.utils.data import Dataset, DataLoader
import random

# For reproducibility
torch.manual_seed(42)
```

166

```
random.seed(42)

# ------------------------------------------------------------
# 1) Simple Note Tokenizer
# ------------------------------------------------------------
class NoteTokenizer:
    '''
    Tokenizes musical notes or events into integer IDs.
    For this demonstration, we create a small vocabulary of note
    ↪  IDs.
    In a real scenario, you could incorporate velocities, durations,
    chords, or instruments, or use MIDI files directly.
    '''
    def __init__(self, min_note=60, max_note=72):
        # We'll assume a range from middle C (60) to C above it (72)
        # in a real scenario, define a broader range or parse actual
        ↪  MIDI data.
        self.min_note = min_note
        self.max_note = max_note
        self.vocab = list(range(self.min_note, self.max_note + 1))
        self.note2id = {}
        self.id2note = {}

        # Build indexing
        idx = 0
        for note in self.vocab:
            self.note2id[note] = idx
            idx += 1
        self.note2id['[PAD]'] = idx
        idx += 1
        self.note2id['[BOS]'] = idx
        idx += 1
        self.note2id['[EOS]'] = idx

        self.id2note = {v: k for k, v in self.note2id.items()}

    def encode(self, notes):
        '''
        Convert a list of notes (integers) into their token IDs.
        If note is out of range, we simply skip it or clamp it.
        '''
        encoded = []
        encoded.append(self.note2id['[BOS]'])
        for note in notes:
            if note < self.min_note:
                note = self.min_note
            elif note > self.max_note:
                note = self.max_note
            encoded.append(self.note2id[note])
        encoded.append(self.note2id['[EOS]'])
        return encoded

    def decode(self, token_ids):
```

167

```
    '''
    Convert token IDs back into notes, ignoring special tokens.
    '''
    notes = []
    for tid in token_ids:
        note = self.id2note[tid]
        if note in ['[BOS]', '[EOS]', '[PAD]']:
            continue
        notes.append(note)
    return notes

    @property
    def vocab_size(self):
        return len(self.note2id)


# --------------------------------------------------------------
# 2) Synthetic Music Data Generation & Dataset
# --------------------------------------------------------------
def generate_random_melody(seq_len=16, min_note=60, max_note=72):
    '''
    Generate a random melody of length seq_len.
    Notes are integers within the given range.
    '''
    return [random.randint(min_note, max_note) for _ in
    ↪  range(seq_len)]


class MusicDataset(Dataset):
    '''
    Holds a collection of random melodies for demonstration.
    Each entry is a list of notes (ints). The dataset returns
    the tokenized input for training.
    '''
    def __init__(self, tokenizer, num_samples=1024, seq_len=16):
        super().__init__()
        self.tokenizer = tokenizer
        self.data = []
        for _ in range(num_samples):
            melody = generate_random_melody(seq_len=seq_len,

                                  ↪  min_note=tokenizer.min_note,

                                  ↪  max_note=tokenizer.max_note)
            self.data.append(melody)

    def __len__(self):
        return len(self.data)

    def __getitem__(self, idx):
        return self.data[idx]

def collate_music_fn(batch):
    '''
```

```
Collate function to pad sequences to the max length in the
↪  batch.
We'll also create a causal mask in the model later.
'''

# We'll encode the batch of melodies here
encoded_batch = []
max_len = 0
for melody in batch:
    encoded = note_tokenizer.encode(melody)
    encoded_batch.append(encoded)
    if len(encoded) > max_len:
        max_len = len(encoded)

# Pad all sequences
padded_batch = []
for seq in encoded_batch:
    if len(seq) < max_len:
        seq = seq + [note_tokenizer.note2id['[PAD]']] * (max_len
        ↪  - len(seq))
    padded_batch.append(seq)

return torch.tensor(padded_batch, dtype=torch.long)


# --------------------------------------------------------------
# 3) Music Transformer Model (Causal)
# --------------------------------------------------------------
class MusicTransformer(nn.Module):
    '''
    A causal Transformer that predicts the next token in a sequence
    of musical notes.
    '''

    def __init__(self, vocab_size, embed_dim=64, num_heads=2,
                 hidden_dim=256, num_layers=2, dropout=0.1,
                 ↪  max_seq_len=128):
        super(MusicTransformer, self).__init__()
        self.vocab_size = vocab_size
        self.embed_dim = embed_dim
        self.embed = nn.Embedding(vocab_size, embed_dim,
        ↪  padding_idx=0)

        # Positional Encoding
        self.pos_emb = nn.Embedding(max_seq_len, embed_dim)

        # Transformer Decoder Layers (using PyTorch's
        ↪  nn.Transformer)
        decoder_layer =
        ↪  nn.TransformerDecoderLayer(d_model=embed_dim,
            nhead=num_heads,
            dim_feedforward=hidden_dim,
            dropout=dropout)
        self.transformer_decoder =
        ↪  nn.TransformerDecoder(decoder_layer,
                num_layers=num_layers)
```

169

```python
    # Output prediction (next-note probabilities)
    self.to_logits = nn.Linear(embed_dim, vocab_size)

def forward(self, tgt):
    '''
    tgt: [batch_size, seq_len] - tokenized sequences
    We create a causal mask so the model sees only past tokens.
    '''
    batch_size, seq_len = tgt.shape

    # Create position IDs [0..seq_len-1]
    positions = torch.arange(0, seq_len,
    ↪  device=tgt.device).unsqueeze(0)  # [1, seq_len]

    # Embed tokens + positional embeddings
    token_emb = self.embed(tgt)  # [batch_size, seq_len,
    ↪  embed_dim]
    pos_emb = self.pos_emb(positions)  # [1, seq_len,
    ↪  embed_dim]

    x = token_emb + pos_emb

    # Convert to shape [seq_len, batch_size, embed_dim]
    x = x.permute(1, 0, 2)

    # Create a causal mask for self-attention
    causal_mask = self.generate_square_subsequent_mask(seq_len,
    ↪  x.device)

    # We pass in x as both 'tgt' and 'memory' because we're
    # doing a purely auto-regressive approach here
    # (no separate encoder). Occupying the 'memory' argument
    # can be done with a zero vector or with x. We'll keep it
    ↪  simple.
    decoded = self.transformer_decoder(x, x,
    ↪  tgt_mask=causal_mask)

    # decoded: [seq_len, batch_size, embed_dim]
    decoded = decoded.permute(1, 0, 2)  # [batch_size, seq_len,
    ↪  embed_dim]

    logits = self.to_logits(decoded)  # [batch_size, seq_len,
    ↪  vocab_size]
    return logits

def generate_square_subsequent_mask(self, sz, device):
    '''
    Generate a causal mask for sequence of length sz.
    A 1 indicates a position that should NOT be accessed
    ↪  (masked).
    '''
```

170

```
    mask = (torch.triu(torch.ones(sz, sz, device=device)) ==
    ↪  1).transpose(0, 1)
    mask = mask.float().masked_fill(mask == 1, float('-inf'))
    return mask

# ----------------------------------------------------------------
# 4) Training and Generation
# ----------------------------------------------------------------
def train_model(model, dataloader, optimizer, criterion, device):
    model.train()
    total_loss = 0.0
    for batch_seq in dataloader:
        batch_seq = batch_seq.to(device)

        # Shift inputs and targets by one to do next-token
        ↪  prediction
        # We predict batch_seq[:, 1:] from batch_seq[:, :-1]
        inp = batch_seq[:, :-1]
        tgt = batch_seq[:, 1:]

        optimizer.zero_grad()
        logits = model(inp)
        # Flatten for cross-entropy
        # logits: [batch_size, seq_len-1, vocab_size]
        # tgt:    [batch_size, seq_len-1]
        logits_reshaped = logits.reshape(-1, model.vocab_size)
        tgt_reshaped = tgt.reshape(-1)

        loss = criterion(logits_reshaped, tgt_reshaped)
        loss.backward()
        optimizer.step()

        total_loss += loss.item()

    return total_loss / len(dataloader)

def generate_sequence(model, start_notes, max_length=32,
↪  device='cpu'):
    '''
    Autoregressively generate a sequence of notes from the model.
    start_notes: list of integer note IDs (tokenized).
    '''
    model.eval()
    output_seq = torch.tensor([start_notes], dtype=torch.long,
    ↪  device=device)

    with torch.no_grad():
        for _ in range(max_length):
            inp = output_seq.clone()
            logits = model(inp)
            # Take last time step's logits
            next_token_logits = logits[:, -1, :]
            # Sample from distribution (or take argmax for greedy)
```

171

```python
        prob = nn.functional.softmax(next_token_logits, dim=-1)
        next_token = torch.multinomial(prob, num_samples=1)

        output_seq = torch.cat([output_seq, next_token], dim=1)

        # Stop if we predict [EOS]
        if next_token.item() == note_tokenizer.note2id['[EOS]']:
            break

    return output_seq.squeeze(0).tolist()


# -------------------------------------------------------------
# 5) Main Execution
# -------------------------------------------------------------
if __name__ == "__main__":
    # 1) Instantiate tokenizer over a note range
    note_tokenizer = NoteTokenizer(min_note=60, max_note=72)

    # 2) Create dataset & dataloader
    dataset = MusicDataset(note_tokenizer, num_samples=2048,
    ↪    seq_len=16)
    dataloader = DataLoader(dataset, batch_size=32, shuffle=True,
                            collate_fn=collate_music_fn)

    # 3) Define model, loss, optimizer
    device = torch.device("cuda" if torch.cuda.is_available() else
    ↪    "cpu")
    model = MusicTransformer(vocab_size=note_tokenizer.vocab_size,
                             embed_dim=64,
                             num_heads=2,
                             hidden_dim=256,
                             num_layers=2,
                             dropout=0.1,
                             max_seq_len=64).to(device)

    criterion =
    ↪    nn.CrossEntropyLoss(ignore_index=note_tokenizer.note2id['[PAD]'])
    optimizer = optim.AdamW(model.parameters(), lr=1e-3)

    # 4) Train
    num_epochs = 5
    for epoch in range(num_epochs):
        train_loss = train_model(model, dataloader, optimizer,
        ↪    criterion, device)
        print(f"Epoch {epoch+1}/{num_epochs} - Loss:
        ↪    {train_loss:.4f}")

    print("Training complete. Now generating a new melody:")

    # 5) Generate a short melody
    # Start with a random few notes
    start_melody = generate_random_melody(seq_len=4,
                     min_note=note_tokenizer.min_note,
```

```
                    max_note=note_tokenizer.max_note)
start_tokens = note_tokenizer.encode(start_melody)
generated_token_ids = generate_sequence(model, start_tokens,
 ↪  max_length=32, device=device)

# Decode to get final note sequence
generated_notes = note_tokenizer.decode(generated_token_ids)
print("Start melody (notes):", start_melody)
print("Generated melody (notes):", generated_notes)
```

Key Implementation Details:

- **Note Tokenization**: We use a class `NoteTokenizer` to map notes to IDs within a fixed range. Special tokens like `[BOS]`, `[EOS]`, and `[PAD]` are added.

- **Synthetic Dataset**: The `MusicDataset` class generates random note sequences (each an integer list). This is for demonstration, though real use-cases usually parse MIDI files.

- **Causal Transformer**: The `MusicTransformer` model uses a decoder-only structure from PyTorch's `nn.TransformerDecoder` layers. A causal mask is applied so the model only attends to past tokens for next-note prediction.

- **Positional Embedding**: A learnable embedding (`pos_emb`) is added to each token embedding to encode the time-step information.

- **Training Loop**: In `train_model`, we split each sequence into (input, target) pairs by shifting one position for next-token prediction. We use cross-entropy loss and `AdamW` optimization.

- **Sequence Generation**: The `generate_sequence` function autoregressively predicts tokens, appending them one at a time until we reach the max length or an `[EOS]` token.

Chapter 22

Style Transfer with Transformers

Style transfer systems transform text or images from one style to another. In text, examples include converting informal sentences to formal style or altering sentiment. In images, it can emulate the style of famous paintings. For text-based style transfer, fine-tune a Transformer encoder-decoder model on paired examples—original text mapped to stylized text. If paired data is scarce, use back-translation or denoising approaches to refine content. For image style transfer, feed image patches into a Vision Transformer that acts as an encoder, then pass the embeddings to a generative decoder trained on style-image pairs. Advanced systems mix multiple styles, using attention to isolate style-specific parameters. You can also add a discriminator network that helps ensure the generated output preserves content while adopting the desired style.

Python Code Snippet

```
import torch
import torch.nn as nn
import torch.optim as optim
from torch.utils.data import Dataset, DataLoader
import torchvision.transforms as T
from PIL import Image
import random

# For reproducibility
```

```
torch.manual_seed(42)
random.seed(42)

# -------------------------------------------------------------
# 1) Synthetic Text Data for Style Transfer + Simple Tokenizer
# -------------------------------------------------------------

class SimpleTokenizer:
    """
    A very basic tokenizer that splits on whitespace.
    In real scenarios, you might use SentencePiece, BPE, or
    ↪ WordPiece.
    """
    def __init__(self):
        self.token2id = {"[PAD]":0, "[BOS]":1, "[EOS]":2, "[UNK]":3}
        self.id2token = {0:"[PAD]", 1:"[BOS]", 2:"[EOS]", 3:"[UNK]"}
        self.vocab_size = 4  # Will grow as we add tokens

    def fit(self, sentences):
        # Collect all unique tokens
        for s in sentences:
            for token in s.split():
                if token not in self.token2id:
                    idx = self.vocab_size
                    self.token2id[token] = idx
                    self.id2token[idx] = token
                    self.vocab_size += 1

    def encode(self, sentence, max_len=20):
        tokens = sentence.split()
        encoded = [self.token2id.get(t, 3) for t in tokens]  # 3 is
        ↪ [UNK]
        # Add [BOS] and [EOS]
        encoded = [1] + encoded + [2]
        # Truncate or pad
        encoded = encoded[:max_len]
        encoded += [0]*(max_len - len(encoded))
        return encoded

    def decode(self, ids):
        tokens = [self.id2token.get(i, "[UNK]") for i in ids]
        # Remove any [PAD], [BOS], [EOS] for readability
        cleaned = [t for t in tokens if t not in ["[PAD]", "[BOS]",
        ↪ "[EOS]"]]
        return " ".join(cleaned)


def generate_text_pairs(num_pairs=2000):
    """
    Generates synthetic text pairs to simulate style transfer.
    Example: informal -> formal
    We'll pick random phrases to form source-target pairs.
    """
```

```python
    informal_phrases = [
        "hey how r u",
        "wanna hang out",
        "lol that was crazy",
        "dunno what to do",
        "this is so cool",
        "let's do that tmrw",
    ]

    formal_phrases = [
        "Hello, how are you?",
        "Would you like to meet up?",
        "That was quite surprising.",
        "I am not certain about the plan.",
        "This is impressive indeed.",
        "Shall we proceed tomorrow?",
    ]

    source_sentences = []
    target_sentences = []

    for _ in range(num_pairs):
        # randomly pick an informal phrase
        s = random.choice(informal_phrases)
        # map it to a random formal phrase
        t = random.choice(formal_phrases)
        source_sentences.append(s)
        target_sentences.append(t)

    return source_sentences, target_sentences


# ----------------------------------------------------------------
# 2) Text Dataset and Collate Function
# ----------------------------------------------------------------

class StyleTransferTextDataset(Dataset):
    """
    Holds pairs of (source_sentence, target_sentence).
    We'll transform them into token IDs using the tokenizer.
    """
    def __init__(self, source_texts, target_texts, tokenizer,
    ↪  max_len=20):
        self.source_texts = source_texts
        self.target_texts = target_texts
        self.tokenizer = tokenizer
        self.max_len = max_len

    def __len__(self):
        return len(self.source_texts)

    def __getitem__(self, idx):
        src = self.source_texts[idx]
```

176

```
            tgt = self.target_texts[idx]
            return src, tgt


def collate_text_fn(batch_data, tokenizer, max_len=20):
    """
    Collate function that tokenizes and pads each pair:
    (source, target) -> (input_ids, target_ids).
    """
    sources, targets = zip(*batch_data)
    input_ids = [tokenizer.encode(s, max_len) for s in sources]
    target_ids = [tokenizer.encode(t, max_len) for t in targets]
    return (
        torch.tensor(input_ids, dtype=torch.long),
        torch.tensor(target_ids, dtype=torch.long)
    )



# --------------------------------------------------------------
# 3) A Simple Transformer Encoder-Decoder for Text
# --------------------------------------------------------------
class PositionalEncoding(nn.Module):
    """
    Inject some information about the relative or absolute
    position of the tokens in the sequence.
    """
    def __init__(self, d_model, max_len=5000):
        super(PositionalEncoding, self).__init__()
        pe = torch.zeros(max_len, d_model)
        position = torch.arange(0, max_len,
        ↪ dtype=torch.float).unsqueeze(1)
        div_term = torch.exp(torch.arange(0, d_model, 2).float()
                            * (-torch.log(torch.tensor(10000.0)) /
                               ↪ d_model))
        pe[:, 0::2] = torch.sin(position * div_term)
        pe[:, 1::2] = torch.cos(position * div_term)
        self.pe = pe.unsqueeze(1)  # shape: [max_len, 1, d_model]

    def forward(self, x):
        # x shape: [seq_len, batch_size, d_model]
        seq_len = x.size(0)
        return x + self.pe[:seq_len, :]


class TransformerStyleTransfer(nn.Module):
    """
    A basic seq2seq model with one transformer encoder
    and one transformer decoder, each composed of multiple layers.
    """
    def __init__(self, vocab_size, d_model=64, nhead=4,
                 num_encoder_layers=2, num_decoder_layers=2,
                 ↪ dim_feedforward=128):
        super(TransformerStyleTransfer, self).__init__()
```

177

```python
        self.d_model = d_model
        self.embedding = nn.Embedding(vocab_size, d_model,
        ↪  padding_idx=0)

        self.pos_encoder = PositionalEncoding(d_model)
        self.pos_decoder = PositionalEncoding(d_model)

        encoder_layers = nn.TransformerEncoderLayer(d_model, nhead,
                                                    dim_feedforward,
                                                    ↪  dropout=0.1)
        self.encoder = nn.TransformerEncoder(encoder_layers,
        ↪  num_encoder_layers)

        decoder_layers = nn.TransformerDecoderLayer(d_model, nhead,
                                                    dim_feedforward,
                                                    ↪  dropout=0.1)
        self.decoder = nn.TransformerDecoder(decoder_layers,
        ↪  num_decoder_layers)

        # Final linear layer to map decoder outputs to vocab
        self.output_fc = nn.Linear(d_model, vocab_size)

    def forward(self, src, tgt):
        """
        src: [batch_size, src_seq_len]
        tgt: [batch_size, tgt_seq_len]
        """
        # Embedding
        # Transform to shape [seq_len, batch_size, d_model] for
        ↪  transformer
        src_emb = self.embedding(src).permute(1, 0, 2)   #
        ↪  [src_seq_len, batch_size, d_model]
        tgt_emb = self.embedding(tgt).permute(1, 0, 2)   #
        ↪  [tgt_seq_len, batch_size, d_model]

        # Positional encoding
        src_emb = self.pos_encoder(src_emb)
        tgt_emb = self.pos_decoder(tgt_emb)

        # Generate key padding masks
        src_padding_mask = (src == 0)   # [batch_size, src_seq_len]
        tgt_padding_mask = (tgt == 0)   # [batch_size, tgt_seq_len]

        # The transformer requires shape: [batch_size, seq_len]
        # but the arguments are reversed in the transforms, so
        # careful with referencing.

        memory = self.encoder(src_emb,
                              src_key_padding_mask=src_padding_mask)

        # The transformer decoder also needs a subsequent mask for
        ↪  autoregressive
```

```python
    # generation. For training, we can provide the entire target
    ↪    to the decoder,
    # but let's illustrate the concept with a triangular mask
    ↪    for the target.

    seq_len = tgt.size(1)
    tgt_mask = nn.Transformer.generate_square_subsequent_mask(
    seq_len).to(tgt.device)

    decoder_out = self.decoder(
        tgt_emb, memory,
        tgt_mask=tgt_mask,
        memory_key_padding_mask=src_padding_mask,
        tgt_key_padding_mask=tgt_padding_mask
    )  # [tgt_seq_len, batch_size, d_model]

    # Map decoder outputs to vocab
    logits = self.output_fc(decoder_out)  # [tgt_seq_len,
    ↪    batch_size, vocab_size]

    # Return shape to [batch_size, tgt_seq_len, vocab_size]
    logits = logits.permute(1, 0, 2)
    return logits


# --------------------------------------------------------------
# 4) Image Style Transfer Skeleton with Vision Transformer-like
↪    Encoder
# --------------------------------------------------------------
class VisionTransformerStyleEncoder(nn.Module):
    """
    This is a simplified vision-transformer-like encoder
    that splits an image into patches and processes them with
    ↪    attention.
    We'll only define a skeleton for demonstration purposes.
    """
    def __init__(self, patch_size=16, in_channels=3, embed_dim=64,
    ↪    nhead=4,
                 num_layers=2, feedforward_dim=128):
        super(VisionTransformerStyleEncoder, self).__init__()
        self.patch_size = patch_size
        self.embed_dim = embed_dim

        # Project each flattened patch to embed_dim
        self.projection =
        ↪    nn.Linear(patch_size*patch_size*in_channels, embed_dim)

        encoder_layer = nn.TransformerEncoderLayer(embed_dim, nhead,
        ↪    feedforward_dim)
        self.encoder = nn.TransformerEncoder(encoder_layer,
        ↪    num_layers)
        self.pos_encoder = PositionalEncoding(embed_dim)
```

179

```python
def forward(self, img):
    """
    img: [batch_size, 3, height, width]
    We'll convert it to [num_patches, batch_size, embed_dim]
    for the transformer encoder.
    """
    b, c, h, w = img.shape
    # number of patches
    patch_h = h // self.patch_size
    patch_w = w // self.patch_size

    patches = []
    for i in range(patch_h):
        for j in range(patch_w):
            patch = img[:, :,
             ↪  i*self.patch_size:(i+1)*self.patch_size,

                                ↪  j*self.patch_size:(j+1)*self.patch_size]
            patch = patch.reshape(b, -1)  # Flatten
            patches.append(patch)

    # Stack patches along dimension 0 => shape [num_patches,
    ↪  batch_size, patch_dim]
    patches = torch.stack(patches, dim=0)

    # Linear projection
    projected = self.projection(patches)  # [num_patches,
    ↪  batch_size, embed_dim]
    encoded = self.pos_encoder(projected)

    encoded = self.encoder(encoded)  # [num_patches, batch_size,
    ↪  embed_dim]
    return encoded


class VisionDecoderSkeleton(nn.Module):
    """
    A placeholder for a decoded style image representation.
    We'll simply output a fixed shape as an example.
    """
    def __init__(self, embed_dim=64, out_channels=3, patch_size=16,
                 height=128, width=128):
        super(VisionDecoderSkeleton, self).__init__()
        self.height = height
        self.width = width
        self.patch_size = patch_size
        self.out_channels = out_channels
        self.embed_dim = embed_dim

        # A naive feed-forward approach to decode each patch
        self.decoder_fc = nn.Linear(embed_dim,
        ↪  patch_size*patch_size*out_channels)
```

```python
def forward(self, encoded_sequence):
    """
    encoded_sequence: [num_patches, batch_size, embed_dim]
    We'll decode each patch and then reconstruct the image grid.
    """
    num_patches, bsz, _ = encoded_sequence.shape
    # decode
    decoded_patches = self.decoder_fc(encoded_sequence)    #
    ↪    [num_patches, batch_size,
    ↪    patch_size*patch_size*out_channels]

    # rearrange patches
    patch_h = self.height // self.patch_size
    patch_w = self.width // self.patch_size

    # Each patch is [bsz, patch_size*patch_size*out_channels]
    # We'll reshape to [bsz, out_channels, patch_size,
    ↪    patch_size]
    decoded_patches = decoded_patches.view(num_patches, bsz,
                                self.out_channels,
                                self.patch_size,
                                self.patch_size)

    # Now we reassemble (patch_h * patch_w) patches back into
    ↪    images
    patches_per_row = patch_w
    patches_per_col = patch_h

    # Let's create a placeholder to hold final images
    # [bsz, out_channels, height, width]
    out_images = torch.zeros(bsz, self.out_channels,
                        self.height, self.width,
                        device=encoded_sequence.device)

    p_i = 0
    for i in range(patches_per_col):
        for j in range(patches_per_row):
            out_images[:, :,
            ↪    i*self.patch_size:(i+1)*self.patch_size,

                        ↪    j*self.patch_size:(j+1)*self.patch_size]
                        ↪    = decoded_patches[p_i]
            p_i += 1

    return out_images


# ----------------------------------------------------------------
# 5) Training Routines for Text Style Transfer
# ----------------------------------------------------------------
def text_style_transfer_train_one_epoch(model, dataloader,
↪    optimizer, criterion, device):
    model.train()
```

```
    total_loss = 0
    for src, tgt in dataloader:
        src, tgt = src.to(device), tgt.to(device)
        optimizer.zero_grad()
        # Shift the target so that the model predicts next tokens
        # except we can feed the entire tgt for simplicity
        logits = model(src, tgt[:, :-1])  # teacher forcing
        ↪ approach
        # We compute the loss against the next token in target
        loss = criterion(logits.reshape(-1, logits.size(-1)), tgt[:,
        ↪ 1:].reshape(-1))

        loss.backward()
        optimizer.step()
        total_loss += loss.item()
    return total_loss / len(dataloader)


def text_style_transfer_evaluate(model, dataloader, criterion,
↪ device):
    model.eval()
    total_loss = 0
    with torch.no_grad():
        for src, tgt in dataloader:
            src, tgt = src.to(device), tgt.to(device)
            logits = model(src, tgt[:, :-1])
            loss = criterion(logits.reshape(-1, logits.size(-1)),
            ↪ tgt[:, 1:].reshape(-1))
            total_loss += loss.item()
    return total_loss / len(dataloader)


def text_inference(model, src_sentence, tokenizer, max_len=20,
↪ device=torch.device("cpu")):
    """
    Generate stylized text from a source input using greedy
    ↪ decoding.
    """
    model.eval()
    src_ids = tokenizer.encode(src_sentence, max_len=max_len)
    src_tensor = torch.tensor([src_ids],
    ↪ dtype=torch.long).to(device)

    # We'll build the target one token at a time
    generated = [1]  # [BOS]
    with torch.no_grad():
        for _ in range(max_len):
            tgt_tensor = torch.tensor([generated],
            ↪ dtype=torch.long).to(device)
            logits = model(src_tensor, tgt_tensor)
            # Take the last token from logits
            next_token_logits = logits[0, -1, :]  # [vocab_size]
            next_token = torch.argmax(next_token_logits).item()
```

182

```
            generated.append(next_token)
            if next_token == 2:   # [EOS]
                break

    return tokenizer.decode(generated)


# ------------------------------------------------------------------
# 6) Main Execution Demo (Text Style Transfer)
# ------------------------------------------------------------------
if __name__ == "__main__":
    device = torch.device("cuda" if torch.cuda.is_available() else
    ↪  "cpu")

    # 6.1) Generate synthetic data
    src_texts, tgt_texts = generate_text_pairs(num_pairs=500)

    # Fit tokenizer
    tokenizer = SimpleTokenizer()
    tokenizer.fit(src_texts + tgt_texts)

    # Split train/test
    data_size = len(src_texts)
    train_size = int(data_size * 0.8)
    train_src = src_texts[:train_size]
    train_tgt = tgt_texts[:train_size]
    test_src  = src_texts[train_size:]
    test_tgt  = tgt_texts[train_size:]

    # Create dataset objects
    train_dataset = StyleTransferTextDataset(train_src, train_tgt,
    ↪  tokenizer)
    test_dataset  = StyleTransferTextDataset(test_src, test_tgt,
    ↪  tokenizer)

    # Data loaders
    batch_size = 32
    train_loader = DataLoader(train_dataset, batch_size=batch_size,
    ↪  shuffle=True,
                              collate_fn=lambda bd:
                              ↪  collate_text_fn(bd, tokenizer,
                              ↪  max_len=20))
    test_loader = DataLoader(test_dataset, batch_size=batch_size,
    ↪  shuffle=False,
                             collate_fn=lambda bd:
                             ↪  collate_text_fn(bd, tokenizer,
                             ↪  max_len=20))

    # 6.2) Initialize model
    model = TransformerStyleTransfer(
        vocab_size=tokenizer.vocab_size,
        d_model=64,
        nhead=4,
```

```python
    num_encoder_layers=2,
    num_decoder_layers=2,
    dim_feedforward=128
).to(device)

# 6.3) Define optimizer and loss
optimizer = optim.Adam(model.parameters(), lr=1e-3)
criterion = nn.CrossEntropyLoss(ignore_index=0)  # ignore [PAD]
↪   tokens

# 6.4) Train loop
epochs = 5
for epoch in range(epochs):
    train_loss = text_style_transfer_train_one_epoch(model,
    ↪   train_loader, optimizer, criterion, device)
    val_loss = text_style_transfer_evaluate(model, test_loader,
    ↪   criterion, device)
    print(f"Epoch [{epoch+1}/{epochs}] Train Loss:
    ↪   {train_loss:.4f}, Val Loss: {val_loss:.4f}")

# 6.5) Quick inference demo
sample_src = "dunno what to do"
styled_text = text_inference(model, sample_src, tokenizer,
↪   max_len=20, device=device)
print(f"Source: {sample_src}")
print(f"Stylized output: {styled_text}")

# 6.6) Skeleton for image style transfer usage:
# Example usage (not a complete training script):
# Suppose we have an image loaded by PIL or other library:
# sample_image = Image.open("some_image.jpg")
# transform = T.Compose([T.Resize((128, 128)), T.ToTensor()])
# tensor_image = transform(sample_image).unsqueeze(0)  # [1, 3,
↪   128, 128]

# vit_encoder = VisionTransformerStyleEncoder().to(device)
# vit_decoder = VisionDecoderSkeleton().to(device)

# # Convert image to device
# tensor_image = tensor_image.to(device)

# # Encode
# encoded_feats = vit_encoder(tensor_image)
# # In practice, you'd have a separate style decoder or combine
# # these features with style embedding in a generative
↪   approach.

# # Decode
# reconstructed = vit_decoder(encoded_feats)
# # 'reconstructed' is a rough output image,
# # you would typically train a model end-to-end to produce
↪   stylized images.
```

Key Implementation Details:

- **Text Style Transfer Pipeline**: We simulate text style transfer from an informal sentence to a more formal one via a sequence-to-sequence Transformer in `TransformerStyleTransfer`.

- **Tokenization**: The class `SimpleTokenizer` is used to convert input sentences into integer token IDs, demonstrating a minimal approach for subword or whitespace tokenization.

- **Transformer Encoder-Decoder**: The model includes distinct encoder and decoder layers, each composed of multi-head attention and feed-forward sublayers. Positional encodings help the model learn sequence order.

- **Training Loop**: The functions `text_style_transfer_train_one_epoch` and `text_style_transfer_evaluate` illustrate supervised seq2seq learning with cross-entropy loss.

- **Greedy Decoding**: The function `text_inference` demonstrates how to generate stylized text by iteratively predicting each next token until `[EOS]` is reached.

- **Vision Transformer Skeleton**: Basic classes `VisionTransformerStyleEncoder` and `VisionDecoderSkeleton` outline a patch-splitting step and a transformer-based encoding-decoding for image style transfer. A fully functional image style transfer would involve training with style-image pairs and potentially adding adversarial/discriminator components.

Chapter 23

Semantic Search and Retrieval with Transformers

Semantic search matches user queries to relevant documents or passages beyond simple keyword lookup. To build such a system, you can use Transformer-based bi-encoders (e.g., Sentence-BERT) that produce vector embeddings for queries and documents. Then, similarity scores are computed via dot product or cosine similarity, enabling fast approximate nearest-neighbor search in a vector index. Another approach uses cross-encoders, where the query and candidate passage are processed together, providing more accurate but slower re-ranking. Innovative retrieval augmentation combines a bi-encoder for recall with a cross-encoder for final ranking, benefiting both speed and accuracy. Further refinements include domain-adaptive pre-training on relevant corpora. This approach works well for question answering, recommendation, or content filtering, where semantic similarity is more relevant than exact keyword matching.

Python Code Snippet

```
import torch
import torch.nn as nn
import torch.optim as optim
import random
```

```python
# For reproducibility
torch.manual_seed(42)
random.seed(42)

# ----------------------------------------------------------
# 1) Simple Tokenizer
# ----------------------------------------------------------
class SimpleTokenizer:
    '''
    A naive tokenizer that splits by whitespace. In real scenarios,
    a subword tokenizer (e.g., BPE) or a pre-trained tokenizer would
    ↪ be used.
    '''
    def __init__(self):
        self.word2idx = {}
        self.idx2word = {}
        self.pad_token = "[PAD]"
        self.unk_token = "[UNK]"

    def fit(self, texts, vocab_size=50):
        # Count word frequencies
        freq = {}
        for txt in texts:
            for token in txt.split():
                freq[token] = freq.get(token, 0) + 1

        # Sort by frequency descending
        sorted_words = sorted(freq.items(), key=lambda x: x[1],
        ↪ reverse=True)
        # Reduce to vocab_size, reserve space for special tokens
        trunc_words = sorted_words[: (vocab_size - 2)]

        # Build the dictionaries
        self.word2idx = {self.pad_token: 0, self.unk_token: 1}
        idx = 2
        for w, _ in trunc_words:
            self.word2idx[w] = idx
            idx += 1
        self.idx2word = {v: k for k, v in self.word2idx.items()}

    def encode(self, text):
        # Convert to indices
        tokens = text.split()
        encoded = [self.word2idx.get(t,
        ↪ self.word2idx[self.unk_token]) for t in tokens]
        return encoded

    def decode(self, encoded_seq):
        return " ".join([self.idx2word.get(idx, self.unk_token) for
        ↪ idx in encoded_seq])

    def pad_batch(self, batch_of_ids, max_len=20):
```

187

```python
        padded = []
        for seq in batch_of_ids:
            if len(seq) < max_len:
                seq = seq + [self.word2idx[self.pad_token]] *
                ↪ (max_len - len(seq))
            else:
                seq = seq[:max_len]
            padded.append(seq)
        return torch.tensor(padded, dtype=torch.long)


# ----------------------------------------------------------
# 2) A Minimal Transformer Encoder for Embedding
# ----------------------------------------------------------
class SimpleTransformerEncoder(nn.Module):
    '''
    A minimal Transformer encoder that outputs a single embedding
    per input sequence (using mean pooling over token embeddings).
    Demonstrates how a Transformer backbone might be adapted for
    semantic embedding tasks.
    '''
    def __init__(self, vocab_size, embed_dim=32, num_heads=2,
                 feedforward_dim=64, num_layers=2, dropout=0.1):
        super(SimpleTransformerEncoder, self).__init__()

        self.embedding = nn.Embedding(vocab_size, embed_dim,
        ↪ padding_idx=0)

        encoder_layer = nn.TransformerEncoderLayer(
            d_model=embed_dim,
            nhead=num_heads,
            dim_feedforward=feedforward_dim,
            dropout=dropout
        )
        self.transformer_encoder =
        ↪ nn.TransformerEncoder(encoder_layer, num_layers)

    def forward(self, input_ids):
        '''
        input_ids: [batch_size, seq_len]
        Transformer expects (seq_len, batch_size, embed_dim).
        Return shape: [batch_size, embed_dim]
        '''
        embedded = self.embedding(input_ids)            #
        ↪ [batch_size, seq_len, embed_dim]
        embedded = embedded.permute(1, 0, 2)            # [seq_len,
        ↪ batch_size, embed_dim]
        encoded = self.transformer_encoder(embedded)    # [seq_len,
        ↪ batch_size, embed_dim]
        # Mean pool across seq_len dimension
        mean_encoding = torch.mean(encoded, dim=0)      #
        ↪ [batch_size, embed_dim]
        return mean_encoding
```

```
# -----------------------------------------------------------
# 3) Semantic Search Utility Functions
# -----------------------------------------------------------
def build_document_embeddings(model, tokenizer, documents,
↪ max_len=20, device="cpu"):
    '''
    Given a list of documents, returns a tensor of embeddings.
    '''
    # Encode and pad documents
    encoded_docs = [tokenizer.encode(doc) for doc in documents]
    padded_docs = tokenizer.pad_batch(encoded_docs, max_len=max_len)

    with torch.no_grad():
        padded_docs = padded_docs.to(device)
        embeddings = model(padded_docs)
    return embeddings

def semantic_search(query, model, tokenizer, doc_embeddings,
↪ documents, max_len=20, top_k=3, device="cpu"):
    '''
    Compute the embedding for the query, compare against
    ↪ doc_embeddings,
    and return top_k matching documents (by cosine similarity).
    '''
    # Encode the query
    query_ids = tokenizer.encode(query)
    query_ids = tokenizer.pad_batch([query_ids],
    ↪ max_len=max_len).to(device)

    with torch.no_grad():
        query_emb = model(query_ids)    # [1, embed_dim]

        # Normalize embeddings for cosine similarity
        # (Alternatively, dot product or other metrics could be
        ↪ used)
        doc_norms = doc_embeddings / (doc_embeddings.norm(dim=1,
        ↪ keepdim=True) + 1e-8)
        query_norm = query_emb / (query_emb.norm(dim=1,
        ↪ keepdim=True) + 1e-8)

        scores = torch.mm(query_norm, doc_norms.t()).squeeze(0)    #
        ↪ [num_docs]
        # Get top_k indices
        top_indices = torch.topk(scores, k=top_k).indices

    # Return top-k documents
    results = [(documents[idx], float(scores[idx])) for idx in
    ↪ top_indices]
    return results

# -----------------------------------------------------------
# 4) Main Block: Build Model, Generate Embeddings, Query
# -----------------------------------------------------------
```

189

```
if __name__ == "__main__":
    # Sample documents
    documents = [
        "Transformers are great at natural language processing
        ↪   tasks",
        "PyTorch provides modules for building transformer models",
        "Semantic search uses vector similarity to rank documents",
        "Many modern search engines leverage transformer
        ↪   embeddings",
        "Domain-specific pretraining can improve retrieval
        ↪   relevance",
        "Cross-encoders can re-rank results for more accurate
        ↪   matching",
        "Vector indexes allow approximate nearest neighbor queries",
        "Fine-tuning transforms general embeddings to
        ↪   domain-specific tasks",
    ]

    # Create and fit tokenizer
    tokenizer = SimpleTokenizer()
    tokenizer.fit(documents, vocab_size=50)

    # Initialize the Transformer-based embedding model (randomly,
    ↪   for demo)
    device = torch.device("cuda" if torch.cuda.is_available() else
    ↪   "cpu")
    model = SimpleTransformerEncoder(
        vocab_size=len(tokenizer.word2idx),
        embed_dim=32,
        num_heads=2,
        feedforward_dim=64,
        num_layers=2,
        dropout=0.1
    ).to(device)

    # Build document embeddings
    with torch.no_grad():
        doc_embeddings = build_document_embeddings(model, tokenizer,
        ↪   documents, max_len=12, device=device)

    # Let's test a few queries
    queries = [
        "What tasks are transformers good for?",
        "How to build a transformer?",
        "Nearest neighbor approaches for search."
    ]

    for q in queries:
        results = semantic_search(q, model, tokenizer,
        ↪   doc_embeddings, documents, max_len=12, top_k=3,
        ↪   device=device)
        print(f"\nQuery: {q}")
        for rank_idx, (doc_text, score) in enumerate(results):
```

190

```
print(f"  Rank {rank_idx+1} | Score: {score:.4f} | Doc:
↪ {doc_text}")
```

Key Implementation Details:

- **Tokenizer**: We define a naïve whitespace-based tokenizer in
  `SimpleTokenizer` that maps words to integer indices, reserving special tokens for padding and unknown words.

- **Transformer Encoder**: The `SimpleTransformerEncoder`
  uses PyTorch's `nn.TransformerEncoder` as a multi-head attention mechanism. The output is mean-pooled across the sequence dimension to produce a single embedding vector for the entire text.

- **Building Document Embeddings**: In
  `build_document_embeddings`, we batch-encode a set of documents, generate embeddings, and store them for later retrieval.

- **Semantic Search**: The `semantic_search` function embeds
  a query, computes its similarity (cosine) to each document embedding, and returns the top matches.

- **Random Initialization vs. Pretrained**: This snippet illustrates the architecture. For production-grade systems, a pretrained model like Sentence-BERT typically replaces the randomly initialized model, then is fine-tuned for your domain.

- **Retrieval**: We demonstrate how to retrieve the top-K similar documents for several sample queries by calculating cosine similarities with the stored document embeddings.

Chapter 24

Transformer-based Recommendation Systems

Recommendation systems inform users about products, movies, or content they might enjoy. A Transformer can model user-item interactions over time, capturing evolving preferences. Start by encoding user history as a sequence of item embeddings, potentially including metadata. The self-attention mechanism reveals how earlier interactions influence the next suggestion. Fine-tune the model to predict the next item the user will engage with, employing cross-entropy or other ranking-based losses. Incorporate user attributes, item categories, or contextual signals (time of day, device type) through additional embeddings. For advanced approaches, combine multi-modal data, such as textual reviews or product images, feeding them through specialized encoders. You might also apply knowledge distillation from a larger language model that has seen more user-generated data, refining personalization insights.

Python Code Snippet

```
import torch
import torch.nn as nn
import torch.optim as optim
from torch.utils.data import Dataset, DataLoader
import random
```

```python
# For reproducibility
torch.manual_seed(42)
random.seed(42)

# ----------------------------------------------------------------
# 1) Synthetic Data Generation
# ----------------------------------------------------------------
def generate_synthetic_user_data(num_users=50, num_items=200,
                                  max_seq_len=10,
                                  ↪ num_sequences=1000):
    '''
    This function generates a synthetic set of user interactions
    ↪ with items.
    Each sample represents a partial interaction history
    (e.g., 5 items) plus the next item to be recommended.
    '''
    user_histories = []
    user_attributes = []
    next_items = []

    for _ in range(num_sequences):
        user_id = random.randint(0, num_users - 1)

        # Generate a random sequence length
        seq_len = random.randint(1, max_seq_len)

        # Interaction history (list of item IDs)
        items = [random.randint(0, num_items - 1) for _ in
        ↪ range(seq_len)]

        # Next item user engaged with
        next_item = random.randint(0, num_items - 1)

        # We'll store user_id as a separate 'attribute'
        # for demonstration of additional embeddings
        user_histories.append(items)
        user_attributes.append(user_id)
        next_items.append(next_item)

    return user_histories, user_attributes, next_items


# ----------------------------------------------------------------
# 2) PyTorch Dataset & DataLoader
# ----------------------------------------------------------------
class RecommendationDataset(Dataset):
    '''
    Each record returns:
        - interaction_history (list of item IDs)
        - user_attribute (e.g., user ID)
        - next_item (the training target)
    '''
```

```python
    def __init__(self, histories, attributes, next_items,
                 max_seq_len=10, pad_token=999999999):
        self.histories = histories
        self.attributes = attributes
        self.next_items = next_items
        self.max_seq_len = max_seq_len
        self.pad_token = pad_token   # Large number representing
        ↪    'PAD'

    def __len__(self):
        return len(self.histories)

    def __getitem__(self, idx):
        return (
            self.histories[idx],
            self.attributes[idx],
            self.next_items[idx]
        )


def collate_fn(batch_data):
    '''
    Collate function to handle:
     - Padding of variable-length item histories
     - Stacking attributes and labels
    '''
    histories, user_attrs, next_items = zip(*batch_data)

    max_len = max(len(seq) for seq in histories)
    max_len = min(max_len, 20)   # Keep a safe upper bound

    padded_histories = []
    for seq in histories:
        if len(seq) < max_len:
            seq = seq + [999999999]*(max_len - len(seq))   # Pad
            ↪    index
        else:
            seq = seq[:max_len]
        padded_histories.append(seq)

    return (
        torch.tensor(padded_histories, dtype=torch.long),
        torch.tensor(user_attrs, dtype=torch.long),
        torch.tensor(next_items, dtype=torch.long)
    )


# ----------------------------------------------------------------
# 3) Transformer-based Model
# ----------------------------------------------------------------
class TransformerRecommender(nn.Module):
    '''
    This model uses two embedding layers:
```

194

```
    - Item embedding for items in the user history
    - User embedding for user-related attributes
Then processes item sequences with a Transformer Encoder,
optionally combined with a user embedding for personalization.
Finally, predicts the next item via a softmax layer.
'''
def __init__(self, num_items, num_users, embed_dim=32,
            num_heads=2, hidden_dim=64, num_layers=2,
            dropout=0.1, pad_idx=999999999):
    super(TransformerRecommender, self).__init__()

    self.embed_dim = embed_dim
    self.pad_idx = pad_idx

    # Embeddings
    self.item_embedding = nn.Embedding(num_items+1, embed_dim,
                                    padding_idx=pad_idx)
    self.user_embedding = nn.Embedding(num_users, embed_dim)

    # Transformer Encoder
    encoder_layer = nn.TransformerEncoderLayer(
        d_model=embed_dim,
        nhead=num_heads,
        dim_feedforward=hidden_dim,
        dropout=dropout
    )
    self.transformer_encoder = nn.TransformerEncoder(
        encoder_layer, num_layers=num_layers
    )

    # Final classification (predict the next item)
    self.fc = nn.Linear(embed_dim, num_items)
    self.dropout = nn.Dropout(dropout)

def forward(self, items, users):
    '''
    items: [batch_size, seq_len]
    users: [batch_size]
    '''
    # items => [batch_size, seq_len] -> item_embedding =>
    ↪ [batch_size, seq_len, embed_dim]
    item_embedded = self.item_embedding(items)

    # We'll expand user embedding across sequence length
    user_embedded = self.user_embedding(users)  # [batch_size,
    ↪ embed_dim]
    user_embedded = user_embedded.unsqueeze(1).repeat(1,
    ↪ items.size(1), 1)

    # Combine item + user embedding
    combined_embedding = item_embedded + user_embedded

    # Permute to [seq_len, batch_size, embed_dim]
```

```python
        combined_embedding = combined_embedding.permute(1, 0, 2)

        # Make an attention mask for padded tokens
        pad_mask = (items == self.pad_idx).transpose(0, 1)   #
        ↪ [seq_len, batch_size]

        # Pass through transformer
        encoded_seq = self.transformer_encoder(
            combined_embedding,
            src_key_padding_mask=pad_mask
        )   # [seq_len, batch_size, embed_dim]

        # Pooling (take the representation of the last token or
        ↪ average)
        # We'll use average pooling here
        encoded_mean = torch.mean(encoded_seq, dim=0)   #
        ↪ [batch_size, embed_dim]
        encoded_mean = self.dropout(encoded_mean)

        # Predict next item
        logits = self.fc(encoded_mean)   # [batch_size, num_items]
        return logits


# --------------------------------------------------------------
# 4) Training and Evaluation
# --------------------------------------------------------------
def train_model(model, dataloader, optimizer, criterion, device):
    model.train()
    total_loss = 0.0
    for batch_items, batch_users, batch_next in dataloader:
        batch_items = batch_items.to(device)
        batch_users = batch_users.to(device)
        batch_next  = batch_next.to(device)

        optimizer.zero_grad()
        logits = model(batch_items, batch_users)
        loss = criterion(logits, batch_next)
        loss.backward()
        optimizer.step()

        total_loss += loss.item()

    return total_loss / len(dataloader)


def evaluate_model(model, dataloader, device):
    model.eval()
    total_correct = 0
    total_count = 0
    with torch.no_grad():
        for batch_items, batch_users, batch_next in dataloader:
            batch_items = batch_items.to(device)
```

196

```
            batch_users = batch_users.to(device)
            batch_next  = batch_next.to(device)

            logits = model(batch_items, batch_users)
            preds = torch.argmax(logits, dim=1)
            total_correct += (preds == batch_next).sum().item()
            total_count   += batch_next.size(0)
    return total_correct / total_count


# -------------------------------------------------------------
# 5) Main Execution
# -------------------------------------------------------------
if __name__ == "__main__":
    # Generate synthetic data
    user_histories, user_attrs, next_items =
    ↪   generate_synthetic_user_data(
        num_users=50,
        num_items=300,
        max_seq_len=10,
        num_sequences=2000
    )

    # Split data into train/test
    train_size = int(0.8 * len(user_histories))

    train_histories = user_histories[:train_size]
    train_attrs     = user_attrs[:train_size]
    train_next      = next_items[:train_size]

    test_histories  = user_histories[train_size:]
    test_attrs      = user_attrs[train_size:]
    test_next       = next_items[train_size:]

    # Create Dataset objects
    train_dataset = RecommendationDataset(train_histories,
    ↪   train_attrs, train_next)
    test_dataset  = RecommendationDataset(test_histories,
    ↪   test_attrs, test_next)

    # Dataloaders
    train_loader = DataLoader(train_dataset, batch_size=32,
    ↪   shuffle=True,
                              collate_fn=collate_fn)
    test_loader  = DataLoader(test_dataset, batch_size=32,
    ↪   shuffle=False,
                              collate_fn=collate_fn)

    # Initialize model
    device = torch.device("cuda" if torch.cuda.is_available() else
    ↪   "cpu")
    model = TransformerRecommender(
        num_items=300,
```

```
    num_users=50,
    embed_dim=32,
    num_heads=2,
    hidden_dim=64,
    num_layers=2,
    dropout=0.1
).to(device)

# Optimizer and loss
optimizer = optim.AdamW(model.parameters(), lr=1e-3)
criterion = nn.CrossEntropyLoss()

# Training loop
num_epochs = 5
for epoch in range(num_epochs):
    train_loss = train_model(model, train_loader, optimizer,
    ↪  criterion, device)
    accuracy   = evaluate_model(model, test_loader, device)
    print(f"Epoch {epoch+1}/{num_epochs}, Loss:
    ↪  {train_loss:.4f}, Test Accuracy: {accuracy:.4f}")

print("Training complete. The Transformer-based recommendation
↪  model is ready for inference.")
```

Key Implementation Details:

- **Synthetic Data Generation**: We create random user-item interaction sequences with `generate_synthetic_user_data`, simulating a scenario where each user has interacted with a sequence of items, followed by the next item to predict.

- **Dataset and Collate Function**: The class `RecommendationDataset` and `collate_fn` handle data preparation, including padding item sequences so they fit into a batch.

- **TransformerRecommender**: The model uses separate embedding layers for items and users, combines them, and passes the results to `nn.TransformerEncoder` for sequence encoding. The final linear layer (`self.fc`) predicts the next item the user might interact with.

- **Loss and Optimization**: We use cross-entropy with `nn.CrossEntropyLoss` to train the network, since we treat next-item prediction as a classification problem.

- **Training and Evaluation**: The `train_model` function back-propagates cross-entropy loss, while `evaluate_model` computes accuracy based on correct next-item predictions.

- **Extensibility**: One could incorporate user-specific metadata or item features (e.g., product images, textual descriptions) by adding specialized encoders and fusing the representations with item history embeddings.

Chapter 25

Tabular Data Analysis with Transformers

Transformers can be adapted to tabular data, often found in spreadsheets or relational databases. Each row becomes a sequence, with columns serving as tokens. Encode numeric columns using embeddings (e.g., binning or continuous projections), while categorical columns use standard token embeddings. Positional or column-based embeddings differentiate each field. A Transformer encoder processes these token embeddings, capturing relationships between columns and potential missing values. Train it for classification or regression tasks with a final feedforward head. For an innovative twist, combine tabular embeddings with text or image features if rows contain references to external data. You can also use masked column prediction as a pretraining objective, similar to masked language modeling, allowing the model to learn patterns from unlabeled tabular records.

Python Code Snippet

```
import torch
import torch.nn as nn
import torch.optim as optim
from torch.utils.data import Dataset, DataLoader
import numpy as np
import random

# ------------------------------
```

```
# 1) Synthetic Data Generation
# -------------------------
def generate_synthetic_tabular_data(num_rows=1000):
    """
    Generate synthetic tabular data with both numeric and
    ↪  categorical features.

    Returns:
        numeric_data: numpy array of shape [num_rows,
        ↪  num_numeric_cols]
        cat_data: numpy array of shape [num_rows, num_cat_cols]
        labels: numpy array of shape [num_rows] (binary
        ↪  classification)
    """
    random.seed(42)
    np.random.seed(42)

    num_numeric_cols = 3    # e.g. 3 numeric features
    num_cat_cols = 2        # e.g. 2 categorical features
    numeric_data = np.random.randn(num_rows, num_numeric_cols) * 5.0
    ↪  + 10.0

    # Let's create simple categorical data with limited categories
    cat_data = np.random.randint(0, 5, size=(num_rows,
    ↪  num_cat_cols))

    # Binary labels based on some synthetic rule for demonstration
    # e.g. if mean of numeric_data + sum of cat_data is above a
    ↪  threshold => label = 1
    thresholds = np.mean(numeric_data, axis=1) + np.sum(cat_data,
    ↪  axis=1)
    labels = (thresholds > (np.mean(thresholds))).astype(int)

    return numeric_data, cat_data, labels


# ---------------------------------------------
# 2) Dataset & Utilities for Tabular Data
# ---------------------------------------------
class TabularDataset(Dataset):
    """
    PyTorch Dataset for tabular data. Each item consists of:
     - numeric features
     - categorical features
     - label (for classification)
    """
    def __init__(self, numeric_data, cat_data, labels):
        self.numeric_data = numeric_data
        self.cat_data = cat_data
        self.labels = labels

    def __len__(self):
        return len(self.labels)
```

```python
    def __getitem__(self, idx):
        return (self.numeric_data[idx], self.cat_data[idx],
        ↪  self.labels[idx])

def tabular_collate_fn(batch_data):
    """
    Collate function to stack numeric data, cat data, and labels
    into tensors. This function will be used in the DataLoader.
    """
    numeric_batch = []
    cat_batch = []
    label_batch = []

    for numeric, cat, label in batch_data:
        numeric_batch.append(numeric)
        cat_batch.append(cat)
        label_batch.append(label)

    numeric_batch = torch.tensor(np.array(numeric_batch),
    ↪  dtype=torch.float)
    cat_batch = torch.tensor(np.array(cat_batch), dtype=torch.long)
    label_batch = torch.tensor(label_batch, dtype=torch.long)
    return numeric_batch, cat_batch, label_batch

# ------------------------------------------------------
# 3) Transformer Model Definition for Tabular Data
# ------------------------------------------------------
class TabularTransformer(nn.Module):
    """
    A Transformer-based architecture for tabular data.
    - Numeric columns are projected into embeddings.
    - Categorical columns are embedded using nn.Embedding.
    - Positional (column) embeddings help the model recognize each
    ↪  column position.
    - Data is stacked as a sequence of (num_total_cols) tokens,
    ↪  feeding into Transformer layers.
    """
    def __init__(
        self,
        num_numeric_cols,
        num_cat_cols,
        cat_cardinalities,
        d_model=32,
        nhead=2,
        num_layers=2,
        dim_feedforward=64,
        dropout=0.1,
        num_classes=2
    ):
        super(TabularTransformer, self).__init__()
        self.num_numeric_cols = num_numeric_cols
        self.num_cat_cols = num_cat_cols
        self.num_total_cols = num_numeric_cols + num_cat_cols
```

```python
        self.d_model = d_model

        # 1) Numeric projection: Linear layer to project each
        ↪   numeric column into d_model
        self.numeric_proj = nn.Linear(1, d_model)

        # 2) Categorical embeddings: Each category has its own
        ↪   embedding dimension
        #    We'll keep them the same size, d_model, for simplicity.
        self.cat_embeddings = nn.ModuleList([
            nn.Embedding(cardinality, d_model) for cardinality in
            ↪   cat_cardinalities
        ])

        # 3) Positional (Column) embeddings: for each column index
        ↪   in the sequence
        #    We have (num_total_cols) positions, each with embedding
        ↪   dimension d_model.
        self.pos_embedding = nn.Embedding(self.num_total_cols,
        ↪   d_model)

        # 4) Transformer Encoder
        encoder_layer = nn.TransformerEncoderLayer(
            d_model=d_model,
            nhead=nhead,
            dim_feedforward=dim_feedforward,
            dropout=dropout,
            batch_first=False  # We'll permute to [seq_len, batch,
            ↪   dim] format
        )
        self.transformer_encoder =
        ↪   nn.TransformerEncoder(encoder_layer,
        ↪   num_layers=num_layers)

        # 5) Classification head
        self.fc = nn.Linear(d_model, num_classes)

    def forward(self, numeric_data, cat_data):
        """
        numeric_data: [batch_size, num_numeric_cols]
        cat_data: [batch_size, num_cat_cols]
        """
        batch_size = numeric_data.size(0)

        # For numeric columns: we treat each column as 1 feature =>
        ↪   project to d_model
        numerics_emb_list = []
        for col_idx in range(self.num_numeric_cols):
            col_vals = numeric_data[:, col_idx].unsqueeze(-1)  #
            ↪   [batch_size, 1]
            proj = self.numeric_proj(col_vals)  # [batch_size,
            ↪   d_model]
            numerics_emb_list.append(proj)
```

203

```python
    # For categorical columns: embed them
    cat_emb_list = []
    for cat_idx in range(self.num_cat_cols):
        col_vals = cat_data[:, cat_idx]  # [batch_size]
        emb = self.cat_embeddings[cat_idx](col_vals)  #
        ↪  [batch_size, d_model]
        cat_emb_list.append(emb)

    # Concatenate all embeddings along sequence dimension =>
    ↪  shape: [batch_size, num_total_cols, d_model]
    combined_emb = torch.stack(numerics_emb_list + cat_emb_list,
    ↪  dim=1)

    # Add positional embeddings for each column position
    # We'll create a position index [0..num_total_cols-1],
    ↪  repeated for batch
    positions = torch.arange(0, self.num_total_cols,
    ↪  device=combined_emb.device)
    pos_emb = self.pos_embedding(positions)  # shape:
    ↪  [num_total_cols, d_model]
    pos_emb = pos_emb.unsqueeze(0).repeat(batch_size, 1, 1)  #
    ↪  broadcast [batch_size, num_total_cols, d_model]

    # Final input to transformer: combined_emb + positional
    ↪  embedding
    transformer_input = combined_emb + pos_emb  # [batch_size,
    ↪  num_total_cols, d_model]

    # Transformer expects [seq_len, batch_size, d_model] by
    ↪  default, so permute
    transformer_input = transformer_input.permute(1, 0, 2)  #
    ↪  [num_total_cols, batch_size, d_model]

    encoded = self.transformer_encoder(transformer_input)  #
    ↪  [num_total_cols, batch_size, d_model]

    # Mean pool over the columns in the sequence dimension
    encoded_mean = torch.mean(encoded, dim=0)  # [batch_size,
    ↪  d_model]

    # Classification output
    logits = self.fc(encoded_mean)  # [batch_size, num_classes]
    return logits

# --------------------------
# 4) Training & Evaluation
# --------------------------
def train_one_epoch(model, dataloader, optimizer, criterion,
↪  device):
    model.train()
    total_loss = 0.0
```

```
    for numeric_batch, cat_batch, label_batch in dataloader:
        numeric_batch = numeric_batch.to(device)
        cat_batch = cat_batch.to(device)
        label_batch = label_batch.to(device)

        optimizer.zero_grad()
        logits = model(numeric_batch, cat_batch)
        loss = criterion(logits, label_batch)
        loss.backward()
        optimizer.step()

        total_loss += loss.item()

    return total_loss / len(dataloader)

def evaluate(model, dataloader, device):
    model.eval()
    correct = 0
    total = 0
    with torch.no_grad():
        for numeric_batch, cat_batch, label_batch in dataloader:
            numeric_batch = numeric_batch.to(device)
            cat_batch = cat_batch.to(device)
            label_batch = label_batch.to(device)

            logits = model(numeric_batch, cat_batch)
            preds = torch.argmax(logits, dim=1)
            correct += (preds == label_batch).sum().item()
            total += label_batch.size(0)
    return correct / total

# --------------------------
# 5) Main Execution
# --------------------------
if __name__ == "__main__":
    # Generate synthetic tabular data
    numeric_data, cat_data, labels =
    ↪ generate_synthetic_tabular_data(num_rows=2000)

    # Split into train/test
    split_idx = int(0.8 * len(labels))
    train_numeric = numeric_data[:split_idx]
    test_numeric = numeric_data[split_idx:]

    train_cat = cat_data[:split_idx]
    test_cat = cat_data[split_idx:]

    train_labels = labels[:split_idx]
    test_labels = labels[split_idx:]

    # We assume each categorical column can have up to 5 categories
    ↪ (from data gen)
```

```python
cat_cardinalities = [5, 5]  # two cat columns, each with
↪    cardinality = 5

# Create dataset/dataloader
train_dataset = TabularDataset(train_numeric, train_cat,
↪    train_labels)
test_dataset = TabularDataset(test_numeric, test_cat,
↪    test_labels)

train_loader = DataLoader(
    train_dataset,
    batch_size=32,
    shuffle=True,
    collate_fn=tabular_collate_fn
)
test_loader = DataLoader(
    test_dataset,
    batch_size=32,
    shuffle=False,
    collate_fn=tabular_collate_fn
)

# Initialize model
device = torch.device("cuda" if torch.cuda.is_available() else
↪    "cpu")
model = TabularTransformer(
    num_numeric_cols=3,
    num_cat_cols=2,
    cat_cardinalities=cat_cardinalities,
    d_model=32,
    nhead=2,
    num_layers=2,
    dim_feedforward=64,
    dropout=0.1,
    num_classes=2
).to(device)

# Setup optimizer and loss function
optimizer = optim.AdamW(model.parameters(), lr=1e-3)
criterion = nn.CrossEntropyLoss()

# Train for a few epochs
num_epochs = 5
for epoch in range(num_epochs):
    avg_loss = train_one_epoch(model, train_loader, optimizer,
↪    criterion, device)
    acc = evaluate(model, test_loader, device)
    print(f"Epoch {epoch+1}/{num_epochs} - Loss: {avg_loss:.4f},
↪    Test Acc: {acc:.4f}")

print("Training complete. Ready for inference on tabular data.")
```

Key Implementation Details:

- **Data Representation**: Each row is broken into columns, which act as tokens in the Transformer. Numeric columns are projected to an embedding dimension by a linear layer, while categorical columns use traditional embedding lookups.

- **Column Position Embeddings**: Just like positional embeddings in NLP, here we add embeddings that indicate each column's position within the row.

- **Transformer Encoder**: The embedded columns are permuted to shape [seq_len, batch_size, d_model] and passed into `nn.TransformerEncoder` layers.

- **Pooling and Classification**: After encoding, the model pools across the sequence dimension (mean pooling here) and feeds the resulting vector into a fully connected layer for classification.

- **Training and Evaluation**: The `train_one_epoch` function updates model parameters to minimize cross-entropy, while `evaluate` calculates accuracy to gauge performance on held-out data.

Chapter 26

Auto-Regressive Transformers for Sequence Generation

Auto-regressive Transformers process sequences one token at a time, predicting the next token from the previous context. This is foundational for many tasks, including language modeling, code generation, and conditional tasks like text-to-text translations. Construct an auto-regressive Transformer by shifting the input sequence right for the decoder and masking future tokens. During training, each token is predicted from all preceding tokens, optimizing cross-entropy loss. At inference, sampling strategies like beam search, top-k, or nucleus sampling can produce more coherent sequences. Advanced variations add pointers or copying mechanisms to replicate segments directly from the input. Additionally, advanced heads can incorporate coverage vectors, ensuring tokens in the input have been addressed in the output. This architecture provides a flexible foundation for a wide variety of generation tasks.

Python Code Snippet

```
import torch
import torch.nn as nn
import torch.optim as optim
from torch.utils.data import Dataset, DataLoader
import random
```

```python
import math

# ------------------------------------------------
# 1) Simple Data Preparation & Tokenizer
# ------------------------------------------------

class SimpleTokenizer:
    '''
    A minimal tokenizer for demonstration purposes.
    It collects a vocabulary of most frequent words.
    Any word not found in the vocab is mapped to [UNK].
    We also include special tokens [BOS], [EOS], [PAD].
    '''
    def __init__(self, vocab_size=50):
        self.vocab_size = vocab_size
        self.word2id = {}
        self.id2word = {}

    def fit(self, texts):
        # Count frequency of words
        freq = {}
        for txt in texts:
            for word in txt.split():
                freq[word] = freq.get(word, 0) + 1

        # Sort by frequency, keep top words (minus room for special
        ↪  tokens)
        sorted_words = sorted(freq.items(), key=lambda x: x[1],
        ↪  reverse=True)
        truncated = sorted_words[: self.vocab_size - 4]

        unique_words = ["[PAD]", "[BOS]", "[EOS]", "[UNK]"]
        unique_words += [w[0] for w in truncated]

        self.word2id = {w: i for i, w in enumerate(unique_words)}
        self.id2word = {i: w for w, i in self.word2id.items()}

    def encode(self, text):
        # Convert space-separated words to IDs
        tokens = []
        for w in text.split():
            if w in self.word2id:
                tokens.append(self.word2id[w])
            else:
                tokens.append(self.word2id["[UNK]"])
        return tokens

    def decode(self, token_ids):
        # Convert IDs to words
        return " ".join(self.id2word.get(tid, "[UNK]") for tid in
        ↪  token_ids)

    @property
```

209

```python
    def pad_id(self):
        return self.word2id["[PAD]"]

    @property
    def bos_id(self):
        return self.word2id["[BOS]"]

    @property
    def eos_id(self):
        return self.word2id["[EOS]"]

def create_synthetic_text_data(num_samples=1000):
    '''
    Generate random short sequences of text for demonstration.
    We'll form them from a small pool of words.
    Each sequence has a random length between 5 and 12.
    '''
    pool = ["the", "cat", "sat", "on", "mat",
            "dog", "ran", "fast", "rain", "cloud",
            "flower", "chair", "banana", "kitchen", "car",
            "transformers", "are", "really", "cool", "wonderful",
            "amazing", "try", "top", "k", "sampling",
            "beam", "search"]

    all_texts = []

    for _ in range(num_samples):
        length = random.randint(5, 12)
        words = random.choices(pool, k=length)
        text = " ".join(words)
        all_texts.append(text)
    return all_texts

# ---------------------------------------------------
# 2) PyTorch Dataset and Collate Function
# ---------------------------------------------------
class LanguageModelDataset(Dataset):
    '''
    Prepares data for auto-regressive training:
    We'll produce input sequences (with BOS token at front)
    and target sequences (shifted by one token) for each sample.
    '''
    def __init__(self, texts, tokenizer, max_len=20):
        self.texts = texts
        self.tokenizer = tokenizer
        self.max_len = max_len
        self.encoded_texts = []

        for txt in texts:
            token_ids = tokenizer.encode(txt)
            # We add BOS, and will add EOS later if space permits
            token_ids = [tokenizer.bos_id] + token_ids
            # Optionally add an EOS if there's still room
```

```python
        if len(token_ids) < (max_len):
            token_ids.append(tokenizer.eos_id)
        # Truncate/pad
        token_ids = token_ids[:max_len]
        self.encoded_texts.append(token_ids)

    def __len__(self):
        return len(self.encoded_texts)

    def __getitem__(self, idx):
        seq = self.encoded_texts[idx]
        # Auto-regressive target is simply one step ahead
        x = seq[:-1]
        y = seq[1:]
        return x, y

def collate_fn(batch_data):
    '''
    Pad sequences to the same length within the batch.
    x: [batch_size, seq_len], y: [batch_size, seq_len]
    '''
    xs, ys = zip(*batch_data)
    max_len = max(len(seq) for seq in xs)

    # We'll pad to max_len. In a real scenario, we might
    # keep a fixed max_len or dynamically batch. Simplified here.
    padded_x = []
    padded_y = []
    for x, y in zip(xs, ys):
        padded_x.append(x + [tokenizer.pad_id]*(max_len - len(x)))
        padded_y.append(y + [tokenizer.pad_id]*(max_len - len(y)))

    return (torch.tensor(padded_x, dtype=torch.long),
            torch.tensor(padded_y, dtype=torch.long))

# ---------------------------------------------------
# 3) Auto-Regressive Transformer Model
# ---------------------------------------------------

class PositionalEncoding(nn.Module):
    '''
    Standard sinusoidal positional encoding for sequence order,
    added to token embeddings.
    '''
    def __init__(self, d_model, max_len=5000):
        super(PositionalEncoding, self).__init__()

        pe = torch.zeros(max_len, d_model)
        position = torch.arange(0, max_len,
        ↪   dtype=torch.float).unsqueeze(1)
        div_term = torch.exp(torch.arange(0, d_model, 2).float() *
        ↪   (-math.log(10000.0) / d_model))
        pe[:, 0::2] = torch.sin(position * div_term)
```

211

```python
        pe[:, 1::2] = torch.cos(position * div_term)
        pe = pe.unsqueeze(1)  # shape: [max_len, 1, d_model]
        self.register_buffer('pe', pe)

    def forward(self, x):
        # x shape: [seq_len, batch_size, d_model]
        seq_len = x.size(0)
        # Add positional info up to seq_len
        return x + self.pe[:seq_len, :]

class AutoRegTransformer(nn.Module):
    '''
    A single-decoder transformer for auto-regressive language
    ↪  modeling.
    This effectively acts like GPT in a simplified form.
    '''
    def __init__(self, vocab_size, d_model=64, nhead=4,
    ↪  num_layers=2, dim_feedforward=128, dropout=0.1):
        super(AutoRegTransformer, self).__init__()

        self.embedding = nn.Embedding(vocab_size, d_model)
        self.pos_encoder = PositionalEncoding(d_model)

        # We build a TransformerDecoder, but there's no separate
        ↪  encoder.
        # We'll use a dummy placeholder for the 'memory' in
        ↪  decoding.
        decoder_layer = nn.TransformerDecoderLayer(
            d_model=d_model, nhead=nhead,
            dim_feedforward=dim_feedforward,
            dropout=dropout
        )
        self.transformer_decoder = nn.TransformerDecoder(
            decoder_layer, num_layers=num_layers
        )

        self.fc_out = nn.Linear(d_model, vocab_size)
        self.d_model = d_model

    def forward(self, x):
        '''
        x shape: [batch_size, seq_len]
        Return shape: [batch_size, seq_len, vocab_size]
        '''
        # Embed tokens
        embedded = self.embedding(x)  # [batch_size, seq_len,
        ↪  d_model]
        # Convert to shape [seq_len, batch_size, d_model] for
        ↪  Transformer
        embedded = embedded.permute(1, 0, 2)
        # Add pos encoding
        embedded = self.pos_encoder(embedded)
```

```python
        # Generate a causal mask for auto-regression
        seq_len = embedded.size(0)
        tgt_mask = self._generate_causal_mask(seq_len, seq_len,
        ↪  x.device)

        # Because we have no encoder, memory is just zeros or None
        # We'll provide a zero-tensor so PyTorch doesn't complain
        memory = torch.zeros(1, x.size(0), self.d_model,
        ↪  device=x.device)

        # Decode
        decoded = self.transformer_decoder(embedded, memory,
                                           tgt_mask=tgt_mask)
        # decoded shape: [seq_len, batch_size, d_model]

        logits = self.fc_out(decoded)  # [seq_len, batch_size,
        ↪  vocab_size]
        logits = logits.permute(1, 0, 2)  # back to [batch_size,
        ↪  seq_len, vocab_size]
        return logits

    def _generate_causal_mask(self, sz1, sz2, device):
        '''
        Generate an upper-triangular matrix of -inf, with zeros on
        ↪  diag.
        This prevents the model from "seeing" future tokens.
        '''
        mask = (torch.triu(torch.ones(sz1, sz2, device=device)) ==
        ↪  1).transpose(0,1)
        # mask shape = [sz2, sz1]
        # We want upper-triangular to be True -> fill with -inf
        mask = mask.float().masked_fill(mask == 0, float('-inf'))
        mask = mask.masked_fill(mask == 1, float(0.0))
        return mask


# ----------------------------------------------------
# 4) Training and Generation Utilities
# ----------------------------------------------------

def train_loop(model, dataloader, optimizer, criterion, device):
    model.train()
    total_loss = 0
    for x, y in dataloader:
        x, y = x.to(device), y.to(device)
        optimizer.zero_grad()
        logits = model(x)
        # Flatten for cross entropy: [batch_size*seq_len,
        ↪  vocab_size]
        # target shape: [batch_size*seq_len]
        loss = criterion(logits.view(-1, logits.size(-1)),
        ↪  y.view(-1))
        loss.backward()
        optimizer.step()
```

213

```
        total_loss += loss.item()
    return total_loss / len(dataloader)

def evaluate(model, dataloader, criterion, device):
    model.eval()
    total_loss = 0
    with torch.no_grad():
        for x, y in dataloader:
            x, y = x.to(device), y.to(device)
            logits = model(x)
            loss = criterion(logits.view(-1, logits.size(-1)),
            ↪   y.view(-1))
            total_loss += loss.item()
    return total_loss / len(dataloader)

def generate_text(model, tokenizer, prompt, max_new_tokens=20,
↪   device='cpu', top_k=5):
    '''
    A simple top-k sampling text generation.
    We feed in the prompt, then iteratively sample new tokens.
    '''
    model.eval()

    # Encode prompt
    tokens = tokenizer.encode(prompt)
    input_ids = torch.tensor(tokens, dtype=torch.long,
    ↪   device=device).unsqueeze(0)
    # input_ids shape: [1, seq_len]

    # We'll generate step by step
    for _ in range(max_new_tokens):
        with torch.no_grad():
            logits = model(input_ids)
            # logits shape: [1, seq_len, vocab_size]
            # We want only the last token
            last_logits = logits[0, -1, :]

            # top-k
            top_vals, top_inds = torch.topk(last_logits, k=top_k)
            # probabilities
            probs = torch.softmax(top_vals, dim=-1)
            sampled_idx = torch.multinomial(probs, 1).item()
            token_id = top_inds[sampled_idx].item()

            # append token to input_ids
            input_ids = torch.cat([input_ids,
            ↪   torch.tensor([[token_id]], device=device)], dim=1)

            # If we hit EOS, break
            if token_id == tokenizer.eos_id:
                break

    # Convert to list and decode
```

```python
        generated_sequence = input_ids[0].tolist()
        decoded = tokenizer.decode(generated_sequence)
        return decoded


# -------------------------------------------------
# 5) Main Execution
# -------------------------------------------------

if __name__ == "__main__":
    # Seed for reproducibility
    torch.manual_seed(42)
    random.seed(42)

    # Generate synthetic text data
    all_texts = create_synthetic_text_data(num_samples=2000)

    # Build tokenizer
    tokenizer = SimpleTokenizer(vocab_size=100)
    tokenizer.fit(all_texts)

    # Split train/test
    split_idx = int(len(all_texts) * 0.8)
    train_texts = all_texts[:split_idx]
    test_texts = all_texts[split_idx:]

    # Create dataset
    train_dataset = LanguageModelDataset(train_texts, tokenizer,
    ↪    max_len=20)
    test_dataset = LanguageModelDataset(test_texts, tokenizer,
    ↪    max_len=20)

    # Dataloaders
    train_loader = DataLoader(train_dataset, batch_size=32,
    ↪    shuffle=True, collate_fn=collate_fn)
    test_loader = DataLoader(test_dataset, batch_size=32,
    ↪    shuffle=False, collate_fn=collate_fn)

    # Initialize model
    device = torch.device("cuda" if torch.cuda.is_available() else
    ↪    "cpu")
    model = AutoRegTransformer(vocab_size=len(tokenizer.word2id),
    ↪    d_model=64,
                              nhead=4, num_layers=2,
                              ↪    dim_feedforward=128, dropout=0.1)
    model.to(device)

    # Optimizer & Criterion
    optimizer = optim.AdamW(model.parameters(), lr=1e-3)
    criterion = nn.CrossEntropyLoss(ignore_index=tokenizer.pad_id)

    # Train
    epochs = 5
    for epoch in range(epochs):
```

```
train_loss = train_loop(model, train_loader, optimizer,
  ↪  criterion, device)
val_loss = evaluate(model, test_loader, criterion, device)
print(f"Epoch {epoch+1}/{epochs}, Train Loss:
  ↪  {train_loss:.4f}, Val Loss: {val_loss:.4f}")

# Simple text generation
prompt_text = "the cat"
generated = generate_text(model, tokenizer, prompt_text,
  ↪  max_new_tokens=15, device=device, top_k=5)
print(f"Prompt: {prompt_text}")
print(f"Generated: {generated}")
```

Key Implementation Details:

- **Data Generation and Tokenization**: We create synthetic text data via `create_synthetic_text_data` and apply a simplified tokenizer (`SimpleTokenizer`)—in real applications, a sophisticated subword tokenizer (e.g., BPE) is recommended.

- **Auto-Regressive Decoder Setup**: The implementation uses `nn.TransformerDecoder` with a causal mask to ensure the model only attends to past tokens when generating the next token.

- **Positional Encoding**: The `PositionalEncoding` class injects sequence position information into the embeddings, crucial for capturing ordering in the sequence.

- **Training Loop**: In `train_loop`, we predict the next token given all previous tokens. We compute cross-entropy loss and perform backpropagation. The `evaluate` function computes validation loss to monitor performance.

- **Sampling for Generation**: The function `generate_text` relies on top-k sampling to pick the next token from the highest probability candidates, promoting diversity in generated sequences.

- **End-to-End Integration**: The final code block stitches together data loading, model building, training, and text generation, offering a complete pipeline for auto-regressive sequence generation.

Chapter 27

Transformer-based Generative Adversarial Networks

GANs typically comprise a generator and a discriminator network. Here, both can employ Transformers in tasks such as text generation or image synthesis. First, build a generator using a Transformer decoder that produces synthetic sequences token by token. The discriminator, another Transformer, classifies whether a sequence (or image, if tokenized) is real or fake. Training follows an adversarial process, with the generator aiming to fool the discriminator, and the discriminator learning to distinguish real data from generated data. For innovative approaches, incorporate partial conditioning on real sequences or images, letting the generator fill masked patches or tokens. Another tactic is to use multi-head attention in the discriminator to detect nuance in syntactic or visual patterns. This encourages more realistic outputs from the generator.

Python Code Snippet

```python
import torch
import torch.nn as nn
import torch.optim as optim
from torch.utils.data import DataLoader, Dataset
import random
```

```
# ----------------------------------
# 1. Config & Utilities
# ----------------------------------
SEED = 42
random.seed(SEED)
torch.manual_seed(SEED)

VOCAB_SIZE = 20      # small toy vocabulary
SEQ_LEN = 5          # length of sequences
BATCH_SIZE = 16
NUM_BATCHES = 100    # total steps (batches) to train
EMBED_DIM = 32
HIDDEN_DIM = 64
NUM_HEADS = 2
NUM_LAYERS = 2

DEVICE = torch.device("cuda" if torch.cuda.is_available() else
↪    "cpu")

# ----------------------------------
# 2. Synthetic Dataset
# ----------------------------------
class SyntheticSequenceDataset(Dataset):
    """
    Generates random integer sequences as 'real' data.
    Each item is a sequence of length SEQ_LEN,
    with tokens in [2..VOCAB_SIZE-1].
    """
    def __init__(self, total_samples=1000):
        super().__init__()
        self.total_samples = total_samples

    def __len__(self):
        return self.total_samples

    def __getitem__(self, idx):
        # Create random sequence
        seq = [random.randint(2, VOCAB_SIZE - 1) for _ in
↪        range(SEQ_LEN)]
        return torch.tensor(seq, dtype=torch.long)

def real_data_loader(batch_size=BATCH_SIZE, total_samples=1000):
    dataset = SyntheticSequenceDataset(total_samples=total_samples)
    return DataLoader(dataset, batch_size=batch_size, shuffle=True)

# ----------------------------------
# 3. Generator (Transformer Decoder)
# ----------------------------------
class TransformerGenerator(nn.Module):
    """
    A simple Transformer-based generator. It creates random noise
↪    tokens
```

and processes them through a TransformerDecoder to output
↪   synthetic
sequences. In a more advanced approach, you could feed partial
↪   real
sequences or combine embeddings with other sources of
↪   conditioning.
"""

```python
def __init__(self, vocab_size, embed_dim, hidden_dim, num_heads,
↪   num_layers, max_seq_len=SEQ_LEN):
    super(TransformerGenerator, self).__init__()
    self.vocab_size = vocab_size
    self.max_seq_len = max_seq_len

    # Embedding for noise input (each position gets random
    ↪   tokens from [0..1])
    self.noise_embed = nn.Embedding(2, embed_dim)  # 2 =
    ↪   possible noise tokens for demonstration

    # Positional embedding
    self.positional_embed = nn.Embedding(max_seq_len, embed_dim)

    # We use a small TransformerDecoder
    decoder_layer =
    ↪   nn.TransformerDecoderLayer(d_model=embed_dim,
                      nhead=num_heads,
                      dim_feedforward=hidden_dim,
                      dropout=0.1)
    self.transformer_decoder =
    ↪   nn.TransformerDecoder(decoder_layer,
    ↪   num_layers=num_layers)

    # Final linear layer to map to vocab distribution
    self.fc_out = nn.Linear(embed_dim, vocab_size)

def forward(self, batch_size):
    """
    We create a noise sequence of length max_seq_len,
    pass it through the decoder, and output a sequence of
    ↪   logits.
    """
    # Noise input: shape = [batch_size, max_seq_len]
    noise_input = torch.randint(0, 2, (batch_size,
    ↪   self.max_seq_len), dtype=torch.long).to(DEVICE)

    # We do not use an encoder here, so we treat the 'memory' as
    ↪   zeros
    # (in practice, you might have an encoder or some
    ↪   condition).
    fake_memory = torch.zeros(self.max_seq_len, batch_size,
    ↪   EMBED_DIM, device=DEVICE)

    # Embed noise
```

```python
        noise_emb = self.noise_embed(noise_input)   # [batch_size,
        ↪ seq_len, embed_dim]

        # Add positional embeddings
        positions = torch.arange(0, self.max_seq_len,
        ↪ device=DEVICE).unsqueeze(0)   # [1, seq_len]
        pos_emb = self.positional_embed(positions)   # [1, seq_len,
        ↪ embed_dim]
        noise_emb = noise_emb + pos_emb

        # Reshape to [seq_len, batch_size, embed_dim] for the
        ↪ decoder
        noise_emb = noise_emb.permute(1, 0, 2)

        # TransformerDecoder forward pass
        # We pass in noise_emb as "tgt" and fake_memory as "memory"
        decoded = self.transformer_decoder(tgt=noise_emb,
        ↪ memory=fake_memory)   # [seq_len, batch_size, embed_dim]

        # Map to vocab
        decoded = decoded.permute(1, 0, 2)   # [batch_size, seq_len,
        ↪ embed_dim]
        logits = self.fc_out(decoded)        # [batch_size, seq_len,
        ↪ vocab_size]
        return logits

# -------------------------------
# 4. Discriminator (Transformer Encoder)
# -------------------------------
class TransformerDiscriminator(nn.Module):
    """
    A Transformer-based discriminator classifies whether a sequence
    ↪ is real or fake.
    It outputs a single logit per sequence (real or fake).
    """
    def __init__(self, vocab_size, embed_dim, hidden_dim, num_heads,
    ↪ num_layers, max_seq_len=SEQ_LEN):
        super(TransformerDiscriminator, self).__init__()

        self.embed = nn.Embedding(vocab_size, embed_dim)
        self.pos_embed = nn.Embedding(max_seq_len, embed_dim)

        encoder_layer =
        ↪ nn.TransformerEncoderLayer(d_model=embed_dim,
                    nhead=num_heads,
                    dim_feedforward=hidden_dim,
                    dropout=0.1)
        self.transformer_encoder =
        ↪ nn.TransformerEncoder(encoder_layer,
        ↪ num_layers=num_layers)

        # Final classification (binary: real or fake)
        self.fc = nn.Linear(embed_dim, 1)
```

```python
def forward(self, sequences):
    """
    sequences: [batch_size, seq_len]
    Output: [batch_size, 1] (logit for real or fake)
    """
    batch_size, seq_len = sequences.shape
    x = self.embed(sequences)  # [batch_size, seq_len,
    ↪   embed_dim]

    # Add positional embeddings
    positions = torch.arange(0, seq_len,
    ↪   device=sequences.device).unsqueeze(0)  # [1, seq_len]
    x = x + self.pos_embed(positions)  # broadcasting adds
    ↪   across batch dimension

    # Reshape for transformer: [seq_len, batch_size, embed_dim]
    x = x.permute(1, 0, 2)

    # Pass through encoder
    encoded = self.transformer_encoder(x)  # [seq_len,
    ↪   batch_size, embed_dim]

    # Pool the sequence representations, e.g., mean pooling
    encoded = encoded.permute(1, 0, 2)  # [batch_size, seq_len,
    ↪   embed_dim]
    pooled = torch.mean(encoded, dim=1)  # [batch_size,
    ↪   embed_dim]

    logit = self.fc(pooled)  # [batch_size, 1]
    return logit

# ---------------------------------
# 5. Initialize Generator, Discriminator, Optimizers
# ---------------------------------
generator = TransformerGenerator(
    vocab_size=VOCAB_SIZE,
    embed_dim=EMBED_DIM,
    hidden_dim=HIDDEN_DIM,
    num_heads=NUM_HEADS,
    num_layers=NUM_LAYERS
).to(DEVICE)

discriminator = TransformerDiscriminator(
    vocab_size=VOCAB_SIZE,
    embed_dim=EMBED_DIM,
    hidden_dim=HIDDEN_DIM,
    num_heads=NUM_HEADS,
    num_layers=NUM_LAYERS
).to(DEVICE)

g_optimizer = optim.Adam(generator.parameters(), lr=1e-3)
d_optimizer = optim.Adam(discriminator.parameters(), lr=1e-3)
```

221

```python
bce_loss = nn.BCEWithLogitsLoss()

# ------------------------------
# 6. Training Loop
# ------------------------------
# DataLoader for real data
real_loader = real_data_loader(batch_size=BATCH_SIZE,
 ↪  total_samples=NUM_BATCHES * BATCH_SIZE)

d_iter = iter(real_loader)  # We'll iterate over the real data

for step in range(NUM_BATCHES):

    # --------------------------
    # 6.1 Train Discriminator
    # --------------------------

    # Get real data
    try:
        real_seqs = next(d_iter)
    except StopIteration:
        d_iter = iter(real_loader)
        real_seqs = next(d_iter)

    real_seqs = real_seqs.to(DEVICE)  # [batch_size, seq_len]

    # Generate fake data
    fake_logits = generator(batch_size=BATCH_SIZE)  # shape
 ↪  [batch_size, seq_len, vocab_size]
    # Sample from the generator's distribution (argmax or sample)
    fake_seqs = fake_logits.argmax(dim=-1).detach()  # [batch_size,
 ↪  seq_len]

    # Discriminator forward for real data
    d_optimizer.zero_grad()
    real_preds = discriminator(real_seqs)  # [batch_size, 1]
    real_targets = torch.ones((BATCH_SIZE, 1), device=DEVICE)
    real_loss = bce_loss(real_preds, real_targets)

    # Discriminator forward for fake data
    fake_preds = discriminator(fake_seqs)  # [batch_size, 1]
    fake_targets = torch.zeros((BATCH_SIZE, 1), device=DEVICE)
    fake_loss = bce_loss(fake_preds, fake_targets)

    d_loss = real_loss + fake_loss
    d_loss.backward()
    d_optimizer.step()

    # --------------------------
    # 6.2 Train Generator
    # --------------------------
    g_optimizer.zero_grad()
```

222

```
# Generate fake data again (we need new fake logits for
↪  gradient)
fake_logits2 = generator(batch_size=BATCH_SIZE)
fake_seqs2 = fake_logits2.argmax(dim=-1)

# Discriminator's opinion on these new fakes
gen_preds = discriminator(fake_seqs2)
gen_targets = torch.ones((BATCH_SIZE, 1), device=DEVICE)  #
↪  generator wants these to be real
g_loss = bce_loss(gen_preds, gen_targets)
g_loss.backward()
g_optimizer.step()

if (step + 1) % 10 == 0:
    print(f"Step [{step+1}/{NUM_BATCHES}] | D_loss:
    ↪  {d_loss.item():.4f} | G_loss: {g_loss.item():.4f}")

print("Training complete. Generator and Discriminator are ready for
↪  inference or further experimentation.")
```

Key Implementation Details:

- The texttt TransformerGenerator uses a simplified Transformer decoder to produce sequences from random noise. In practice, more sophisticated conditioning (e.g., partial sequences or learned embeddings) can be used.

- The texttt TransformerDiscriminator is a Transformer encoder that classifies entire sequences as real or fake. The output is a single logit indicating genuineness.

- The `bce_loss` (binary cross-entropy) with logits is employed for both the discriminator and generator objectives.

- Real sequences are sampled from a small random integer corpus (**SyntheticSequenceDataset**), while the generator outputs fake sequences via token argmax.

- The end-to-end adversarial training loop optimizes the discriminator to distinguish real sequences from generated (fake) sequences, and the generator to produce sequences the discriminator deems real.

- Emphasis is placed on showing how Transformers can be integrated into both the generator (decoder) and the discriminator (encoder), highlighting how multi-head self-attention can capture global dependencies in both tasks.

Chapter 28

Aspect-Based Sentiment Analysis with Transformers

Aspect-based sentiment analysis (ABSA) goes beyond overall sentiment to evaluate opinions about specific entities or attributes (e.g., food vs. service in restaurant reviews). Collect a dataset where text is annotated with aspects and respective sentiments. Use a Transformer-based span extraction or classification model: the encoder processes the text, while a classification head predicts the sentiment of each aspect. Alternatively, you can explicitly model aspect terms by highlighting them with special attention tokens so the model focuses on relevant text sections. More advanced techniques combine NER or phrase extraction for aspect detection, and then apply a Transformer-based sentiment classifier. This modular pipeline allows domain-specific improvements, such as new embeddings for restaurant, electronics, or service reviews. Output typically includes each aspect with a label such as positive, negative, or neutral.

Python Code Snippet

```
import torch
import torch.nn as nn
import torch.optim as optim
from torch.utils.data import Dataset, DataLoader
```

```python
import random

# For reproducibility
torch.manual_seed(42)
random.seed(42)

# ----------------------------------------------------------------
# 1) Synthetic ABSA Data Generation & Simple Subword Tokenizer
# ----------------------------------------------------------------
class SimpleSubwordTokenizer:
    '''
    Very basic subword tokenizer that splits text by whitespace
    and then merges selected pairs into 'subwords'.
    This is just for demonstration and doesn't implement true BPE.
    '''
    def __init__(self, vocab_size=50):
        self.vocab_size = vocab_size
        self.token2id = {}
        self.id2token = {}

    def fit(self, texts):
        # Collect frequency of each token (word) across all texts
        all_tokens = {}
        for txt in texts:
            for token in txt.split():
                all_tokens[token] = all_tokens.get(token, 0) + 1

        # Sort tokens by frequency, truncate to vocabulary size
        # ↪ minus space for [UNK], [PAD]
        sorted_tokens = sorted(all_tokens.items(), key=lambda x:
        ↪ x[1], reverse=True)
        truncated_tokens = sorted_tokens[:self.vocab_size - 2]

        # Initialize special tokens
        self.token2id = {"[UNK]": 0, "[PAD]": 1}
        idx = 2
        for token, _ in truncated_tokens:
            self.token2id[token] = idx
            idx += 1
        self.id2token = {v: k for k, v in self.token2id.items()}

    def encode(self, text):
        # Convert tokens to IDs with [UNK] for OOV
        tokens = text.split()
        encoded = [self.token2id.get(t, 0) for t in tokens]
        return encoded

    def decode(self, ids):
        tokens = [self.id2token.get(i, "[UNK]") for i in ids]
        return " ".join(tokens)

    def pad(self, encoded_batch, max_len):
        padded_batch = []
```

```
    for seq in encoded_batch:
        if len(seq) < max_len:
            seq = seq + [self.token2id["[PAD]"]] * (max_len -
            ↪  len(seq))
        else:
            seq = seq[:max_len]
        padded_batch.append(seq)
    return padded_batch

def generate_synthetic_absa_data(num_samples=2000):
    '''
    Generate random text data for demonstration of ABSA.
    Each sample has an 'aspect' (e.g., food or service)
    and a random sentiment label (positive or negative).
    We'll embed the aspect in the original text so the model
    can learn to attend to it.
    '''
    possible_aspects = ["food", "service"]
    possible_positive_tokens = ["great", "awesome", "wonderful",
    ↪  "amazing"]
    possible_negative_tokens = ["terrible", "awful", "bad",
    ↪  "horrible"]
    base_phrases = [
        "The atmosphere is nice",
        "I love the ambiance",
        "It was too crowded",
        "The place is very clean",
        "The price is reasonable"
    ]

    texts = []
    aspects = []
    sentiments = []

    for _ in range(num_samples):
        aspect = random.choice(possible_aspects)
        label = random.randint(0, 1)  # 0 = negative, 1 = positive

        # Construct a text that mentions the aspect
        phrase = random.choice(base_phrases)
        if label == 1:
            # Positive
            token = random.choice(possible_positive_tokens)
        else:
            # Negative
            token = random.choice(possible_negative_tokens)

        # E.g. "The atmosphere is nice food was amazing"
        text = f"{phrase} {aspect} was {token}"

        texts.append(text)
        aspects.append(aspect)
        sentiments.append(label)
```

226

```
        return texts, aspects, sentiments

# ----------------------------------------------------------------
# 2) PyTorch Dataset & DataLoader for ABSA
# ----------------------------------------------------------------
class ABSADataset(Dataset):
    def __init__(self, texts, aspects, sentiments, tokenizer,
    ↪  max_len=15):
        self.texts = texts
        self.aspects = aspects
        self.sentiments = sentiments
        self.tokenizer = tokenizer
        self.max_len = max_len

        # We'll encode the entire text.
        # In a real ABSA scenario, one might highlight aspect or
        ↪  handle multiple aspects per text.
        self.encoded_texts = [tokenizer.encode(t) for t in texts]

    def __len__(self):
        return len(self.texts)

    def __getitem__(self, idx):
        return self.encoded_texts[idx], self.aspects[idx],
        ↪  self.sentiments[idx]

def collate_fn_absa(batch_data):
    '''
    Collate function to pad variable-length sequences,
    and return aspect tokens (though we won't use them in a separate
    ↪  embedding here).
    '''
    encoded_lists, aspects, sentiments = zip(*batch_data)
    max_len = min(max(len(seq) for seq in encoded_lists), 15)

    # Pad sequences
    padded_encoded = tokenizer.pad(encoded_lists, max_len)
    return (
        torch.tensor(padded_encoded, dtype=torch.long),
        list(aspects),  # we won't convert aspects to tensor in this
        ↪  simple demonstration
        torch.tensor(sentiments, dtype=torch.long)
    )

# ----------------------------------------------------------------
# 3) Transformer Model Definition
# ----------------------------------------------------------------
class ABSTransformerClassifier(nn.Module):
    '''
    A simple Transformer-based classifier for aspect-level
    ↪  sentiment.
    '''
```

227

```python
    def __init__(self, vocab_size, embed_dim=32, num_heads=2,
                 hidden_dim=64, num_layers=2, num_classes=2,
             ↪  dropout=0.1):
        super(ABSTransformerClassifier, self).__init__()

        self.embedding = nn.Embedding(vocab_size, embed_dim,
        ↪  padding_idx=1)

        encoder_layer = nn.TransformerEncoderLayer(
            d_model=embed_dim,
            nhead=num_heads,
            dim_feedforward=hidden_dim,
            dropout=dropout
        )

        self.transformer_encoder =
        ↪  nn.TransformerEncoder(encoder_layer, num_layers)

        # Classification head
        self.fc = nn.Linear(embed_dim, num_classes)

    def forward(self, x):
        '''
        x: Tensor of shape [batch_size, seq_len]
        The Transformer requires [seq_len, batch_size, embed_dim].
        '''
        # Embedding => shape [batch_size, seq_len, embed_dim]
        embedded = self.embedding(x)

        # Permute to [seq_len, batch_size, embed_dim]
        embedded = embedded.permute(1, 0, 2)

        # Pass through Transformer
        encoded = self.transformer_encoder(embedded)

        # Mean pooling across seq_len
        mean_encoded = torch.mean(encoded, dim=0)

        # Classification layer
        logits = self.fc(mean_encoded)
        return logits


# ----------------------------------------------------------------
# 4) Training and Evaluation Utilities
# ----------------------------------------------------------------
def train_absa_model(model, dataloader, optimizer, criterion,
↪  device):
    model.train()
    total_loss = 0
    for batch_x, _, batch_y in dataloader:
        batch_x = batch_x.to(device)
        batch_y = batch_y.to(device)
```

228

```python
            optimizer.zero_grad()
            outputs = model(batch_x)
            loss = criterion(outputs, batch_y)
            loss.backward()
            optimizer.step()

            total_loss += loss.item()
    return total_loss / len(dataloader)

def evaluate_absa_model(model, dataloader, device):
    model.eval()
    correct = 0
    total = 0
    with torch.no_grad():
        for batch_x, _, batch_y in dataloader:
            batch_x = batch_x.to(device)
            batch_y = batch_y.to(device)

            outputs = model(batch_x)
            preds = torch.argmax(outputs, dim=1)
            correct += (preds == batch_y).sum().item()
            total += batch_y.size(0)
    return correct / total


# ------------------------------------------------------------
# 5) Main Execution Logic (Data Prep, Model Init, Training)
# ------------------------------------------------------------
if __name__ == "__main__":
    # Step A: Generate synthetic data for ABSA
    texts, aspects, sentiments =
    ↪ generate_synthetic_absa_data(num_samples=2000)

    # Step B: Fit the tokenizer
    tokenizer = SimpleSubwordTokenizer(vocab_size=100)
    tokenizer.fit(texts)

    # Step C: Split data into train/test
    train_size = int(0.8 * len(texts))
    train_texts, test_texts = texts[:train_size], texts[train_size:]
    train_aspects, test_aspects = aspects[:train_size],
    ↪ aspects[train_size:]
    train_sentiments, test_sentiments = sentiments[:train_size],
    ↪ sentiments[train_size:]

    # Step D: Create dataset objects
    train_dataset = ABSADataset(train_texts, train_aspects,
    ↪ train_sentiments, tokenizer)
    test_dataset = ABSADataset(test_texts, test_aspects,
    ↪ test_sentiments, tokenizer)

    # Step E: Create dataloaders
    train_loader = DataLoader(train_dataset, batch_size=32,
    ↪ shuffle=True,
```

```
                        collate_fn=collate_fn_absa)
test_loader = DataLoader(test_dataset, batch_size=32,
↪    shuffle=False,
                        collate_fn=collate_fn_absa)

# Step F: Initialize model and training utilities
device = torch.device("cuda" if torch.cuda.is_available() else
↪    "cpu")
model =
↪    ABSTransformerClassifier(vocab_size=len(tokenizer.token2id)).to(device)
optimizer = optim.AdamW(model.parameters(), lr=1e-3)
criterion = nn.CrossEntropyLoss()

# Step G: Training loop
num_epochs = 5
for epoch in range(num_epochs):
    train_loss = train_absa_model(model, train_loader,
↪    optimizer, criterion, device)
    acc = evaluate_absa_model(model, test_loader, device)
    print(f"Epoch {epoch+1}/{num_epochs} | Loss:
↪    {train_loss:.4f}, Accuracy: {acc:.4f}")

print("Training complete. Model is ready for aspect-based
↪    sentiment prediction.")
```

Key Implementation Details:

- **Synthetic ABSA Data**: The function
  generate_synthetic_absa_data creates text samples refer-
  encing an aspect (e.g., "food" or "service") and assigns a
  random sentiment label (positive or negative).

- **Subword Tokenization**: We showcase a simplified version
  of subword tokenization via SimpleSubwordTokenizer, lim-
  iting vocabulary size and assigning token IDs with [UNK] and
  [PAD] as special placeholders.

- **Transformer Encoder**: The core model,
  ABSTransformerClassifier, uses a PyTorch
  nn.TransformerEncoder, which applies multi-head self-attention
  to capture context across entire sequences.

- **Pooling Strategy**: We perform mean pooling over the trans-
  formed output tokens before feeding into the final classification layer self.fc, which predicts sentiment polarity.

- **Training Loop**: We define `train_absa_model` and `evaluate_absa_model` to optimize the Transformer model parameters on cross-entropy loss and evaluate classification accuracy respectively.

- **Single-Aspect Focus**: In this demonstration, each example references one aspect and a single sentiment label. In real ABSA tasks, models often detect multiple aspects and sentiments within a single utterance.

Chapter 29

Zero-Shot Classification with Transformers

Zero-shot classification enables a model to categorize data into classes it has never seen during training, particularly useful for dynamic or long-tail label sets. A Transformer-based encoder (e.g., BART or T5) can embed both the input text and a candidate label description. Scoring involves computing how well the text embedding aligns with the label embedding, often via cosine similarity or a learned matching function. Training can utilize a large language model that has been pre-trained on diverse tasks, so it can generalize to unseen classes given textual descriptions. In advanced setups, prompt engineering provides label descriptions that help the model accurately map new labels to relevant semantic regions. This approach dramatically reduces the need for curated training examples for every new label.

Python Code Snippet

```
import torch
import torch.nn.functional as F
from transformers import AutoTokenizer, AutoModel
import math
import random
```

```python
# For reproducibility
torch.manual_seed(42)
random.seed(42)

#
↪  -------------------------------------------------------------------
# 1) Pretrained Model Loading and Embedding Extraction
#
↪  -------------------------------------------------------------------
class ZeroShotEmbedder:
    '''
    Loads a pretrained Transformer model (e.g., BART or T5 encoder)
    and provides a method to obtain sentence embeddings for both
    ↪  text
    and label descriptions.
    '''

    def __init__(self, model_name="facebook/bart-large"):
        # Initialize tokenizer and model
        self.tokenizer = AutoTokenizer.from_pretrained(model_name)
        self.model = AutoModel.from_pretrained(model_name)
        self.model.eval()  # Set model to eval mode (no dropout
        ↪  etc.)

        # If GPU is available, use it
        self.device = torch.device("cuda" if
        ↪  torch.cuda.is_available() else "cpu")
        self.model.to(self.device)

    def get_embedding(self, text):
        '''
        Given some text, returns the mean-pooled embedding vector
        from the last hidden state of the model's encoder.
        '''
        with torch.no_grad():
            inputs = self.tokenizer(text, return_tensors="pt",
            ↪  truncation=True,
                                    max_length=64)
            # Move inputs to device
            inputs = {k: v.to(self.device) for k, v in
            ↪  inputs.items()}
            # Forward pass through the model
            outputs = self.model(**inputs)

            # For models like BART, outputs.last_hidden_state is
            ↪  [batch_size, seq_len, hidden_dim]
            # We do mean pooling over the seq_len dimension
            last_hidden = outputs.last_hidden_state
            attention_mask = inputs["attention_mask"].unsqueeze(-1).
            expand(last_hidden.size()).float()

            # Compute mean of non-padded embeddings
            sum_embeddings = torch.sum(last_hidden * attention_mask,
            ↪  dim=1)
```

```python
        sum_mask = torch.clamp(attention_mask.sum(dim=1),
        ↪   min=1e-9)
        mean_embeddings = sum_embeddings / sum_mask

        return mean_embeddings

#
↪   -------------------------------------------------------------------
# 2) Zero-Shot Classification Logic
#
↪   -------------------------------------------------------------------
def texttt_zero_shot_classification(embedder, texts,
↪   candidate_labels):
    '''
    This function performs a simple zero-shot classification by
    ↪   comparing
    the embedding of the text to the embeddings of each candidate
    ↪   label
    description. The label that yields the highest cosine similarity
    ↪   is
    deemed the likely correct label.
    '''
    # Pre-compute label embeddings
    label_embeddings = {}
    for label in candidate_labels:
        label_embeddings[label] = embedder.get_embedding(label)

    results = []
    for txt in texts:
        text_embedding = embedder.get_embedding(txt)

        best_label = None
        best_score = -math.inf

        # Compare text embedding to each label embedding
        for label in candidate_labels:
            # Cosine similarity: (A · B) / (||A|| * ||B||)
            # text_embedding and label_embeddings[label] are each
            ↪   shape [1, hidden_dim]
            cos_sim = F.cosine_similarity(text_embedding,
            ↪   label_embeddings[label])
            cos_val = cos_sim.item()
            if cos_val > best_score:
                best_score = cos_val
                best_label = label

        results.append((txt, best_label, best_score))

    return results

#
↪   -------------------------------------------------------------------
# 3) Synthetic Data Generation
```

234

```
#
↪   ------------------------------------------------------------------
def generate_synthetic_documents(num_docs=10):
    '''
    Creates random text samples that might plausibly be about varied
    ↪   topics.
    For demonstration purposes, we won't restrict ourselves to any
    ↪   known labels.
    '''

    corpus = []
    vocab = [
        "deep", "learning", "policy", "soccer", "finance",
        ↪   "investment",
        "government", "election", "algorithm", "robotics",
        ↪   "economy", "players",
        "football", "technology", "protein", "data", "analysis",
        ↪   "training",
        "sports", "innovation", "money", "market", "virtual",
        ↪   "assistant"
    ]

    for _ in range(num_docs):
        doc_length = random.randint(5, 15)
        doc_words = random.choices(vocab, k=doc_length)
        text = " ".join(doc_words)
        corpus.append(text)

    return corpus

#
↪   ------------------------------------------------------------------
# 4) Main Execution Block (Demonstration)
#
↪   ------------------------------------------------------------------
if __name__ == "__main__":
    # Initialize our embedder with a pretrained model (e.g., BART)
    embedder = ZeroShotEmbedder(model_name="facebook/bart-large")

    # Generate synthetic texts
    random_texts = generate_synthetic_documents(num_docs=8)

    # Candidate labels that the model didn't see in a supervised
    ↪   manner
    # (the concept of "sports", "politics", etc. are unknown from a
    # training perspective in a typical zero-shot scenario)
    candidate_labels = [
        "Sports news",
        "Political commentary",
        "Financial report",
        "Technology review"
    ]

    # Perform zero-shot classification
```

235

```
classification_results =
↪  texttt_zero_shot_classification(embedder, random_texts,
↪  candidate_labels)

# Print the results
print("=== Zero-Shot Classification Results ===")
for text, predicted_label, confidence in classification_results:
    print(f"Text: {text}")
    print(f"Predicted Label: {predicted_label} (Cosine Sim:
↪  {confidence:.4f})")
    print("------------------------------------")
```

Key Implementation Details:

- **Pretrained Transformer's Encoder:** We use a large pre-trained model (e.g., BART) via Hugging Face. The embeddings are obtained by mean-pooling the last hidden states, with padding masks accounted for in the pooling.

- **ZeroShotEmbedder Class:** Loads the tokenizer and model, handles device allocation, and provides the `get_embedding` method to convert a string into a dense vector representation.

- **texttt_zero_shot_classification Function:** Given text inputs and candidate label descriptions, it compares each text embedding to each label embedding. The label with the highest cosine similarity is returned.

- **Cosine Similarity & Dot Product:** We use `F.cosine_similarity` to measure how close the text embedding is to each label embedding.

- **Synthetic Data Generation:** The `generate_synthetic_documents` function shows how we might produce simple random texts for demonstration. In production, you would replace this with real data.

- **Overall Flow:** The main block demonstrates how to instantiate the zero-shot embedder, generate random text documents, define candidate labels, and finally classify each document into one of those labels without any additional task-specific training data.

Chapter 30

Conversational Agents with Retrieval-Augmented Transformers

A retrieval-augmented Transformer chatbot can fuse knowledge-base lookups with generative conversation. First, construct a retrieval module that indexes external documents or FAQs in a vector store. Encode the user query using a Transformer encoder and retrieve the top relevant passages. Next, feed these passages into a generative Transformer model (e.g., T5 or GPT-based) as context, instructing it to base its response on the retrieved information. This ensures answers are more grounded in factual data. For improved performance, refine the retrieval system with domain-adaptive pre-training on knowledge articles. Additional enhancements include dynamic re-ranking of retrieved passages with a cross-encoder and using generative constraints to prevent the model from ignoring retrieved text. This method produces coherent, context-aware responses backed by relevant references.

Python Code Snippet

```
import torch
import torch.nn as nn
```

```python
import torch.optim as optim
import torch.nn.functional as F
from torch.utils.data import Dataset, DataLoader
import numpy as np
import random

# For demonstration, we'll use Hugging Face Transformers for
↪ embedding and generation
!pip install transformers   # This is just an example, comment it out
↪ if already installed
from transformers import AutoModel, AutoTokenizer,
↪ AutoModelForCausalLM


###################################################################
# 1) Create a Synthetic Knowledge Base and Transformer-based
↪ Retrieval
###################################################################

class SimpleKnowledgeBase:
    """
    A toy knowledge base storing passages (documents) as text
    ↪ strings.
    We'll embed them with a Transformer encoder to enable retrieval.
    """
    def __init__(self, passages):
        self.passages = passages
        self.embeddings = None

def create_knowledge_base():
    """
    Create a very simple knowledge base with a small set of
    ↪ passages.
    """
    passages = [
        "Transformer models are great for natural language
        ↪ processing tasks.",
        "PyTorch provides a powerful platform for building deep
        ↪ learning models.",
        "Retrieval-augmented generation uses a knowledge base to
        ↪ ground responses.",
        "Domain-adaptive pretraining can improve performance in
        ↪ specialized contexts.",
        "Generative constraints help ensure the model accurately
        ↪ uses retrieved information."
    ]
    return SimpleKnowledgeBase(passages)

###################################################################
# 2) Embedding Utility via a Transformer Encoder (e.g., BERT)
###################################################################

class EmbeddingEncoder:
    """
```

238

```
    This class uses a pretrained Transformer encoder (from Hugging
    ↪  Face)
    to generate embeddings for text. We'll default to
    ↪  'bert-base-uncased'.
    """

    def __init__(self, model_name="bert-base-uncased",
    ↪  device="cpu"):
        self.tokenizer = AutoTokenizer.from_pretrained(model_name)
        self.model = AutoModel.from_pretrained(model_name)
        self.model.to(device)
        self.model.eval()
        self.device = device

    def encode_texts(self, texts, batch_size=2):
        """
        Encode a list of texts into embeddings.
        """
        all_embeddings = []
        for i in range(0, len(texts), batch_size):
            batch_texts = texts[i: i+batch_size]
            encodings = self.tokenizer(
                batch_texts,
                return_tensors='pt',
                truncation=True,
                padding=True,
                max_length=128
            )
            input_ids = encodings["input_ids"].to(self.device)
            attention_mask =
            ↪  encodings["attention_mask"].to(self.device)

            with torch.no_grad():
                outputs = self.model(input_ids,
                ↪  attention_mask=attention_mask)
                # We'll pool by taking the mean of the last hidden
                ↪  state
                last_hidden_state = outputs.last_hidden_state
                # [batch_size, seq_len, hidden_dim] => mean over
                ↪  seq_len => [batch_size, hidden_dim]
                embeddings = last_hidden_state.mean(dim=1)
            all_embeddings.append(embeddings.cpu())
        return torch.cat(all_embeddings, dim=0)

def build_kb_embeddings(knowledge_base, encoder):
    """
    Build embeddings for each passage in the knowledge base.
    """
    kb_texts = knowledge_base.passages
    kb_embs = encoder.encode_texts(kb_texts)
    knowledge_base.embeddings = kb_embs

################################################################
# 3) Retrieval Function
```

239

```
################################################################

def retrieve_top_k(query, knowledge_base, encoder, k=2):
    """
    Given a user query, embed it using the same encoder,
    compute cosine similarities with knowledge base embeddings,
    and return the top-k matching passages.
    """
    query_emb = encoder.encode_texts([query])   # shape [1,
    ↪  hidden_dim]
    kb_embs = knowledge_base.embeddings   # shape [num_passages,
    ↪  hidden_dim]

    # Compute cosine similarity
    query_norm = F.normalize(query_emb, p=2, dim=1)
    kb_norm = F.normalize(kb_embs, p=2, dim=1)

    similarities = torch.matmul(query_norm, kb_norm.transpose(0, 1))
    ↪  # [1, num_passages]
    # Get top-k
    top_k_scores, top_k_indices = torch.topk(similarities, k, dim=1)

    retrieved_passages = []
    for idx in top_k_indices[0]:
        retrieved_passages.append(knowledge_base.passages[idx])
    return retrieved_passages

################################################################
# 4) Generative Transformer Model (e.g., GPT-2) for Conversation
################################################################

class GenerativeTransformer:
    """
    We use a pretrained GPT-2 (or distilgpt2) from Hugging Face to
    ↪  generate text.
    """
    def __init__(self, model_name="distilgpt2", device="cpu"):
        self.tokenizer = AutoTokenizer.from_pretrained(model_name)
        # Ensure the tokenizer can handle [PAD] token
        if "pad_token" not in self.tokenizer.special_tokens_map:
            self.tokenizer.pad_token = self.tokenizer.eos_token

        self.model =
        ↪  AutoModelForCausalLM.from_pretrained(model_name)
        self.model.to(device)
        self.device = device
        self.model.eval()

    def generate_response(self, context, max_length=50,
    ↪  temperature=0.7, top_k=50):
        """
        Generate a response given some context (prompt).
        """
```

```
        encodings = self.tokenizer.encode(context,
        ↪   return_tensors='pt').to(self.device)
        with torch.no_grad():
            output_sequences = self.model.generate(
                input_ids=encodings,
                max_length=max_length,
                temperature=temperature,
                top_k=top_k,
                do_sample=True,
                pad_token_id=self.tokenizer.eos_token_id
            )
        gen_text = self.tokenizer.decode(output_sequences[0],
        ↪   skip_special_tokens=True)
        # We only want the part that comes after the context
        return gen_text[len(context):].strip()


###############################################################
# 5) End-to-End Chatbot Pipeline
###############################################################


def texttt_chat_with_retrieval_augmented_transformer(query,
↪   knowledge_base, encoder, generator):
    """
    Combines retrieval with generative response:
    1) Retrieves top passages from knowledge base
    2) Feeds them as context to the generative model
    3) Returns a final response
    """
    retrieved_passages = retrieve_top_k(query, knowledge_base,
    ↪   encoder, k=2)
    # Construct a prompt or context for generation
    # We'll do a simple approach: put retrieved passages before user
    ↪   question
    combined_context = (
        "Knowledge Base Passages:\n"
        + "\n".join(retrieved_passages)
        + "\n\nUser Query: " + query
        + "\nChatbot Answer:"
    )
    response = generator.generate_response(combined_context)
    return response


###############################################################
# 6) Main Execution (Initialization and Example)
###############################################################


if __name__ == "__main__":
    # Device setting
    device = torch.device("cuda" if torch.cuda.is_available() else
    ↪   "cpu")

    # 1) Create a knowledge base
    kb = create_knowledge_base()
```

```
# 2) Create an embedding encoder and build embeddings
encoder = EmbeddingEncoder(model_name="bert-base-uncased",
↪  device=device)
build_kb_embeddings(kb, encoder)

# 3) Create a generative transformer
generator = GenerativeTransformer(model_name="distilgpt2",
↪  device=device)

# 4) Example usage: user query
example_query = "How can I use a knowledge base in a
↪  transformation model?"

# 5) Generate a retrieval-augmented response
bot_reply =
↪  texttt_chat_with_retrieval_augmented_transformer(example_query,
↪  kb, encoder, generator)
print("USER QUERY:\n", example_query)
print("BOT REPLY:\n", bot_reply)
```

Key Implementation Details:

- **Knowledge Base and Embeddings**: A small toy knowledge base is constructed in `SimpleKnowledgeBase`, and `EmbeddingEncoder` uses a Transformer encoder (e.g., BERT) to embed each passage.

- **Retrieval Step**: `retrieve_top_k` function compares the embedded user query against knowledge base embeddings via cosine similarity, retrieving the top matching passages.

- **Generative Transformer**: `GenerativeTransformer` wraps a GPT-style model to generate responses from combined retrieval context and user query.

- **Interaction Pipeline**: The function `texttt_chat_with_retrieval_augmented_transformer` orchestrates retrieval and generative steps, creating a context from the top passages and user query, steering the Transformer's response.

- **End-to-End Integration**: In the main block, the code builds embeddings for the knowledge base, retrieves relevant information for a given query, and produces a final chatbot-style reply using a retrieval-augmented approach.

Chapter 31

Question Generation for Educational Use with Transformers

Transformer-based question generation converts statements or passages into questions for quizzes or study aids. Deploy an encoder-decoder model: the encoder processes a passage, and the decoder produces a question. Training data typically consists of source text (context) paired with questions about that text. An advanced step is to specify target answer spans in the source, prompting the model to produce a question whose answer matches that span. This can be achieved by highlighting or tagging the critical portion of the text. Innovative methods add difficulty or cognitive level embeddings—ranking questions by difficulty to adapt to learner needs. You could also integrate domain-specific styles, such as generating multiple-choice questions or short answers for specialized fields like medical or legal education.

Python Code Snippet

```
import torch
import torch.nn as nn
import torch.optim as optim
from torch.utils.data import Dataset, DataLoader
import random
```

```python
# For reproducibility
torch.manual_seed(42)
random.seed(42)

# ------------------------------------------------------------
# 1) Synthetic Data Generation & Simple Subword Tokenizer
# ------------------------------------------------------------
class SimpleSubwordTokenizer:
    '''
    Basic subword tokenizer that splits text by whitespace
    and builds a minimal vocabulary. For demonstration only.
    '''
    def __init__(self, vocab_size=50):
        self.vocab_size = vocab_size
        self.token2id = {}
        self.id2token = {}

    def fit(self, texts):
        all_tokens = {}
        for txt in texts:
            for token in txt.split():
                all_tokens[token] = all_tokens.get(token, 0) + 1
        # Sort by frequency, keep top N
        sorted_tokens = sorted(all_tokens.items(), key=lambda x:
        ↪ x[1], reverse=True)
        truncated_tokens = sorted_tokens[:self.vocab_size - 4]

        # Reserve special tokens
        self.token2id = {"[PAD]": 0, "[SOS]": 1, "[EOS]": 2,
        ↪ "[UNK]": 3}
        idx = 4
        for token, _ in truncated_tokens:
            self.token2id[token] = idx
            idx += 1

        self.id2token = {v: k for k, v in self.token2id.items()}

    def encode(self, text, add_special_tokens=False):
        tokens = text.split()
        encoded = []
        for t in tokens:
            if t in self.token2id:
                encoded.append(self.token2id[t])
            else:
                encoded.append(self.token2id["[UNK]"])
        if add_special_tokens:
            encoded = [self.token2id["[SOS]"]] + encoded +
            ↪ [self.token2id["[EOS]"]]
        return encoded

    def decode(self, ids):
        tokens = [self.id2token.get(i, "[UNK]") for i in ids]
        return " ".join(tokens)
```

```python
    def pad(self, encoded_batch, max_len):
        padded_batch = []
        for seq in encoded_batch:
            if len(seq) < max_len:
                seq = seq + [self.token2id["[PAD]"]] * (max_len -
                ↪   len(seq))
            else:
                seq = seq[:max_len]
            padded_batch.append(seq)
        return padded_batch


def generate_synthetic_data(num_samples=1000):
    '''
    Generate pairs of (context, question) for demonstration.
    '''
    contexts = []
    questions = []
    sample_contexts = [
        "The cat sat on the mat",
        "Transformers excel at many tasks",
        "Paris is the capital of France",
        "Python is a popular language for AI",
        "The sun rises in the east"
    ]
    sample_questions = [
        "Where did the cat sit?",
        "Which model excels at many tasks?",
        "What is the capital of France?",
        "Which language is popular for AI?",
        "Where does the sun rise?"
    ]
    # Randomly sample from these sets
    for _ in range(num_samples):
        idx = random.randint(0, len(sample_contexts) - 1)
        contexts.append(sample_contexts[idx])
        questions.append(sample_questions[idx])
    return contexts, questions

# ------------------------------------------------------------
# 2) PyTorch Dataset & DataLoader
# ------------------------------------------------------------
class QuestionGenerationDataset(Dataset):
    '''
    Stores pairs of context and question text. Encodes them using
    the provided tokenizer.
    '''
    def __init__(self, contexts, questions, tokenizer, max_len=20):
        self.contexts = contexts
        self.questions = questions
        self.tokenizer = tokenizer
        self.max_len = max_len
```

```python
        # Encode contexts without special tokens
        self.encoded_contexts = [tokenizer.encode(ctx,
        ↪   add_special_tokens=False)
                                    for ctx in contexts]
        # Encode questions with [SOS] ... [EOS]
        self.encoded_questions = [tokenizer.encode(q,
        ↪   add_special_tokens=True)
                                    for q in questions]

    def __len__(self):
        return len(self.contexts)

    def __getitem__(self, idx):
        return self.encoded_contexts[idx],
        ↪   self.encoded_questions[idx]

def collate_fn(batch_data):
    '''
    Collate function to handle padding of variable-length sequences
    for contexts and questions.
    '''
    contexts, questions = zip(*batch_data)
    max_len_context = min(max(len(seq) for seq in contexts), 30)
    max_len_question = min(max(len(seq) for seq in questions), 30)

    padded_contexts = tokenizer.pad(contexts, max_len_context)
    padded_questions = tokenizer.pad(questions, max_len_question)

    return (
        torch.tensor(padded_contexts, dtype=torch.long),
        torch.tensor(padded_questions, dtype=torch.long)
    )

# ------------------------------------------------------------
# 3) Encoder-Decoder Transformer Model
# ------------------------------------------------------------
class TransformerQGModel(nn.Module):
    '''
    A simple encoder-decoder Transformer for question generation.
    '''
    def __init__(self, vocab_size, embed_dim=32, num_heads=2,
                    hidden_dim=64, num_layers=2, dropout=0.1):
        super(TransformerQGModel, self).__init__()

        self.embedding = nn.Embedding(vocab_size, embed_dim,
        ↪   padding_idx=0)
        self.pos_encoder = PositionalEncoding(embed_dim, dropout)

        encoder_layer = nn.TransformerEncoderLayer(
            d_model=embed_dim,
            nhead=num_heads,
            dim_feedforward=hidden_dim,
            dropout=dropout
```

246

```
        )
        self.encoder = nn.TransformerEncoder(encoder_layer,
        ↪  num_layers)

        decoder_layer = nn.TransformerDecoderLayer(
            d_model=embed_dim,
            nhead=num_heads,
            dim_feedforward=hidden_dim,
            dropout=dropout
        )
        self.decoder = nn.TransformerDecoder(decoder_layer,
        ↪  num_layers)

        self.fc_out = nn.Linear(embed_dim, vocab_size)

    def forward(self, src, tgt):
        '''
        src: [batch_size, src_len]
        tgt: [batch_size, tgt_len]
        Returns logits of shape [batch_size, tgt_len, vocab_size].
        '''
        # Embed + positional encode
        src_emb = self.pos_encoder(self.embedding(src).permute(1, 0,
        ↪  2))
        tgt_emb = self.pos_encoder(self.embedding(tgt).permute(1, 0,
        ↪  2))

        # Generate source mask and target mask
        src_mask = None  # No mask for entire src
        tgt_mask = nn.Transformer.generate_square_subsequent_mask(
        tgt_emb.size(0)).to(tgt.device)

        memory = self.encoder(src_emb, mask=src_mask)
        output = self.decoder(tgt_emb, memory, tgt_mask=tgt_mask,
        ↪  memory_mask=None)
        # output => [tgt_len, batch_size, embed_dim]
        output = output.permute(1, 0, 2)
        logits = self.fc_out(output)  # [batch_size, tgt_len,
        ↪  vocab_size]
        return logits


class PositionalEncoding(nn.Module):
    '''
    Implement the PE function. This helps the model learn the
    positional relationships of tokens in the sequence.
    '''
    def __init__(self, d_model, dropout=0.1, max_len=5000):
        super(PositionalEncoding, self).__init__()
        self.dropout = nn.Dropout(p=dropout)

        pe = torch.zeros(max_len, d_model)
```

```python
        position = torch.arange(0, max_len,
        ↪    dtype=torch.float).unsqueeze(1)
        div_term = torch.exp(torch.arange(0, d_model, 2).float()
                            * (-torch.log(torch.tensor(10000.0)) /
                            ↪   d_model))
        pe[:, 0::2] = torch.sin(position * div_term)
        pe[:, 1::2] = torch.cos(position * div_term)
        pe = pe.unsqueeze(1)   # [max_len, 1, d_model]
        self.register_buffer('pe', pe)

    def forward(self, x):
        '''
        x => [seq_len, batch_size, d_model]
        '''
        seq_len = x.size(0)
        x = x + self.pe[:seq_len, :]
        return self.dropout(x)


# ----------------------------------------------------------------
# 4) Training and Inference Helpers
# ----------------------------------------------------------------
def train_one_epoch(model, dataloader, optimizer, criterion,
↪   device):
    model.train()
    total_loss = 0.0
    for contexts, questions in dataloader:
        contexts = contexts.to(device)
        questions = questions.to(device)

        # Split questions into inputs (tgt_inp) and targets
        ↪   (tgt_out)
        # We'll shift by one position for teacher forcing
        tgt_inp = questions[:, :-1]
        tgt_out = questions[:, 1:].contiguous()

        optimizer.zero_grad()
        logits = model(contexts, tgt_inp)
        # logits => [batch_size, tgt_len, vocab_size]
        # Flatten logits and targets for cross-entropy
        logits = logits.view(-1, logits.size(-1))
        tgt_out = tgt_out.view(-1)

        loss = criterion(logits, tgt_out)
        loss.backward()
        optimizer.step()

        total_loss += loss.item()
    return total_loss / len(dataloader)

def greedy_decode(model, src, max_len=20):
    '''
    Greedy decoding of questions given a context 'src'.
    src => [1, src_len].
```

```
    '''
    model.eval()
    device = next(model.parameters()).device
    src = src.to(device)
    # Start token index
    sos_idx = tokenizer.token2id["[SOS]"]
    eos_idx = tokenizer.token2id["[EOS]"]

    # Expand batch dimension for single sample
    generated = torch.tensor([[sos_idx]], dtype=torch.long,
    ↪   device=device)
    for _ in range(max_len):
        with torch.no_grad():
            logits = model(src, generated)
            next_token = logits[:, -1, :].argmax(dim=-1).item()
            generated = torch.cat([generated,
            ↪   torch.tensor([[next_token]], device=device)], dim=1)
            if next_token == eos_idx:
                break
    return generated.squeeze(0).tolist()


# ----------------------------------------------------------------
# 5) Main Execution
# ----------------------------------------------------------------
if __name__ == "__main__":
    # Generate synthetic dataset
    contexts, questions = generate_synthetic_data(num_samples=2000)

    # Build tokenizer
    all_texts = contexts + questions
    tokenizer = SimpleSubwordTokenizer(vocab_size=100)
    tokenizer.fit(all_texts)

    # Split data
    train_size = int(len(contexts) * 0.8)
    train_contexts, train_questions = contexts[:train_size],
    ↪   questions[:train_size]
    test_contexts, test_questions = contexts[train_size:],
    ↪   questions[train_size:]

    # Create dataset
    train_dataset = QuestionGenerationDataset(train_contexts,
    ↪   train_questions, tokenizer)
    test_dataset = QuestionGenerationDataset(test_contexts,
    ↪   test_questions, tokenizer)

    # Dataloader
    train_loader = DataLoader(train_dataset, batch_size=32,
    ↪   shuffle=True, collate_fn=collate_fn)
    test_loader = DataLoader(test_dataset, batch_size=32,
    ↪   shuffle=False, collate_fn=collate_fn)

    # Model
```

```
device = torch.device("cuda" if torch.cuda.is_available() else
↪    "cpu")
model =
↪    TransformerQGModel(vocab_size=len(tokenizer.token2id)).to(device)
optimizer = optim.AdamW(model.parameters(), lr=1e-3)
criterion =
↪    nn.CrossEntropyLoss(ignore_index=tokenizer.token2id["[PAD]"])

# Training
num_epochs = 5
for epoch in range(num_epochs):
    epoch_loss = train_one_epoch(model, train_loader, optimizer,
    ↪    criterion, device)
    print(f"Epoch [{epoch+1}/{num_epochs}] - Loss:
    ↪    {epoch_loss:.4f}")

# Quick demonstration of inference on a single sample
sample_context = "Paris is the capital of France"
context_encoded = tokenizer.encode(sample_context,
↪    add_special_tokens=False)
context_tensor = torch.tensor([context_encoded],
↪    dtype=torch.long)

# Generate question
output_ids = greedy_decode(model, context_tensor, max_len=15)
decoded_question = tokenizer.decode(output_ids)
print("Context:", sample_context)
print("Generated Question:", decoded_question)
```

Key Implementation Details:

- **Subword Tokenization**: A simplified tokenizer implementation (SimpleSubwordTokenizer) collects a limited vocabulary and encodes text with optional special tokens (e.g., "[SOS]" and "[EOS]").

- **Encoder-Decoder Transformer**: The core architecture is in TransformerQGModel, which uses nn.TransformerEncoder for encoding the context and nn.TransformerDecoder for generating questions.

- **Positional Encoding**: We apply sinusoidal positional encodings (PositionalEncoding) to embed token position information in both encoder and decoder inputs.

- **Training Procedure**: The train_one_epoch function uses a typical teacher-forcing approach. It shifts the target ques-

250

tion by one token for the decoder input, and optimizes via cross-entropy loss.

- **Greedy Decoding**: The `greedy_decode` function generates tokens one by one, appending the argmax token from the last step's output until it reaches an end-of-sequence token ("[EOS]") or a maximum length.

- **Overall Pipeline**: The end-to-end flow starts with data generation, splitting into train/test, tokenizing, and loading into `QuestionGenerationDataset`. We then train and finally test question generation using a sample context.

Chapter 32

Transformer-Based Summaries for Legal or Medical Documents

Legal contracts and medical texts are lengthy and specialized, requiring domain-specific summarization. Combine domain-adaptive pre-training and a seq2seq Transformer (e.g., BART or T5) to handle legal or medical jargon. Prepare a dataset of document-summary pairs, ensuring the summaries capture relevant clauses or diagnoses. Fine-tune the model with a summarization loss, focusing on brevity and clarity. Complex documents might require chunking them into smaller sections, each summarized individually, before concatenating partial summaries. For advanced implementations, incorporate highlight-based pointers that direct attention to the most pertinent sentences or sections. Additionally, you could condition the summarizer on user-specific queries, tailoring the extracted details. This approach helps professionals sift through massive documents quickly, ensuring crucial information is easily accessible.

Python Code Snippet

```
import torch
import random
import numpy as np
from torch.utils.data import Dataset, DataLoader
```

```
from transformers import BartTokenizerFast,
↪  BartForConditionalGeneration, AdamW
from transformers import get_linear_schedule_with_warmup

# ------------------------------------------------------------
# 1) Synthetic Dataset for Demonstration
# ------------------------------------------------------------
class LegalMedicalSummarizationDataset(Dataset):
    """
    A synthetic dataset emulating legal/medical documents paired
    ↪  with
    short target summaries. In practice, you'd replace this with a
    ↪  real
    domain-specific dataset, possibly combined with domain-adaptive
    ↪  pretraining.
    """
    def __init__(self, tokenizer, num_samples=200,
    ↪  max_source_length=512, max_target_length=128):
        super().__init__()
        self.tokenizer = tokenizer
        self.num_samples = num_samples

        # For demonstration, we create artificial 'docs' and
        ↪  'summaries'
        # In real scenarios, docs might be large passages from legal
        ↪  or medical files.
        self.source_texts = []
        self.target_texts = []

        # We'll produce random text from a small vocabulary to
        ↪  simulate shape & length.
        # We'll label some random "clauses" or "diagnoses" in them.
        vocab = ["patient", "contract", "diagnosis", "clause",
        ↪  "procedure",
                 "treatment", "section", "paraphrase", "agreement",
                 ↪  "dosage",
                 "legal", "medical", "risk", "trial", "finding",
                 ↪  "analysis"]

        for _ in range(num_samples):
            doc_length = random.randint(50, 120)
            # Synthetic "document"
            doc_words = [random.choice(vocab) for __ in
            ↪  range(doc_length)]
            doc_str = " ".join(doc_words)

            # Synthetic "summary"
            # We'll just pick out a few words from the doc to
            ↪  simulate a summary
            summary_length = random.randint(5, 15)
            summary_words = random.sample(doc_words, summary_length)
            summary_str = " ".join(summary_words)
```

```python
            self.source_texts.append(doc_str)
            self.target_texts.append(summary_str)

        # Tokenize once here if desired, or lazily in __getitem__.
        # Doing it in __getitem__ typically allows dynamic
        ↪  padding/collation.
        self.max_source_length = max_source_length
        self.max_target_length = max_target_length

    def __len__(self):
        return self.num_samples

    def __getitem__(self, idx):
        return self.source_texts[idx], self.target_texts[idx]

def collate_fn(batch, tokenizer, max_source_length,
↪  max_target_length):
    """
    Custom collate function to batch-encode the input texts and
    ↪  summaries.
    Trick: we ensure truncation/padding to the specified lengths.
    """
    sources, targets = zip(*batch)

    # Tokenize input (documents)
    model_inputs = tokenizer(
        list(sources),
        max_length=max_source_length,
        padding=True,
        truncation=True,
        return_tensors="pt"
    )

    # Tokenize target (summaries)
    with tokenizer.as_target_tokenizer():
        labels = tokenizer(
            list(targets),
            max_length=max_target_length,
            padding=True,
            truncation=True,
            return_tensors="pt"
        )["input_ids"]

    # The Bart/T5 model typically uses -100 for padded label tokens
    labels[labels == tokenizer.pad_token_id] = -100

    model_inputs["labels"] = labels
    return model_inputs

# -----------------------------------------------------------------
# 2) Model Initialization: BART
# -----------------------------------------------------------------
def create_model_and_tokenizer(model_name="facebook/bart-base"):
```

254

```
"""
Loads a pre-trained BART model and its tokenizer.
For domain adaptation, you would continue pre-training on
large corpora of legal/medical text before fine-tuning on
↪   summaries.
"""

tokenizer = BartTokenizerFast.from_pretrained(model_name)
model = BartForConditionalGeneration.from_pretrained(model_name)
return model, tokenizer

# -----------------------------------------------------------
# 3) Training and Evaluation Routines
# -----------------------------------------------------------
def train_summarizer(model, tokenizer, train_loader, optimizer,
↪   scheduler, num_epochs, device):
    """
    Basic training loop for BART summarization. We feed the inputs
    ↪   and labels
    to the model, compute cross-entropy loss, and optimize while
    ↪   decreasing the
    learning rate over time (scheduler).
    """
    model = model.to(device)
    model.train()

    for epoch in range(num_epochs):
        total_loss = 0.0
        for batch in train_loader:
            # Move batch to device
            for k, v in batch.items():
                batch[k] = v.to(device)

            outputs = model(**batch)
            loss = outputs.loss

            optimizer.zero_grad()
            loss.backward()
            optimizer.step()
            scheduler.step()

            total_loss += loss.item()

        avg_loss = total_loss / len(train_loader)
        print(f"Epoch {epoch+1}/{num_epochs} | Loss:
        ↪   {avg_loss:.4f}")

def generate_summary(model, tokenizer, text, device,
↪   max_length=128):
    """
    Simple utility to generate a summary from a single input text
    using the fine-tuned BART model.
    """
    model.eval()
```

255

```python
    tokens_input = tokenizer(
        [text],
        max_length=512,
        truncation=True,
        return_tensors="pt"
    ).to(device)

    # Generate summary ids
    with torch.no_grad():
        summary_ids = model.generate(
            **tokens_input,
            max_length=max_length,
            num_beams=4,
            early_stopping=True
        )

    # Decode the tokens
    summary_text = tokenizer.decode(summary_ids[0],
    ↪    skip_special_tokens=True)
    return summary_text

# ------------------------------------------------------------
# 4) Main Execution (Data Prep, Training, Demo)
# ------------------------------------------------------------
if __name__ == "__main__":
    # Reproducibility
    random.seed(42)
    np.random.seed(42)
    torch.manual_seed(42)

    device = torch.device("cuda" if torch.cuda.is_available() else
    ↪    "cpu")

    # Create model & tokenizer
    model_name = "facebook/bart-base"
    model, tokenizer = create_model_and_tokenizer(model_name)

    # Create dataset and DataLoader
    dataset = LegalMedicalSummarizationDataset(tokenizer,
    ↪    num_samples=300)
    train_loader = DataLoader(
        dataset,
        batch_size=8,
        shuffle=True,
        collate_fn=lambda b: collate_fn(
            b,
            tokenizer,
            dataset.max_source_length,
            dataset.max_target_length
        )
    )

    # Prepare optimizer & scheduler
```

256

```
optimizer = AdamW(model.parameters(), lr=3e-5,
↪   weight_decay=0.01)
total_steps = len(train_loader) * 3  # e.g. 3 epochs
scheduler = get_linear_schedule_with_warmup(
    optimizer,
    num_warmup_steps=0,
    num_training_steps=total_steps
)

# Training
train_summarizer(model, tokenizer, train_loader, optimizer,
↪   scheduler, num_epochs=3, device=device)

# Demonstrate generation with a random sample
sample_doc = ("This contract section details the procedure and
↪   risk analysis "
                "for the patient diagnosis. Further clauses
↪       describe the legal "
                "agreements and disclaimers. The dosage and
↪       treatment plan appear "
                "in subsequent paragraphs along with the trial
↪       findings.")
generated_sum = generate_summary(model, tokenizer, sample_doc,
↪   device)

print("\nSample Document:")
print(sample_doc)
print("\nGenerated Summary:")
print(generated_sum)
```

Key Implementation Details:

- **Domain-Specific Summarization**: While we demonstrate on synthetic examples, real-world legal or medical texts may require carefully curated datasets. Incorporate specialized vocabulary and domain-adaptive pre-training to capture legal/medical jargon.

- **Pre-Trained Seq2Seq Model**: We utilize BartForConditionalGeneration along with its tokenizer (BartTokenizerFast) from the Hugging Face Transformers library. This approach leverages any pre-existing domain knowledge in the backbone model and fine-tunes it for summarization.

- **Data Collation**: The collate_fn ensures that input and output sequences (documents and summaries) are padded/truncated to fixed sizes. The labels corresponding to padded tokens are set to -100 to avoid penalization during training.

- **Training Scheme**: The training routine `train_summarizer` iteratively processes batches, calculates the cross-entropy loss, and updates model parameters using `AdamW` with a linear scheduler.

- **Inference**: The `generate_summary` function encodes input text, applies the model in evaluation mode, and uses beam search (`num_beams=4`) to produce the final summary tokens, which are then decoded back to text.

- **Flexibility for Advanced Features**: One can easily integrate chunking large documents, highlight-based pointers, user-specific queries, or domain-adaptive pre-training to refine the summarization process for lengthy legal and medical documents.

Chapter 33

Natural Language Interfaces for Databases with Transformers

A Transformer-based natural language interface allows users to query databases using plain English (or other languages). Start by gathering a parallel corpus of user questions paired with the corresponding SQL or structured query. Use an encoder-decoder Transformer: the encoder processes the natural language question, while the decoder produces the SQL query token by token. Fine-tuning leverages cross-entropy loss for each generated SQL token. For advanced features, incorporate schema linking: map table and column names to the user's query tokens, adding attention markers that highlight relevant entities. You can also integrate a schema encoder that provides structural embeddings for tables and columns. This approach automates data exploration, letting non-technical users extract insights from relational databases without writing database-specific syntax.

Python Code Snippet

```python
import torch
import torch.nn as nn
```

```python
import torch.optim as optim
from torch.utils.data import Dataset, DataLoader
import random

#############################################
# 1) Synthetic Parallel Data (Questions->SQL)
#############################################
def generate_text2sql_data():
    """
    Generate a small parallel corpus of user questions mapped to SQL
    ↪ queries.
    Normally, you'd use a real dataset, but here we build a few
    ↪ examples.
    """
    data_pairs = [
        ("How many employees are there",      "SELECT COUNT(*)
         ↪ FROM employees;"),
        ("What is the average salary",         "SELECT AVG(salary)
         ↪ FROM employees;"),
        ("List all products",                  "SELECT * FROM
         ↪ products;"),
        ("Show all customers who bought shoes", "SELECT * FROM
         ↪ customers WHERE product = 'shoes';"),
        ("How many orders are pending",        "SELECT COUNT(*)
         ↪ FROM orders WHERE status = 'pending';")
    ]
    questions  = [pair[0] for pair in data_pairs]
    sql_queries = [pair[1] for pair in data_pairs]
    return questions, sql_queries

####################################
# 2) Simple Tokenizer for Demonstration
####################################
class SimpleTokenizer:
    """
    Very simple tokenizer that splits text by whitespace.
    We create separate vocabularies for questions and SQL.
    This does NOT reflect best practices in production systems.
    """
    def __init__(self, vocab_size=100):
        self.vocab_size = vocab_size
        self.token2id = {}
        self.id2token = {}

    def fit(self, texts):
        """
        Build a minimal vocabulary from the provided texts.
        In real scenarios, you'd implement subword tokenization
        ↪ (BPE, WordPiece, etc.).
        """
        # Count frequencies
        freq_dict = {}
        for txt in texts:
```

260

```
        for tok in txt.split():
            freq_dict[tok] = freq_dict.get(tok, 0) + 1

    # Sort and keep top N, reserving special tokens
    sorted_tokens = sorted(freq_dict.items(), key=lambda x:
    ↪   x[1], reverse=True)
    truncated = sorted_tokens[: (self.vocab_size - 4)]   #
    ↪   Reserve special tokens
    self.token2id = {
        "[PAD]": 0,
        "[UNK]": 1,
        "[BOS]": 2,
        "[EOS]": 3
    }
    idx = 4
    for tok, _ in truncated:
        self.token2id[tok] = idx
        idx += 1

    self.id2token = {v: k for k, v in self.token2id.items()}

def encode(self, text, add_special=True):
    """
    Tokenize and convert to ids. Optionally add BOS/EOS tokens.
    """
    tokens = text.split()
    ids = []
    for t in tokens:
        if t in self.token2id:
            ids.append(self.token2id[t])
        else:
            ids.append(self.token2id["[UNK]"])
    if add_special:
        ids = [self.token2id["[BOS]"]] + ids +
        ↪   [self.token2id["[EOS]"]]
    return ids

def decode(self, ids):
    """
    Convert IDs back to tokens, removing special tokens if
    ↪   present.
    """
    tokens = []
    for i in ids:
        token = self.id2token.get(i, "[UNK]")
        if token not in ["[PAD]", "[BOS]", "[EOS]"]:
            tokens.append(token)
    return " ".join(tokens)

def pad_batch(self, encoded_list, max_len=20):
    """
    Pad sequences to a uniform length for the entire batch.
    """
```

```python
        padded = []
        for seq in encoded_list:
            if len(seq) < max_len:
                seq = seq + [self.token2id["[PAD]"]] * (max_len -
                ↪ len(seq))
            else:
                seq = seq[:max_len]
            padded.append(seq)
        return padded


#############################################
# 3) PyTorch Dataset for Question->SQL Pairs
#############################################
class Text2SQLDataset(Dataset):
    def __init__(self, questions, sql_queries, tokenizer_in,
    ↪ tokenizer_out, max_len=20):
        """
        Each item is (encoded_question, encoded_sql).
        """
        self.questions   = questions
        self.sql_queries = sql_queries
        self.tokenizer_in = tokenizer_in
        self.tokenizer_out = tokenizer_out
        self.max_len = max_len

        self.encoded_in = [self.tokenizer_in.encode(q) for q in
        ↪ self.questions]
        self.encoded_out = [self.tokenizer_out.encode(s) for s in
        ↪ self.sql_queries]

    def __len__(self):
        return len(self.questions)

    def __getitem__(self, idx):
        return self.encoded_in[idx], self.encoded_out[idx]


def collate_fn(data_batch):
    """
    Collate function to pad input/output sequences within each
    ↪ batch.
    """
    in_seqs, out_seqs = zip(*data_batch)
    max_in_len  = max(len(isq) for isq in in_seqs)
    max_out_len = max(len(osq) for osq in out_seqs)

    # For demonstration, let's clamp them to e.g., 25 tokens
    max_in_len  = min(max_in_len, 25)
    max_out_len = min(max_out_len, 25)

    padded_in  = tokenizer_in.pad_batch(in_seqs, max_len=max_in_len)
    padded_out = tokenizer_out.pad_batch(out_seqs,
    ↪ max_len=max_out_len)
```

262

```python
    in_tensor  = torch.tensor(padded_in,  dtype=torch.long)
    out_tensor = torch.tensor(padded_out, dtype=torch.long)
    return in_tensor, out_tensor

############################################
# 4) Encoder-Decoder Transformer Model
############################################
class TransformerSeq2Seq(nn.Module):
    """
    A simple encoder-decoder Transformer for text-to-sql tasks.
    """
    def __init__(
        self,
        vocab_in_size,
        vocab_out_size,
        d_model=32,
        nhead=2,
        num_encoder_layers=2,
        num_decoder_layers=2,
        dim_feedforward=64,
        dropout=0.1,
        pad_idx=0
    ):
        super(TransformerSeq2Seq, self).__init__()

        self.pad_idx = pad_idx

        # Embeddings for encoder/decoder
        self.encoder_embedding = nn.Embedding(vocab_in_size,
        ↪  d_model, padding_idx=pad_idx)
        self.decoder_embedding = nn.Embedding(vocab_out_size,
        ↪  d_model, padding_idx=pad_idx)

        # Positional encoding is often beneficial, but for brevity
        ↪  we're omitting
        encoder_layer = nn.TransformerEncoderLayer(d_model, nhead,
        ↪  dim_feedforward, dropout)
        self.encoder  = nn.TransformerEncoder(encoder_layer,
        ↪  num_encoder_layers)

        decoder_layer = nn.TransformerDecoderLayer(d_model, nhead,
        ↪  dim_feedforward, dropout)
        self.decoder  = nn.TransformerDecoder(decoder_layer,
        ↪  num_decoder_layers)

        # Final linear layer to map decoder outputs to vocabulary
        self.fc_out = nn.Linear(d_model, vocab_out_size)

    def make_src_key_padding_mask(self, src):
        """
        Create a mask for padding tokens in the source sequences.
        src: [batch_size, src_len]
        return: [batch_size, src_len]
```

263

```python
    """
    return (src == self.pad_idx)

def make_tgt_key_padding_mask(self, tgt):
    """
    Create a mask for padding tokens in the target sequences.
    tgt: [batch_size, tgt_len]
    return: [batch_size, tgt_len]
    """
    return (tgt == self.pad_idx)

def generate_square_subsequent_mask(self, sz):
    """
    Generates an upper-triangular matrix of -inf,
    used for masking future tokens in the decoder.
    """
    mask = (torch.triu(torch.ones(sz, sz)) == 1).transpose(0, 1)
    mask = mask.float().masked_fill(mask == 0, float('-inf'))
    mask = mask.masked_fill(mask == 1, float(0.0))
    return mask

def forward(self, src, tgt):
    """
    src: [batch_size, src_len]
    tgt: [batch_size, tgt_len]
    Returns logits with shape [batch_size, tgt_len,
    ↪ vocab_out_size].
    """
    batch_size, src_len = src.shape
    batch_size_t, tgt_len = tgt.shape

    # Create masks
    src_key_padding_mask = self.make_src_key_padding_mask(src)
    ↪ # [batch_size, src_len]
    tgt_key_padding_mask = self.make_tgt_key_padding_mask(tgt)
    ↪ # [batch_size, tgt_len]
    tgt_mask =
    ↪ self.generate_square_subsequent_mask(tgt_len).to(src.device)

    # Embeddings => [batch_size, src_len, d_model]
    enc_embedding = self.encoder_embedding(src)
    # Switch to [src_len, batch_size, d_model] for
    ↪ nn.Transformer
    enc_embedding = enc_embedding.permute(1, 0, 2)

    # Pass through TransformerEncoder
    memory = self.encoder(
        enc_embedding,
        src_key_padding_mask=src_key_padding_mask
    ) # [src_len, batch_size, d_model]

    # Decoder embeddings => [tgt_len, batch_size, d_model]
    dec_embedding = self.decoder_embedding(tgt).permute(1, 0, 2)
```

```python
        # Pass through TransformerDecoder
        outs = self.decoder(
            dec_embedding,
            memory,
            tgt_mask=tgt_mask,
            tgt_key_padding_mask=tgt_key_padding_mask,
            memory_key_padding_mask=src_key_padding_mask
        )  # [tgt_len, batch_size, d_model]

        # Project to vocabulary
        logits = self.fc_out(outs.permute(1, 0, 2))  # [batch_size,
        ↪  tgt_len, vocab_out_size]
        return logits


##############################################
# 5) Training & Evaluation Functions
##############################################
def train_epoch(model, dataloader, optimizer, criterion, device):
    model.train()
    total_loss = 0
    for batch_in, batch_out in dataloader:
        batch_in = batch_in.to(device)
        batch_out = batch_out.to(device)

        # Prepare decoder input and target
        # Typically, we feed in the sequence without the last token,
        # and compare to the sequence without the first token
        dec_in  = batch_out[:, :-1]
        dec_tgt = batch_out[:, 1:]

        optimizer.zero_grad()
        logits = model(batch_in, dec_in)  # logits: [batch_size,
        ↪  seq_len, vocab_out_size]

        # Flatten predictions for cross-entropy
        logits_2d = logits.reshape(-1, logits.size(-1))
        dec_tgt_2d = dec_tgt.reshape(-1)

        loss = criterion(logits_2d, dec_tgt_2d)
        loss.backward()
        optimizer.step()
        total_loss += loss.item()
    return total_loss / len(dataloader)

def evaluate(model, dataloader, tokenizer_out, device):
    """
    Just a simple forward pass to show how we might decode
    ↪  predictions
    in teacher-forcing mode. A real evaluation would use beam search
    or greedy decoding to generate SQL from the question only.
    """
    model.eval()
```

```
total_loss = 0
predictions = []
references = []
criterion =
↳ nn.CrossEntropyLoss(ignore_index=tokenizer_out.token2id["[PAD]"])
with torch.no_grad():
    for batch_in, batch_out in dataloader:
        batch_in = batch_in.to(device)
        batch_out = batch_out.to(device)
        dec_in  = batch_out[:, :-1]
        dec_tgt = batch_out[:, 1:]

        logits = model(batch_in, dec_in)
        logits_2d = logits.reshape(-1, logits.size(-1))
        dec_tgt_2d = dec_tgt.reshape(-1)

        loss = criterion(logits_2d, dec_tgt_2d)
        total_loss += loss.item()

        # Convert first sample in each batch to text for
        ↳ demonstration
        # We'll grab the argmax target from the final dimension
        best_tokens = logits[0].argmax(dim=-1).cpu().numpy()
        predictions.append(tokenizer_out.decode(best_tokens))
        references.append(
            tokenizer_out.decode(batch_out[0].cpu().numpy()))
    avg_loss = total_loss / len(dataloader)
    return avg_loss, list(zip(predictions, references))


############################################
# 6) Main Execution
############################################
if __name__ == "__main__":
    # Random seeds for reproducibility
    torch.manual_seed(42)
    random.seed(42)

    # 1) Create Synthetic Data
    questions, sql_queries = generate_text2sql_data()

    # 2) Fit Two Tokenizers:
    #    one for the 'natural language' side, one for the 'SQL' side
    tokenizer_in  = SimpleTokenizer(vocab_size=50)
    tokenizer_out = SimpleTokenizer(vocab_size=50)
    tokenizer_in.fit(questions)
    tokenizer_out.fit(sql_queries)

    # 3) Create Dataset / DataLoader
    dataset = Text2SQLDataset(questions, sql_queries, tokenizer_in,
    ↳ tokenizer_out)
    dataloader = DataLoader(dataset, batch_size=2, shuffle=True,
    ↳ collate_fn=collate_fn)
```

```
# 4) Initialize Model
device = torch.device("cuda" if torch.cuda.is_available() else
↪  "cpu")
model = TransformerSeq2Seq(
    vocab_in_size=len(tokenizer_in.token2id),
    vocab_out_size=len(tokenizer_out.token2id),
    d_model=32,
    nhead=2,
    num_encoder_layers=2,
    num_decoder_layers=2,
    dim_feedforward=64,
    dropout=0.1,
    pad_idx=tokenizer_in.token2id["[PAD]"]
).to(device)

# 5) Define optimizer, loss
optimizer = optim.AdamW(model.parameters(), lr=1e-3)
criterion =
↪  nn.CrossEntropyLoss(ignore_index=tokenizer_out.token2id["[PAD]"])

# 6) Train loop
epochs = 10
for epoch in range(epochs):
    epoch_loss = train_epoch(model, dataloader, optimizer,
    ↪  criterion, device)
    val_loss, sample_preds = evaluate(model, dataloader,
    ↪  tokenizer_out, device)
    print(f"Epoch [{epoch+1}/{epochs}] - Train Loss:
    ↪  {epoch_loss:.3f}, Eval Loss: {val_loss:.3f}")
    # Show a couple of example predictions vs references
    for pred, ref in sample_preds[:2]:
        print(f"  Predicted: {pred} | Reference: {ref}")
    print("-----")

print("Training complete. You can now try generating SQL from
↪  your natural language questions!")
```

Key Implementation Details:

- The class SimpleTokenizer illustrates a very basic tokenization approach, splitting text by spaces. In production, subword tokenization (like Byte Pair Encoding) is recommended
  to handle rare or unknown tokens more gracefully.

- The main model TransformerSeq2Seq leverages PyTorch's
  built-in Transformer encoder and decoder to convert a source
  sequence (the user question) into a target sequence (the SQL
  query).

267

- Source and target sequences are preprocessed with padding masks and (optional) causal masks so that the decoder does not attend to future positions.

- Training is performed via cross-entropy loss on the shifted target (teacher forcing), where the model predicts the next token based on current inputs and past outputs.

- The evaluation section includes a simple demonstration of how the model's logits can be converted to actual tokens with an argmax operation, highlighting how decoding might work in practice. For a full production system, beam search or other decoding strategies are often employed.